Beyond Me

Doing the Impossible
with the Purposes of God

A Biblical Approach

Revised Edition

Saye Didi Dolopei
Senior Pastor of Good Word Ministries, UK

Aleph World Press
United Kingdom

Published by **Aleph World** Press
www.alephworld.co.uk
Durham, UK

Beyond Me:
Doing the Impossible with the Purposes of God
by Saye Didi Dolopei

First Published 2010
ISBN: 978-1-6095751-5-1

Revised Second Edition 2013
ISBN: 978-0-9926055-0-6

Unless otherwise indicated, Bible quotations are taken from The New King
James Version. Copyright © 1994 by Thomas Nelson, Inc.

Printed in the United Kingdom

Endorsements

❖❖❖

One thing you will find immediately attractive and special about this book, is how the author meticulously draws on the power and insight of the Bible, in order to make them very accessible to readers. As you read, you will have enough Scriptures to lift you up, and to fill your day as if you were reading a daily devotional as well. His approach is profound and, the book is filled with incredible wisdom throughout. Each page, engages the reader as you peel through each chapter.

This book is certainly not about opinion; it is a pack of practical truth and everyday wisdom for people of purpose desiring to do great things for God. If you thought it was over for you, or if you are about to call it quit, this book will inspire you to do it again.

Rev. K. D. Hollis
Senior Pastor & General Overseer Church of the Living
God, Philadelphia, Pennsylvania, USA

****

An important book, for such a time as this! You cannot ignore the depth of practical and living biblical wisdom, and principles, that are unearthed by this book. It certainly will stand the test of time, given its huge prophetic implications.

Pastor A. Danso Ampomah
Senior Pastor, God Solution Centre,
London, United Kingdom

****

A relevant book that will engage and challenge any person, who is presently considering their personal purpose, and how best they can fulfil the purposes of God for their life. This is one book about purpose that does not try too hard, and taps from the very *Source* of purpose. It teems with brilliant nuggets of living truths about purpose, hope, and life in general. I definitely recommend it.

Rev. Bernard O. Appiah
Pastor, Author and CEO FFC-United Kingdom

For David, after he had served the purpose of God in his own generation, fell asleep and was laid with his fathers and saw corruption.
                              - Act 13:36 (NASB)

I make known the end from the beginning, from ancient times, what is still to come. I say: My purpose will stand, and I will do all that I please. From the east I summon a bird of prey; from a far-off land, a man to fulfil my purpose. What I have said, that will I bring about; what I have planned, that will I do.
                              - Isaiah 46:10,11(NIV)

Who (God) has saved us and called us with a holy calling, not according to our works, but according to His own purpose and grace which was given to us in Christ Jesus before time began.
                              - 2 Timothy 1:9

But with God all things are possible.
                              - Matthew 19:26

May He (God) grant you according to your heart's desire, and fulfil all your purpose.
                              - Psalm 20:4

Then I heard a voice from heaven saying to me, "Write: 'Blessed are the dead who die in the Lord from now on.'"
"Yes," says the Spirit, "that they may rest from their labours, and their works follow them."
                              - Revelations 14:13

Dedication

❖❖❖

To my wife, a wonderful woman, increasingly driven by God's purpose; who has greatly helped shape my own purpose in life.

May our God and the Lord Jesus Christ grant you according to your heart's desire and fulfil all your purpose in life.

Thank you for loving me and standing with me in God's Kingdom building agenda.

Contents

❖❖❖

Foreword

❖❖❖

A Word about this Revised Edition

We are still very excited about the initial ideas, thoughts, and principles that led us to write the early edition of 'Beyond Me'. However, it has been a couple of years since it was written, and like the nature of every book, it never ceases to be the author's *baby*. As such, a book although deemed to be complete when physically published, is really never completely finished, at least in the mind of the author. It continues to grow and to expand equally in the mind of the author as his or her own experience in life also evolves and expands.

This has been the case with 'Beyond Me'. It has never ceased to be our *baby*, which we've always felt we could look after by adding exciting new ideas, and also by tweaking some others for the sake of further clarity, and our aim to continue to build a more wide-ranging view on the subject of personal purpose and the purposes of God, as we see it from God's point of view.

Of course, we know that a subject as vast as personal purpose or the purposes of God can never be comprehensively covered in a single volume, no matter how large a scope it attempts. However, our intension is to ensure that this present volume remains fresh and relevant in its focus, to be able to as possible, speak to many people of diverse backgrounds and persuasions. That is why it became necessary to incorporate very subtle additions, based on some new truths we have learned, in order to further enrich the reader's experience and to strengthen some ideas for today's application, without taking away from the main thrust of the book.

In fact, the more we think about the subject of personal purpose and the purposes of God, the more convinced we are that the very ideas, thoughts and principles captured in this present volume are most helpful and key, for anyone who is interested in the journey of discovering or pursuing personal purpose and the purposes of God for their life.

Some of what we have now learned, which also have become part of our own experience on this journey, we have selflessly decided to include as additional ideas to strengthen previous thought along the same line. For example, we found out that one of our cherished experiences was the area of *Service* (either to God or His people), and how astoundingly indispensable it is when discovering and pursuing personal purpose and the purposes of God.

Other improvements include correction of basic typographical errors, the re-arrangement and proper stringing of chapters for better correlation of thoughts, the rephrasing of some phraseology, reformatting of fonts and pages, for compactness. Also, we could have introduced a new subtitle like *Winning with God's Purposes*, which is appropriate, but the original subtitle *Doing the Impossible with the Purposes of God* really captures the overarching feel, atmosphere, direction, content and message the book conveys.

We maintained the major title *Beyond Me,* not for any sentimental reasons, except that in our view, it captures and represents the very essence and reality of personal purpose alongside the purposes of God. One thing is certain, that if you are familiar with life's many typical challenges and opportunities, the title, *Beyond Me* will come as no special revelation. However, we chose it as a suitable title because it embodies the true characterisation of *purpose* in real life scenarios, and also helps portray its clearly gripping subtlety and the increasing effect of *purpose* on human beings, as our greatest life-long pursuit even after reconciling with our Maker in true relationship through the Lord and Saviour, Jesus Christ.

You might also notice that the publishing agency has changed, and the introduction to the book has been expanded quite a bit to help lead readers directly into the main issues of the book. All of these were steps consciously taken with the hope that you will find the book helpful, accessible, and also be blessed by its content overall.

Introduction

❖❖❖

Purpose and Observable Marks of Purpose

For David, after he had served the purpose of God in his own generation, fell asleep and was laid with his fathers and saw corruption.(Act 13:36 (NASB)

The question is usually asked, 'so, what is my purpose, and how does this play out on life's vast stage? ' This crucial question leads to many things, however, it is mainly our open but quiet admission of the fact that life is more than it appears, and that we all normally bear compelling inner desires to reach for more than just physical existence and to find our life's purpose.

In a sense, the question of life's purpose filters down to the question of, "Who am I?". The same question also connects to other bigger questions including the question of source and origin, "Where did I come from?". Of course, these are questions that urgently beg answers no matter who asks them, but again they are probably life's most gripping questions which, when properly channelled, will drive us to God who ultimately knows what our life is all about, and what our life's purpose should be.

Incidentally, it is under such probing circumstance that many have made the crucial discovery of not only their relationship with God, but also their purpose and life's possibilities in and through God.

Equally so, in time, they have also along with their discovery come into a new realisation that the most important things in life are the purposes of God, which admittedly are more important than our greatest plans. In addition, they also realise that with and through God's purposes they too can achieve their plans and fulfil their purpose in life. This realisation only leads to one dominant truth, that ultimately, in so far as we commit ourselves to discovering and carrying out God's purposes, we will inevitably discover our life's purpose and fulfil them by the grace that God provides.

Of course, whether one is only now trying to discover their purpose, or is at the verge of plunging right into it, or even already pursing their purpose, which they believe has been given by God, the odds and challenges to the discovery and faithful fulfilment of one's purpose come with tremendous highs and lows. It is never easy. People will often find out, as they carefully take time to enquire more deeply about life, that to make real sense of life, they must go beyond themselves and search for God's purposes. They must deliberately reach out for the purposes of God and then find out just how their own life fits into God's purposes.

To ignite the flame toward discovering one's purpose, questions of purpose including *Why am I here?*, must be carefully pursued. Unfortunately, some people are either reluctant or unwilling to commit and to ask themselves such relevant questions, which lead to the discovery of life's purpose. Isn't it interesting, that John the Baptist knew exactly who he was and why he came (John 3:26-36).

The imperative of asking challenging and uncomfortable questions in relation to life's purpose lies in the fact that, such questions lead us into other important discoveries necessitated by God's wisdom and grace for an exciting relationship, in which God reveals Himself and all that He wants us to know and to do. By revealing His purposes, and by us first establishing God's purposes through His revelation to us, we then find life's true depth, beauty, meaning, and its bountiful treasures. This also helps us to appreciate why things are the way they are, and to understand our difference from others. Equally important is that, understanding God's purpose for us helps us to persevere and go on even when it seems okay to quit, because of life's challenges. On a more practical note, and without a shadow of doubt, the purposes of God give us the reason to live and the desire to wake up, get up and do something with life. But, in the absence of a clear direction of God's purpose for our life, or even failing to seek and to establish God's purposes for us, we will soon realise that there is nothing more painful as "succeeding in life without God". The same is true about doing everything, except the will and purposes of God. It is simply disastrous, and the most miserable failure ever, no matter the height we climb or the depth we descend in the name of succeeding on our own.

If we intend to find true pleasure or happiness, and to make sense of life's challenges, by riding upon them to the heights God has in His mind for us, then we must start by first seeking and establishing what really is God's purpose for us. This is the reason why the Bible repeatedly emphasises the importance of the purposes of God, although it also admits that the purposes of God are 'beyond us', so to speak.

Nowhere in the Bible is this truth more clearly defined and emphasised than in Proverbs 19:21, which says *"there are many plans in a man's heart, nevertheless the Lord's counsel (purpose) that will stand"*. What does that mean? That essentially, God's purposes are all that matter and apprehending what His purposes are will definitely make life and living a lot easier. It also implies that we are made for His purposes and our lives are beyond ourselves (see Isaiah. 43:7, 21).

With that kind of understanding, we know that whatever God does is according to His purposes and plans for our lives. Secondly, God will work His purposes and plans through our lives. So, if God would choose to do something on earth or even work His will in us, He will have to orchestrate situations and use one of us, who are called according to His purposes (Romans 8:28). This is simply called the *manifold wisdom of God* (Ephesians 3:10) by which God works His purposes. Someone or some occasions must serve to bring His purposes to pass, a choice which is always beyond us.

To this end, Paul rightly observed *God saved us and called us with a holy calling, not according to our works, but according to His own purpose and grace which was given to us in Christ Jesus before time began (2Tim. 1:9).*

What is Purpose?

By the way, purpose is usually a call to *give* or to *donate*, and a person of purpose always seeks every opportunity to fulfil such a call in *giving* and *donating*, obviously, what they've received (1Cor. 11:23; 1Cor. 4:7, 1Cor. 15:1-5 Gen. 12:1-2). Also, your personal purpose is always tied in with, and relates directly to serving your generation faithfully with the gifts and abilities God has given you. Even more specifically, it involves using your gifts and talents in positively influencing your circle of influence. This is done for God's glory and in conformity with His perfect will and His agenda on earth, including the betterment of humanity.

Purpose generally relates to the area of your *pain* and the *pain* of others, giving you the unequal privilege to use your derived experience and talents, directly or indirectly, to help those who are in need. God, in His divine wisdom, has placed in the trajectory of your life's path certain people, in order for them to generously benefit through your service as a result of what God has made you, given you, or allowed you to experience and to have. For example Abraham was blessed to be a blessing (Gen. 12:2). The Lord Jesus, as our High Priest, is able to sympathise with us and take compassion on us because in the days of His flesh, He also was tempted in all points as we are, although without sin, and likewise suffered in His flesh (Heb. 4:14-5:1-10).

A key text that helps to explain personal purpose and God's purposes for our lives is Acts 13:36, which affirms that *'David served his own generation by the will and purpose of God'*. The NASB translation of the same text reads, *"For David, after he had served the purpose of God in his own generation, fell asleep, and was laid among his fathers and underwent decay."*Equally relevant to the subject of purpose is Matthew 20:28, which asserts that Jesus came to *serve* and to *give*.

Also Genesis 12:2 lets us know that Abraham is blessed to be a blessing, and Numbers 18:7 clearly states that the priesthood is a gift for service.

The preceding scriptural references are by no means exhaustive, because there are myriad of other crucial and relevant texts available. However, those we've referenced at least give us a good glimpse into the nature and definition of purpose. Of course, 2Timothy 1:9 must also be mentioned here for its implicit reference to the source and origin of our purposes and the fact that they do not stem from personal efforts, but according to the grace and purpose of God, given to us in Christ before time began.

Again, purpose could be viewed in terms of a divine call to give, donate or contribute something of value and significance, which also assumes a generous nature of 'self-sacrifice' from a person of purpose, who willingly seeks avenues to serve notwithstanding the demands and challenges. Regardless of the personal sacrifice involved, such people are often compensated with a huge sense of personal fulfilment, which makes their sacrifice not only worthy, but also relatively and seemingly easy.

The word 'easy' in this case is being used with extreme care, and it is probably safer to say, their reward of personal fulfilment make them want to do what they know to do best, and sometimes they might even look to be addicted to their purpose. A good example of this is an exceptional family referred to as *the household of Stephanas*, mentioned in 1Corinthians 16:15, who became addicted to the ministry (service) of the saints. Surely, purpose can be a great invigorator!

In Romans 1:9-15, Paul cannot wait to get to Rome so as to impart some spiritual gifts to those in Rome. Likewise, in 1 Cor. 15:1-5, Paul passes on what he has received, the gospel. He served the Corinthian church with the gift that had been entrusted to him, for the benefit of all and sundry. In Romans 9:3, we see a remarkable indication of self-sacrifice from Paul in line with pursuing his purpose, when he wished that he himself were accursed from Christ for his brethren, his countrymen according to the flesh.

Moses also saw his life's purpose in carrying out God's purposes. He served his generation sacrificially and faithfully at the will and command of God Almighty. He was willing even to 'donate 'his life for the sake of others, the congregation of Israel (Exodus 32:31-33).

Now then, if you were asked similar to the way that Elisha asked a beleaguered widow in 2Kings 4:1-1, *"what do you have in your house?"* Can you think about something that, no matter how little, could change and improve your life situation, as well as others around you? Furthermore, what can you identify as your 'little jar of oil' in your *house* which you could use to get you out of debt, and others out of a *slavery* situation? What is it that you have been given to give and to donate? Why don't you begin today by giving it, using it and putting it to work for the benefit of others around you? Serve using that which you have received and have been given to bring glory to God. Do so with all the grace and strength God has given you, and be glad about it. John the Baptist's greatest joy was fulfilled in serving, and seeing Jesus step into His own purpose (John 1:26-30).

What a joy to know that just serving the demands of one's purpose, no matter the sacrifice involved, can make one glad and offer a great sense of personal fulfilment. Paul also is glad and rejoices and accepts the magnanimous expectation and challenge of being able to be poured out as a drink offering on the sacrifice and service of the faith of others. Then, he called on the same people to also be glad and to rejoice with him as well, suggesting that Paul was doing a good thing, fulfilling his purpose which he would not shy away from (Phil. 2:17-8).

Think about great men and women and their achievements, which we celebrate and remember with utter gratitude, counting them men and women who fulfilled their purpose in life. What exactly is the common thread that we often pin them to, and what is the denominator common to them all? Is it how long they lived? Or, is it not that they all served in one way or another? Certainly, it is the fact that they discovered their purpose and gave themselves to it entirely through their laudable sacrificial services in their time, to serve God and their generation. That is what set them apart, and it is for the same reason which they are remembered. Indeed, their enviable contributions to the welfare and wellbeing of the rest of humanity, made possible by their belief and trust in God, caused them to be remembered with great admiration.

Of course, our ultimate example, the Lord Jesus Christ, who had an earthly life in the flesh for about thirty-three years served and as He himself puts it, "For even the Son of Man did not come to be served, but to serve, and to give His life a ransom for many"(Mark 10:45). If the servant is not greater than the master, like the Lord Jesus claimed, then as our purpose on earth we also ought to serve, and to do so faithfully and positively with the gifts, talents and blessings God has given to us. That's the legacy and example to emulate and to bequeath to others who need to know and to benefit from our purpose of being.

Now, while there could be various ways of looking at and defining purpose, we will attempt a few based on biblical examples and principles. First, Purpose is a discoverable, God-given "cause" comparable in worth to the price of the life of the pursuer.

Regarding this truth, Paul was not only eager to discover God's cause (reason) for taking hold of him and for separating him from his mother's womb, he forsook every other thing that was initially to his personal credit. To the extent that even if required, Paul would die for what he later discovered as his life's purpose on earth, to make Christ known, to preach the Gospel of Jesus Christ and at all cost to bring countless many to the saving knowledge of God Almighty (Phil. 3:1-14; Gal. 1:11-16; Acts 21:13; Rom.15:19; 2Tim 4:7). Even the Lord Jesus had to lay down His life for His sheep, attesting that His purpose was equivalent to the price of His life (John 10-11-18).

This first definition of purpose cuts right down to the heart of purpose, and explains why people who have discovered their God-given purpose are willing to go the extra mile. The reasons are that, they have settled in themselves to identify with their purpose and taken the appropriate steps to literally become one with it. It is from this perspective that one can begin to understand the riveting passion of Paul regarding his purpose in Philippians 1:12-25, part of which he declares, *"for to me, to live is Christ, and to die is gain"*. Also in Acts 21:13, *"What do you mean by weeping and breaking my heart? For I am ready not only to be bound, but also to die at Jerusalem for the name of the Lord Jesus"*, Paul said.

Second, Purpose is the primary goal in life (albeit God-given) to which all other goals are only secondary.

Third, Purpose is the one goal in life that a person discovers that gives rise to and makes other supportive goals meaningful, substantive and even possible, but without which one will be thought of as having not fully lived to their potential.

Regarding the second and third definitions of purpose, again Paul sets for us a good benchmark in principle and practice, when he says in Philippians 3:12-15, *...but this one thing I do ...I press toward the goal for the prize of the upward call of God in Christ Jesus.* The Lord Jesus even puts it in a better light for us in His epic advice to Martha, the sister of Mary, who was said to be encumbered and distracted by many things and much serving. The words of His advice are found in Luke 10:38-42, saying, *And Jesus answered and said to her, "Martha, Martha, you are worried and troubled about many things. But one thing is needed, and Mary has chosen that good part, which will not be taken away from her.*

Observable Marks of Purpose

Three key observable 'marks' and attributes of personal purpose: First, people of purpose *make*. They create in others and in places God's desires and positively influence people they encounter, whether by proxy or from afar. In Matthew 28:19 Jesus' instruction to His disciples was simply, Go and *Make....*

Second, people of purpose *give or donate*. They give, donate, or contribute what they have received from God in the form of gifts, talents and blessings, including themselves, to a worthy cause in helping another or humanity as a whole. Unfortunately, in the story of Luke 16:20-31, titled the Rich man and Lazarus, the Rich man missed this powerful truth and found himself in hell. In Romans 9:3 Paul takes this point of 'giving' and 'donating' seriously when he says, *'for I could wish that I myself were accursed from Christ for my brethren, my countrymen according to the flesh.* Even Jesus our Lord had as the basis of His purpose on earth two main things, to *give* and to *serve*, Mark 10:45. Most importantly He concludes that the final judgement will include questions of *service*, and 'sacrifice' for others (Mtt. 25:36). The Lord also admonished His disciples commanding, *freely you received, freely give* (Mtt 10:8). In other words, "give as freely as you received".

Without exaggerating, I would say in respect to the second observable mark of purpose, that people of purpose are definitely a gift to the world and the earth (cf. Ephesians 4:7-14). Again, people who discover their purposes and pursue them faithfully, know that they only make a living by what they get, but make life by what they give or donate to their world, with the clear understanding that life is measured in 'donation' and not duration or mere 'accumulation'.

Remember, we are blessed to be a blessing:

> *Then Jesus, looking at him, loved him, and said to him, "One thing you lack: Go your way, sell whatever you have and give to the poor, and you will have treasure in heaven; and come, take up the cross, and follow Me" (Mark 10:21).*

Third, any personal purpose on earth is therefore subsumed under *service.* Jesus came to serve and to do the will of the Father (Mark 10:45, Mtt 20:28 and Heb. 10:7). David served, and Paul served (Acts 13:36; Phil 2:17; 2Tim. 4:6, 7). Moses served his generation sacrificially and faithfully. He was willing to donate his life for the sake of others (Ex. 32:31-33). John the Baptist was a man of purpose who knew what his life was about; he served (Jn 1:19-28).

Apostle James summarises pure and undefiled religion before God and the Father to be simply to visit orphans and widows in their trouble, *and* to keep oneself unspotted from the world (James 1:27). James suggests here that, even the most sophisticated religion is nothing but altogether useless and without purpose if, it does not serve those in need.

The clearest and I believe the most pointed description of the issues of judgment, found in Matthew 25, ultimately pertains to matters of service and serving, and also considers those two to be the believer's primary purpose on earth. *Then the King will say to those on His right hand, 'Come, you blessed of My Father, inherit the kingdom prepared for you from the foundation of the world: for I was hungry and you gave Me food; I was thirsty and you gave Me drink; I was a stranger and you took Me in (Matt 25:34-35).*

What to Expect

The main thrust of this book, centres on practical life applications relevant to our daily challenge of trying to locate and to elegantly fulfil our God-assigned purposes on earth. In reality, the book is about the dynamic power of purpose working for even the most unlikely candidate, which causes them to achieve great things with God. It also seeks to address issues with regards to the appropriate behaviour under purpose, which without doubt influences the outcome of one's pursuit, along the line of their God-given purposes. Great attention is given to subjects like provisions God has already placed in His purposes to effectively enable, and to sufficiently provide for those pursuing their God given purposes.

We also mainly considered in some detail the life of the Apostle Paul, his intriguing call and subsequent journey to Rome under strange arrangements with an impossible promise in Acts 23:11. This then sets the tone for the subject of purpose which is the main concern of this book. By drawing on Paul's exclusive experience brought into the broader context of Scriptures, while looking at other important heroes of the Faith, we are able to delineate essential principles about the purposes of God. We then allow those principles to inform our own personal struggles in grappling with the purposes of God, prophecies, and our own plans, amid daunting obstacles and oppositions of life in general.

From the life, perspectives and conclusions reached primarily based on the strengths and weaknesses of people of faith, but especially Paul, who you will encounter as you read, the book advises on why quitting your purpose is inexcusable. It illustrates the wisdom and the powerful potential awaiting anyone who dares obey God's command, and describes the vast opportunity for things to do and not to do, when walking in the purposes of God.

You will find it helpful as you read that, one of life's greatest ironies is that many times when we are planning to give up hope, God is just about to open brand new chapters. Assuming that someone should, or if by reason of difficult situations, our early doom is pronounced; often we find out that God Almighty is about to do something new with us, usually greater in measure and intensity compared to what we've always known and done. This entirely has nothing to do with us – has no reference to our age, strength, weakness or background, but everything to do with the purposes of God. And if that is true, then, I propose to you that purpose is everything!

With purpose, God can do with you what you yourself or others thought was totally impossible. Your purposes especially those that come from God can be a great invigorator and a wonderful motivator. They can take you to heights God has for you to climb, and victoriously across every valley you have to cross on purpose. It is our prayer that you will fulfil your God-ordained purpose.

That's our prayer for you as you read this book, which we truly believe is God's idea for any person who has a desire to see God Almighty consistently glorified on earth and in their own life. In the end, we hope every one of us can be so precise about our purpose and then pursue our destiny in God like Paul, or even like John the Baptist, who will be forever remembered for his great confession concerning himself and why he came to earth:

> *...When the Jews sent priests and Levites from Jerusalem to ask him, "Who are you?" He confessed, and did not deny, but confessed, "I am not the Christ." And they asked him, "What then? Are you Elijah?" He said, "I am not." "Are you the Prophet?" And he answered, "No." Then they said to him, "Who are you, that we may give an answer to those who sent us? What do you say about yourself?" He said: "I am 'The voice of one crying in the wilderness: "Make straight the way of the Lord," 'as the prophet Isaiah said." ...And they asked him, saying, "Why then do you baptize if you are not the Christ, nor Elijah, nor the Prophet?" John answered them, saying, "I baptize with water, but there stands One among you whom you do not know. It is He who, coming after me, is preferred before me, whose sandal strap I am not worthy to loose." (John 1:19-27)*

It will help to remember that your purpose is more than your job. It is a worthwhile service rooted in a genuine conviction or passion that is of God. It is something you must do that truly is the will of God for your life, which grips and calls you to an irresistible sense of duty, with measurably beneficial outcome to a person, a group of people, or to nations. In a more remarkable way, persons of purpose are usually *victims* of their God-given convictions, something that more or less defines them. Like Paul, they are willing to sacrificially *die* in many ways to their selfish personal ambitions, in order to *live* for their purpose. Like Joseph the son of Jacob, purpose could begin with an *ordinary dream* that might require painful personal sacrifices, but which ends with the salvation of his own relatives, friends, enemies, and a million others. Yet, no matter the sacrifices involved, you will discover that finding and following your God-given purpose is utterly beyond price, and life is worth living because of it! So start now.

Light from the Dark:
Just When You Thought it
Was Over

❖❖❖

Opening New Chapters

Unto the upright there arises light in the darkness... (Ps 112:4). The Lord will perfect that which concerns me... (Ps 138:8). Being confident of this very thing, He who has begun a good work in you will complete it until the day of Jesus Christ. (Phil 1:6)

You probably know about Naomi, the woman from Bethlehem, who lost her husband, Elimelech and her two sons, Mahlon and Chilion. When there was great famine in their country, Elimelech and Naomi moved, together with their sons, to Moab for greener pastures. Unfortunately after ten years of their sojourn, they all died leaving Naomi with two young widows, the wives of Mahlon and Chilion.

Desperate, discouraged and despondent, Naomi made the decision to run back home after she heard that at least the Lord had begun to feed her people back in Judah. She was not necessarily planning for a better life after her unfortunate situation in Moab.

Naomi just wanted to survive on the quiet until her time was due to join her family in the after-life. She had decided to live the rest of her life being alone, and advised the young widows to stay in their own country. Naomi thought perhaps men might still find her young in-laws attractive and they would be able to raise families of their own. She gave the two women all she had left, her blessings for a new start in life. But for herself, Naomi saw no hope, not even in Judah, her own country that she was now heading to. She even changed her name from Naomi (meaning, *Pleasant*) to one she made up for herself, Mara (meaning, *Bitter*). In her own words, she firmly told the two young women, Orpah and Ruth,

> ... *"turn back, my daughters; why will you go with me? Are there still sons in my womb, that they may be your husbands?* [12] *Turn back, my daughters, go - for I am too old to have a husband. If I should say I have hope, if I should have a husband tonight and should also bear sons,* [13] *would you wait for them till they were grown? Would you restrain yourselves from having husbands? No, my daughters; for it grieves me very much for your sakes that the hand of the Lord has gone out against me!"* [14] *Then they lifted up their voices and wept again; and Orpah kissed her mother-in-law, but Ruth clung to her.* [15] *And she said, "Look, your sister-in-law has gone back to her people and to her gods; return after your sister-in-law."* (Ruth 1:11-15)

Somehow, one of the young women, Orpah, made the difficult choice to leave her mother-in-law and to return to her own people. We are told that she *kissed her mother-in-law farewell*. Note, contrary to popular opinion, I do not think Orpah's kiss was a kiss of betrayal, but one of affection and respect for her mother-in-law, and also her careful circumspection under the situation.

Remember Orpah was young and the love of her life was dead. Obviously, she was still grieving her husband's sudden death. I believe Orpah's mother-in-law saw and considered their plight. Orpah and Ruth had stayed with Naomi even after the death of their husbands, something which only happens out of great commitment and admiration in this case.

If we will consider the merit of their case, first, Naomi was too old to give them other sons, and even if she had sons, they will be too young to marry the widows. Secondly, they were Moabites and except for divine intervention, the widows had no easy prospects of marrying men from Judah, who were under covenant to marry one of theirs. To make things worse, Naomi did not paint too good a picture of what lay ahead for her in-laws or for herself. So, the present state of things meant, Naomi a widow returning to no inheritance will be terribly burdened with looking after two foreign widows as well as herself.

Appreciating their present dilemma, and the prospect of imminent difficulties ahead, I believe Orpah would have thought, one person going with Naomi will be enough burden, and since Ruth was bent on going at all cost, Orpah decided to give her the chance. So, in a sense, *Orpah represents to me, someone who is sensitive to other people's need, putting theirs before hers.* Her calculated concerns for her mother-in-law's own unfortunate circumstance, coupled with her desire to grant Ruth the chance to serve their mother-in-law, was responsible for the hard and difficult decision to separate from her in-laws at the last minute.

Orpah was without doubt a gracious woman who created chance and opportunities for others. Just suppose that Orpah went with Ruth and Naomi, it might have been a very difficult thing for Naomi to decide which one of her daughters-in-law to put forward to Boaz. Chances were that, Ruth could have married someone else, but not Baoz thereby inadvertently jeopardizing the birth of Obed, the grandfather of David.

In the end we know that, through God's intervention, something good came out of the whole situation with Naomi. Her husband and children were not raised from the dead, but the Lord God appointed a new chapter in her life with countless new pages, beginning with the selfless love, sweet fellowship and wonderful service from Ruth coming alongside Naomi. In the course of time Ruth gave birth, and Naomi literally re-gained hope, life and ultimately her personal purpose by entirely giving herself to God's purposes. From being bitter she became happy, holding Obed in her bosom. She was even considered the mother of Obed. That's just what it is, when the Bible says, *"all things work together for good..."* (Romans 8:28). Hard to comprehend, but true to the core for those that wait on the Lord, *it is never over until God says so.* Even if it means the Lord having to insert new pages here and there to give your story a perfect and purposeful finish design to complete His purposes for you, He will.

Please hold on and don't quit just yet, because your God says, *"I know the thoughts that I think toward you, says the Lord, thoughts of peace and not of evil, to give you a future and a hope."* *Jeremiah 29:11*. Again, "There is hope in your future, says the Lord...."Jer.31:17. A word from God in this fashion is something to cheer up and be happy about. You can when you consider that the person saying cheer up is able to make all grace to abound to you for every good work in, for, and with you *(2 Corinthians 9:8)*. God literally fights for you and He holds your future.

Unlike Paul the Apostle, who you will encounter very soon, Naomi, Ruth and Orpah, were not in a physical prison. However, their crises represented a form of prison intended to bind and to incarcerate them for life. They could have remained arrested in their state of hopelessness, if that was all they knew God had for them. But before long, Ruth and Naomi saw that God had a great plan and a purpose for them beyond themselves and beyond all they had initially anticipated. While their experience in Moab decisively ended a chapter of their lives, their decision to move back to Judah started a new chapter.

Similarly, while Paul's imprisonment was terrifyingly scary and, without much prospect for future ministry, it was only the end of one chapter and the beginning of a new chapter, in view of the purposes of God for him. In fact, it was never God's idea that Paul would perish in prison or at the hand of his accusers in Jerusalem.

It is Not Over

But the following night the Lord stood by him and said, "Be of good cheer, Paul; for as you have testified for Me in Jerusalem, so you must also bear witness at Rome." (Acts 23:11)

In a few places in the Gospels, the Lord Jesus Christ encouraged people under different circumstances to *be of good cheer*. Clearly, *good cheer* represented different things with respect to individual circumstances. But, in Acts 23:11, the command to '*be of good cheer*' couldn't have come at a more extraordinary time in the life and ministries of Apostle Paul.

Without doubt, Paul was in a pretty precarious and life-threatening situation. He had miraculously but narrowly eluded possible conviction by the Jewish Sanhedrin, before which he had been vehemently accused of sedition. We are told that Paul could have easily been 'torn into pieces' due to violent mob action among the Pharisees and Sadducees over what to do with Paul. One part accused him of blasphemy, that he broke laid-down religious laws which was punishable by death, while the other half defended him over matters of belief in death and resurrection. Seeing how unsettled things had turned, the army commander quickly ordered his troop to swiftly take Paul away to the barracks, and to take him into custody for his own safety.

While in custody, about the second night of his imprisonment, and probably while he was fast asleep trying to recover from his ordeal, he might have tried to convince himself that finally the end has come. It was easy for him to think that way because his situation seemed to have followed the words of prophecies he got previously before arriving at Jerusalem. It is possible that Paul was quickly reminded about the prophecies of Agabus, the warnings from Phillip's daughters, and the Caesarean church regarding possible beating, binding, imprisonment and imminent death (Acts 21:8-15). He might have told himself, 'yes, *Aga* said it was going to be this bad when I got to Jerusalem.'

While he was thinking these thoughts and I believe feeling down and despondent, the Lord appeared standing right over him and commanded him to *"be of good cheer."* That's why I said I think he was suffering a low-moment in prison, because the message of the Lord was intentionally meant to lift him up: *Paul, be happy - take courage, "it is not over yet because you must do this again in Rome, testifying about Me."*

In Paul's own words according to Acts 20:22-25, he was compelled by the Holy Spirit to go to Jerusalem, the very place where beatings and threats of death awaited him. Clearly, he was unsure if he was going to survive his ordeal. So when he sent for the elders of the Church of Ephesus, he told them he knew none of them would ever see him again. For a fact, no one expecting a good outcome from their trip would speak the way Paul did.

Surely, Paul was convinced that the final chapter of his life and ministry would end with his visit to Jerusalem. His words were,

> *"And now, compelled by the Spirit, I am going to Jerusalem, not knowing what will happen to me there. I only know that in every city the Holy Spirit warns me that prison and hardships are facing me. However, I consider my life worth nothing to me, if only I may finish the race and complete the task the Lord Jesus has given me—the task of testifying to the gospel of God's grace." Now I know that none of you among whom I have gone about preaching the kingdom will ever see me again (Acts 20:22-25 NIV).*

Paul concluded his final chapter before he even began to write it. He expected nothing but a possible end of his life at Jerusalem. But you see, God always knows how to open and add new pages to the chapters of our lives. Therefore, we cannot conclude decisively on matters of our life and future before God actually gives His verdict.

It is amazing how God always preserves and sustains His people by the power of His spoken and written Word. David says in Psalm 119:49 *"Remember the word to Your servant, upon which You have caused me to hope"*. God's Word is so powerful that when it is released, even death, the major enemy of life is postponed.

Essentially, nothing can undermine the promise of the Word until it comes to fruition. Two men in Scripture, Simeon and Enoch could not see death at the Word of the Lord.

And, behold, there was a man in Jerusalem, whose name was Simeon; and the same man was just and devout, waiting for the consolation of Israel: and the Holy Ghost was upon him. ²⁶And it was revealed unto him by the Holy Ghost, that he should not see death, before he had seen the Lord's Christ. ²⁷And he came by the Spirit into the temple: and when the parents brought in the child Jesus, to do for him after the custom of the law, ²⁸Then took he him up in his arms, and blessed God, and said, ²⁹Lord, now lettest thou thy servant depart in peace, according to thy word: ³⁰For mine eyes have seen thy salvation, ³¹Which thou hast prepared before the face of all people (Luke 2:25-31-KJV)

By faith Enoch was taken away so that he did not see death, "and was not found, because God had taken him"; for before he was taken he had this testimony, that he pleased God (Hebrews 11:5).

You will Testify

You shall laugh at destruction and famine, and you shall not be afraid of the beasts of the earth (Job 5:22).

So, the Lord told Paul to get up and cheer up. In a way, He was asking Paul to stop being depressed about something which he had obviously been forewarned about. Agabus the prophet prophesied what was awaiting Paul at Jerusalem, so he should have known that unavoidable difficulties were before him. Also, he had the Lord's assurance from his prison cell when He told him, *Paul – I promise this thing you are going through will not destroy you as you think. You certainly cannot die or in fact, they cannot kill you until I permit them. You have my word for it because you still need to get to Rome to testify! (Acts 23:11 – my paraphrase).*

When the Almighty God speaks to you from the middle of your "prison", that you will testify or bear witness, it's a time to start dancing and shouting. "Prisons" are opened at the word of God!

In fact, *get ecstatic* and begin to laugh at your trouble (Job 5:22). You know why? Because you've got a more sure word over and against your problem, and every problem must bow and exit at the word of the Lord. When the Lord says, *you will testify*, it means He has already gone ahead of you, so whatever yoke or prison presently barring you, must lose their grip and be broken so that you can go ahead and testify.

It is like when God told Moses to tell Pharaoh, 'Let my people go that they may worship me on this mountain' (Exod 4:22,23; chpt 5). Well, the Lord said it and went ahead to wait for His people to come through with their sacrifices of praise and thanksgiving! When Pharaoh insisted he would not let God's people go, Pharaoh had one option, either to 'let them go or for him to'; 'move from their way or be removed'. Don't forget you have God's promise according to Isaiah 55:11 that His word "… shall not return to Him void, but it shall accomplish what He please, and it shall prosper in the thing for which He sent it." So, God's word prevailed against Pharaoh and his chariots, and the children of God went out in victory just as the Lord had said.

My friend, what has the Lord said or told you lately? Can I tell you, it will happen just as He said it would! No matter the circumstances, you cannot die until God's word and promises for you are fulfilled. Let's see if Paul will testify as the Lord said, or if it was all final and over for Paul and his ministry.

Our Desires and the Purposes of God

You have caused men to ride over our heads; we went through fire and through water; but You brought us out to rich fulfilment (Psalms 66:12).

So far, Paul has been thoroughly consoled by the words of the Lord. The fact that the Lord had visited him in prison was not only a good thing, but also a good reason to take courage and to be strong.

After the Lord visited him in prison, Paul might have thought to himself, "Yes, I'm in God's perfect will." Or he might have thought, 'I brought this trouble on myself for dismissing earlier warnings', but in any case it was turning out for a worthy purpose.

Although Paul was in prison, from the midst of the same prison he received an assurance about fulfilling his life-long dream of going to Rome. Talk about God ordering the steps of the righteous, this was a perfect example (Psalms. 37:23). Isn't it written as well that, 'God grants and watches over the desires of His people to perform them' and He also would 'perfect His cause concerning His people (Psalms 138:8).

Now, in the most unusual way Paul was beginning to see the unfolding of the fulfilment of his life-long desire and prayer to visit Rome (Rom. 1:15; 15:22; Acts 19:21). Rome was the one place he had always greatly desired to go, but had never been able to. As he completed his course here on earth, Paul very much wished to add Rome to the list of places where he ministered. He prayed about visiting Rome, and attempted on a few occasions to go but was fiercely opposed and hindered, in some cases by Satan.

Granted that, some years and probably many years had already passed when Paul prayed and waited without any real certainties of visiting Rome. Yet, his dream and desire for Rome came at last in the most inconspicuous manner, attesting that God knows exactly how to bring us into our dreams and His purposes.

First, I thank my God through Jesus Christ for you all, that your faith is spoken of throughout the whole world. [9] For God is my witness, whom I serve with my spirit in the gospel of His Son, that without ceasing I make mention of you always in my prayers, [10] making request if, by some means, now at last I may find a way in the will of God to come to you (Roman 1:15).

For this reason I also have been much hindered from coming to you. [23] But now no longer having a place in these parts, and

having a great desire these many years to come to you, ^{24}
whenever I journey to Spain, I shall come to you, For I hope to see
you on my journey, and to be helped on my way there by you, if
first I may enjoy your company for awhile. (Roman 15:22-24)

When these things were accomplished, Paul purposed in the Spirit,
when he had passed through Macedonia and Achaia, to go to
Jerusalem, saying, "After I have been there, I must also see
Rome." (Acts 19:21)

Wisdom for Personal Purpose: Here are four dominant wisdom
keys from Paul's desire for Rome and the circumstances leading to
his trip to Rome:

I. It is one thing to desire but it is another thing when it comes to
the fulfilment of our desires. We have control over what we
desire but not necessarily how and when that desire comes to
fruition. (Proverb 19:21)

II. Concerning our desires, we can plan, pray, hope, and work
towards them, but we need to always wait on the Lord. And just
because our desires seem to delay in coming to pass, it is no
proof that our desires are wrong. Neither does it mean that they
are not God's plans for us, or that God has forgotten about us.

It took Paul many years of waiting, praying and yearning,
planning, and even reaching for his desire to minister in Rome.
He sought very hard to find a 'way in the will of God'.
However, it was going to happen totally beyond the scope of
Paul's own imagination and power to accomplish his desire.
The truth is, desire will always be granted as the Lord designs.
Ours is to write it, work it and wait on it.

> *Then the Lord answered me and said: "Write the vision and*
> *make it plain on tablets, that he may run who reads it. For the*
> *vision is yet for an appointed time; but at the end it will speak,*
> *and it will not lie. Though it tarries, wait for it; because it*
> *will surely come, It will not tarry. (Habakkuk. 1:2-3)*

My Personal Story: When most of my childhood friends had opportunity to live and to study in Western nations, it seemed I was the only person destined to stay just around the Western African region. I had lived in Liberia, Ivory Coast and Ghana, and been to Togo, but never beyond. I heard reports of the many wonderful things my friends were doing and having. Meanwhile, I got *stuck* in Ghana. To admit, I wasn't so keen on travelling to the West and I loved Ghana, because God had already truly blessed me there. But there was, and probably still is today, a common notion that unless one travels to the West, they still hadn't fully realized good life and exposure.

During this period, I remember receiving a letter from an American family who helped me while in Bible College. In their letter they said to me that, if coming to the West was part of my destiny, God would make it happen. That one line of the entire letter was what someone needed to tell me. Ever since I read it, it has been with me even up to today. It has been for me one of my greatest lessons regarding the plans and purposes of God concerning His people and their own desire.

Today, I live in Britain as a citizen and have visited a number of Western nations, exceeding some friends who travelled before I did. When it was time for me to travel to the West from Africa, it was absolutely effortless. Obtaining my citizenship was equally hassle-free. I did not have to queue or appeal for or against anything. The Lord made it possible and caused all things to conspire in my favour because my time came according to the will and purposes of God.

III. The third wisdom key pertains to possible hindrances and oppositions to our desires. This applies to important areas of life and our desires. Whether it is marriage, a career pursuit, ministerial endeavour, spiritual revival; resettling in another country, trusting God for family member salvation, or even setting up a new business; a change in financial or relationship situation, or even the pursuit of happiness, these are all desires at different levels that will require us finding 'a way in the will of God'.

Our desires, and in effect every good desire will have to go through periods of opposition and possible hindrances, and there is nothing wrong with that. Again, whether our desires experience hindrances or not, it is almost a matter of course that they may take time and sometimes a lot of praying and waiting with opposition, but they will come to pass.

For a great and effective door has opened to me, and there are many adversaries (1 Corinthians 16:9). I will be glad and rejoice in Your mercy, for You have considered my trouble; You have known my soul in adversities, [8] And have not shut me up into the hand of the enemy; You have set my feet in a wide place (Psalms 31:7,8).

Leading to the fourth wisdom key, let me add that Paul's angelic visitation in his prison became a crucial point of great assurance. Hopefully, thereafter he began to see himself in Rome already getting on with his itineraries, because the Lord had assured him that he must get to Rome. All of this worked perfectly in favour of Paul's desire and his many years of tedious longing and planning for Rome. That was a miracle considering that Paul, through all of his terrible ordeals including his arrest and imprisonment at Jerusalem, had lost hope of ever seeing Rome in his lifetime. Then, suddenly, he was told by an angel, he must testify in Rome also.

IV. Do you know it is easy to get a miracle from God when our desire falls in line with His purposes? God needed Paul to testify in Rome, and Paul always had a desire to go to Rome. We see similar situation in First Samuel chapters 1and 2, in which God needed a replacement for Eli, the 'backslidden' Priest, and Hannah who was barren also needed a boy child. Because Hannah's desire 'collided' with God's purpose at the time, God then granted Hannah her desire because she promised to give her child back to God for His service.

Again, in Isaiah 6:6-8, when God was looking for a man to send, Isaiah, although he felt unfit, unworthy and unprepared, because he was willing, God healed his weakness and sent him as a prophet to the nations. If you want a miracle, ask or locate what God is saying or doing, or seek where God is going at any given time; make yourself ready, avail yourself, show up and God will use you or send you. Desire what God wants to give, do or use, and you've got your miracle!

But in a great house there are not only vessels of gold and silver, but also of wood and clay, some for honour and some for dishonour. Therefore if anyone cleanses himself from the latter, he will be a vessel for honour, sanctified and useful for the Master, prepared for every good work. [22] Flee also youthful lusts; but pursue righteousness, faith, love, peace with those who call on the Lord out of a pure heart. (2 Timothy 2:20)

God's Divine Design, His Purposes and You: His Ways - Not Yours

❖❖❖

The Road to Rome

Then I said, 'Behold, I have come - in the volume of the book it is written of Me - to do Your will, O God.'" (Hebrew 10:7)

The road to Rome for many will be the road leading to our desires and ultimately the purposes of God for our lives. It leads from a *prison* with a promise from God, delivered by God's servant or an angel, like we had in the case of Paul. First, just because you heard from God through His servant or an angel does not mean it will be all smooth sailing. Spiritually speaking, and by reason of faith, whatever God told you or promised means it is already done. However, in the physical, whatever you were told in promise has to be first processed, delivered and then received. Therefore, when God promised Paul that he will have to bear witness of Him in Rome, in God's mind, that is exactly what Paul was doing in Rome, witnessing, but in the physical, Paul was yet to get to Rome.

In fact, it seemed a long way before Paul even began to think about the possibility of appearing in Rome. Hence, in most cases, the promises of faith, one's own desire, and purpose usually work this way; *you are there, but not quite there yet.* Like Paul, although your purpose and assignment are already foretold, you still have to travel the road to Rome. And the road to Rome lies ahead not behind, so you must go forward. Although the road to Rome is entirely unfamiliar and you have never been that way before, you must still travel the road to get to Rome.

This I believe was Paul's greatest anxiety, despite His faith in God and the fact that he had God's words of assurance on his side. How long, how tedious or treacherous will his journey be, and who will take him and how he was going to get there might have been some genuine questions he had to ask himself. How was Paul going to get to Rome, and what would it take?

Interestingly, the Scripture does not say that the Lord mentioned any other detail of Paul's eventual journey to Rome. So, Paul to a large extent had to grapple with the uneasy suspense surrounding the detail of what form his journey to Rome might take. Of course this was nothing new, but something most people faced with Paul's dilemma would often attempt to do; to try to form and conjecture some detail about what probably lies ahead of them. Why do people like such details? It is a simple human psychology. People naturally fear the unknown. But also, it's so natural with people to avoid and to resist any surprise or suspense that might take away from them the power of control. Generally, human beings whether men or women have great need to be in control. So, when faced with situations that take control away from us, it frustrates us because it works against our ego, and unsettles our delicately 'balanced world'.

Another reason why we prefer to feed on a lot of details is in fact that we love to ride on a good degree of safety. 'Playing it safe' appeals to most people who are often risk averse. For this very reason, and the common belief that, *'seeing is believing',* many detest matters of faith, and for the majority of people, just believing without seeing a thing with the natural eyes is almost like telling them to go across a busy highway blind folded.

But, the truth is, despite our fear and hesitation, when it comes to God and His dealing with His children and those He calls with special purposes, God requires them to leave the *control* over to Him. He literally wants them to attempt every aspect of their journey in faith, as it were, *crossing the busy highway blind folded* but allowing Him to lead them safely to their destination.

Travelling the Road to Rome: the White Cane Principle

Speaking of 'playing it safe' and our unwillingness to venture into the unknown, I will share with you a true story my wife told me about a wonderful man who suffers from vision impairment. This man lived on one of the rounds my wife covered when she was a post-woman. She told me how this man was so alert and how often confident he appeared when he came to his door to receive his parcel. Although he could not see anything physically, he did not hesitate to put his hand out to receive his delivery. She told me, many times as she left his door, she couldn't help thinking, *what if...,* and *what if ...?*

But this is what was extremely remarkable about this visually challenged man. Under his circumstance, he was very independent, and could walk the streets of our city totally unaided except for his white cane. With his cane he navigated the footpaths, sidewalks, crossed the main roads and streets confidently. He did not allow the fear of the *unknown or unseen* to stop him from attempting to live his life to the fullest. He took himself where he wanted to go.

What is there to learn from the attitude of this visually impaired man? It is simple, faith will take you where you don't know nor can see. And when it comes to the promises and purposes of God, faith is of paramount importance. You cannot walk with God, or attain any of His promises or even fulfil His purposes for your life without applying faith. *For without faith it is impossible to please God... (Hebrews 11:6).*

Anyone having to travel *the Road to Rome* will need to travel it like a physically visually impaired person who uses their *white cane* to navigate the unknown and unseen. *For we walk by faith not by sight (2 Corinthians 5:7).* Have you received a word of promise and purpose from God? Then, get your 'white cane' and trust your 'post woman's delivery'. You don't and might even not yet see anything of your desire physically, but you have the Word of God which is your sceptre and a 'white cane'. Of course, you also probably have a man of God in your life who is your 'postman' who delivers your parcels. Just step out in faith.

What is faith? Faith is total confidence in and total surrender to God, and daring to take obedient actions in view of our total trust and confidence in the integrity of our Father, God. Faith means responding boldly to the love and grace of God, and *"...faith is the substance of things hoped for, the evidence of things not seen. (Hebrew 11:1).* The second verse of Hebrews 11 is so crucial and gives a compelling reason for stepping out boldly in faith regarding what you need from God. It says, *"For by it (faith) the elders obtained a good testimony."* Only steps taken in faith guarantee a *good report.* Such steps do succeed and prevail even within impossible situations because even a little step in faith pleases God, to which He also responds generously.

The Bible says that, the only thing that pleases God is *faith*, and also all things are possible to those who believe (Mark 9:23). Let's agree that those who believe are simply people of faith, meaning they are convinced, persuaded and confident regarding the power, ability and promises of God, and as a result they please God. When Peter stepped out of the boat and walked on the water, it was faith. He believed his Master, meaning he was persuaded and confident that if the Lord commanded him to come then he could also step over the raging water of the sea without sinking.

Every Christian is admonished time and time again, *for we walk by faith, not by sight (2 Corinthians 5:7).* We are also told in 2 Chronicles 20:20, *believe in the Lord your God, and you shall be established; believe His prophets, and you shall prosper."*

Having faith and exercising the faith that God has given us is never optional. It is the only way to get to your *Rome* and to achieve your desire and purpose in life. Consider the visually impaired man I mentioned earlier. When he needed to get to the town or to pay a visit to the hospital or even to visit a newly opened supermarket that everyone was talking about in our city, he went even under treacherous winter weather trusting his cane and instinct to get him there. If he had decided never to venture out, being scared and full of fear of strangers and the thoughts of what might go wrong in the streets, he would have been in the least, very miserable because every street has its share of tangible uncertainties.

More than White Cane

The *white cane* and the natural instinct are a great asset to anyone who suffers from visual impairment. They complement each other and work hand-in-hand. Just as it is in the physical so it is in the spiritual, and we can learn a great deal of spiritual lessons about the wonderful combination of the *white cane* and natural instinct. Without doubt, together the two make their user very versatile in navigating the paths and streets of life. However, natural instinct is like the use of our natural mind compared to the use of our spiritual eyes.

Therefore, natural instinct has great limitations without the 'white cane'. Here is why; because the paths and streets of life are never ever the same, and relying on your natural instinct alone means setting yourself up for bumping into other streets users and into unforeseen obstacles newly erected and positioned along footpaths, sidewalks and thoroughfares. Such obstacles are almost always unexpected, unannounced and sometimes put in place by well-meaning people who don't see them as threats because they simply take things for granted.

But for the visually impaired, unexpected and unannounced objects planted in their usual pathways are some of the greatest threats to their wellbeing and freedom.

Because they have no control over who does what on our streets, the wisest and safest option to adopt and adapt is not to rely on the natural instinct alone. As powerful as it may be, it tends to draw too much on experience and familiarity, and does not always trigger to pre-empt or hint changes in situations and circumstances as we expect. Your best and most reliable options therefore will be to stay with what works even when things change.

The *white cane* may not necessarily pre-empt changes unless changes in the form of new postings along usual paths come into close range. However, the *white cane* is adapted to assist its user to detect present and imminent danger. Compared to natural instinct, the *white cane* is more reliable and hardly would fail to detect the unexpected which lies in the way, and helps its users to avoid approaching dangers and possible collision in their way.

Similarly, your *white cane* helps you to navigate your way around obstacles and hindrances that stand in your way. Even though you hold them in your hands and carry them about, *white canes* are like your pathfinders and instructors telling you if it is safe to keep going, to break, or to turn. They work like a compass that locates a landmark from which you determine where you are, and want to possibly be. Hence, the *white cane* is so useful.

I have made some comparison between the use and importance of the *white cane* and our natural instinct to underscore an important fact of life. That all of humanity, especially those who are called by God with specific purposes, could somewhat be likened to the physically visually impaired on the streets of life, travelling the *Road to Rome.* To arrive safely at our destinations, we cannot just solely depend on our natural instinct, as some unfortunately do. It will require the combination of both the natural instinct as in the use of our natural minds for planning, but then mainly the use of the *white cane,* as in the use of the Word of God and faith, which are a safe and sure way to get to where God wants us to be.

Let the road get rocky, things shift and change, but the Word of God abides forever and remains very versatile to help us navigate our way around the obstacles of life (Matt 24:35).

Let the road be hard and long, we will certainly overcome and attain our destination by faith. *And this is the victory that has overcome the world - our faith (1 John 5:4).* Our minds and of course our natural instinct may fail and get us into trouble sometimes, but the Word of God will dig us out of those very troubles. The Word of God remains our light in dark places, and it is the shepherd's Rod that pulls us back in line when we break ranks. The Word is our staff that assures and comforts us through the dangers of the unforeseen, the unknown and our Lord Himself is He who directs our very path (Psalms 23).

Hear how the Word of God ties all this together:

Yea, though I walk through the valley of the shadow of death, I will fear no evil; For You are with me; Your rod and Your staff, they comfort me. (Psalms 23:4)

Heaven and earth will pass away, but My words will by no means pass away. (Matt. 24:35)

Your word is a lamp to my feet and a light for my path. (Psalms 119:105)

The entrance of Your words gives light; It gives under- standing to the simple. (Psalms 119:130)

Sanctify them by Your truth. Your word is truth (John 17:17). Then Jesus said to those Jews who believed Him, "If you abide in My word, you are My disciples indeed. And you shall know the truth, and the truth shall make you free." (John 8:31,32)

How can a young man cleanse his way? By taking heed according to Your word. Your word I have hidden in my heart, that I might not sin against You. (Psalms 119:9 & 11)

Trust in the Lord with all your heart, And lean not on your own understanding; In all your ways acknowledge Him, And He shall direct your paths (Proverbs 3:5,6)

God will Qualify You

God promotes conquerors! Despite Paul's initial excitement about going to Rome, there were real obstacles and hurdles to overcome. Paul definitely received God's word and promise concerning Rome, and that same word became Paul's *white cane*. He had never been a stranger to obstacles and oppositions, except that going to Rome was new and different. Certainly, Paul had already had his fair share of difficult oppositions in life while trying to do God's will and trying to get on with God's purposes.

Reading through most of his letters we glean that Paul himself considered his difficult past and experiences to be perfect training grounds to prepare him for his future challenges. He learned a great deal from his past experiences and managed to come to definite conclusions about real hindrances that stand in the way of personal desires and God's purposes for His people. In Romans 8:37-38 and 2 Corinthians 11:22-30, Paul makes reference to his challenges and to some extent, infers about other difficulties he had to endure while trying to fulfil his God given purpose:

Yet in all these things we are more than conquerors through Him who loved us. [38] For I am persuaded that neither death nor life, nor angels nor principalities nor powers, nor things present nor things to come, [39] nor height nor depth, nor any other created thing, shall be able to separate us from the love of God which is in Christ Jesus our Lord. (Romans 8:37-38)

Are they Hebrews? So am I. Are they Israelites? So am I. Are they the seed of Abraham? So am I. [23] Are they ministers of Christ? I speak as a fool - I am more: in labours more abundant, in stripes above measure, in prisons more frequently, in deaths often. From the Jews five times I received forty stripes minus one. [25] Three times I was beaten with rods; once I was stoned; three times I was shipwrecked; a night and a day I have been in the deep; [26] in journeys often, in perils of waters, in perils of robbers, in perils of my own countrymen, in perils of the Gentiles, in perils in the city, in perils in the wilderness, in perils in the sea, in perils among false brethren; [27] *in weariness and toil, in sleeplessness often, in hunger and thirst, in fastings often, in cold and nakedness - besides the other things, what comes upon me daily: my deep concern for all the churches.* [29] *Who is weak, and I am not weak? Who is made to stumble, and I do not burn with indignation?* [30] *If I must boast, I will boast in the things which concern my infirmity. (2 Corinthians 11:22-30)*

Let me just remind you before we go any further, that our God will not just thrust you onto the *Road to Rome* without initial training for the road ahead. He prepares you through life's little experiences for the big event, so that you can have an advantage, and the wisdom of hindsight. This may be an equivalent of your curriculum vitae (CV) when you apply for a job or seek promotion.

Your CV for the *Roman Road* or the road to Rome always ensures that you already have answers to questions like: 'What have you been through?' 'How did you make it through?' 'And what skills do you bring to your new task and assignment of God?'

David, the youngest son of Jesse, an astute shepherd boy had a similar CV when he appeared before King Saul. David's CV qualified him to face Goliath. When he was before King Saul, he courageously presented himself as the one who could 'cut down' Goliath whom everyone else was cowering away from. He said to Saul, who initially had some reservations about David:

"Your servant used to keep his father's sheep, and when a lion or a bear came and took a lamb out of the flock, [35] *I went out after it and struck it, and delivered the lamb from its mouth; and when it arose against me, I caught it by its beard, and struck and killed it.* [36] *Your servant has killed both lion and bear; and this uncircumcised Philistine will be like one of them, seeing he has defied the armies of the living God."* [37] *Moreover David said, "The Lord, who delivered me from the paw of the lion and from the paw of the bear, He will deliver me from the hand of this Philistine." And Saul said to David, "Go, and the Lord be with you!" (1 Samuel 17:34-37).*

How does all of what we've said so far relate to you?

First, if God brought you before a challenge, it simply means you can overcome that challenge. Remember 1Corinthians 10:13, *No temptation has overtaken you except such as is common to man; but God is faithful, who will not allow you to be tempted beyond what you are able, but with the temptation will also make the way of escape, that you may be able to bear it.*

Second, God always qualifies those He chooses for His purposes through life's situations. Your qualifying training meets the requirement for where He intends to take you in the future. So don't dismiss today's challenges and victories. Like David, you need the acquired skills and expertise for future victories and challenges when they present themselves. (See 2 Timothy 2:20-21; Isaiah 48:10-11; Proverbs 17:3)

The Thoughts of God

Sometime ago, the Lord taught me something about how He goes about His business of dealing with His children in relation to His purposes. My lesson came from a popular verse of Isaiah 55 which is regularly quoted, often without due regard for what exactly the Father really means after He breathed those powerful words. What He tells us in that little passage is so profound that when you get it, you will do anything the Lord commands you to do and go anywhere He asks you to go. Not only that, but you will also begin to appreciate the wisdom of God for your life in every situation you find yourself in. Most certainly, grasping the true revelation of the text will be a great source of peace and rest in any stormy trial.

Let's hear exactly what that passage says. It says,

> *"For My thoughts are not your thoughts, nor are your ways My ways," says the Lord.* [9] *"For as the heavens are higher than the earth, so are My ways higher than your ways, And My thoughts than your thoughts.*

"For as the rain comes down, and the snow from heaven, And do not return there, But water the earth, And make it bring forth and bud, That it may give seed to the sower And bread to the eater, [11] So shall My word be that goes forth from My mouth; It shall not return to Me void, But it shall accomplish what I please, And it shall prosper in the thing for which I sent it (Isaiah 55:8-11)

Such a terse passage, but eternally huge, and for me it powerfully pulls together other texts and thoughts of the Bible. For example when God says that *His word never returns to Him void or empty, but always accomplishes what He pleases (Isaiah 55:11)*, do you know what that means? Well, He doesn't have to negotiate His desires, thoughts or actions with any other, and absolutely nothing can hinder His purpose and cause (Job 42:2). He is so free to do as He likes anytime, anywhere, anyhow and with whomever or whatever He chooses. Yes, that's our God; that's the God of Abraham, Isaac and Jacob, the Almighty God to whom all of creation bows; the Sovereign One.

This relates to you as well. That whatever the Lord has decided concerning you, nobody can decide otherwise. Doors He has already opened before you are opened and those He has shut are shut unless He opens them again for whatever reason that He finds pleasing. So, don't worry too much about what your enemy or Satan is planning or doing. If the Lord does not permit them, (which I know He won't) they cannot even come near you. That's the reason why the Psalmist says in Psalm 91:5-8,

You shall not be afraid of the terror by night, Nor of the arrow that flies by day, [6] Nor of the pestilence that walks in darkness, Nor of the destruction that lays waste at noonday. [7] A thousand- may fall at your side, and ten thousand at your right hand; But it shall not come near you. [8] Only with your eyes shall you look, And see the reward of the wicked.

And again,

I lay down and slept; I awoke, for the Lord sustained me. I will not be afraid of ten thousands of people who have set themselves against me all around (Ps 3:5-6).

Are you getting excited already?! I still need to tell you what the Lord showed me and why I pulled out the passage in Isaiah 55:8-11 in the first place. This is all happening in verse 8, and I'd like you to read it again because it is so easy to misread or misquote it thinking that you already know what it says. Here it is; *"For My thoughts are not your thoughts, nor are your ways My ways," says the Lord.* Hope you got it this time.

Okay, let's break it down. The first part of the text regards the 'thoughts of God' and He is categorically clear that His thoughts are not ours. Let's put it this way; God's thoughts are only God's thoughts and not human's thoughts. So then, whenever God thinks or bears a thought, it is God's thought and that thought is only God's. His thoughts are thoughts that are absolutely His, the way He alone thinks. Therefore it is very logical to say that His thoughts are not ours, period. I know what you are thinking, but think about this also. Can you think and bear thoughts as almighty as the Almighty God would?

I know we have *the mind of Christ (1 Corinthians 2:16)*, but the mind of Christ is not our mind, it is *the Mind of Christ!* Notice that the same verse that says we have the mind of Christ also raises a serious rhetorical question; *who has known the mind of the Lord that he may instruct Him?"*. I will leave it at this point, but only to stress the fact that, God's thoughts are His thoughts and are not like any other you know, except for those He has revealed and acted upon for His purposes.

Yet still, our God abides sovereign and above all, to be able to think and to bear thoughts in ways that we are not necessarily familiar with. Neither can we pin Him to a certain way of thinking regarding His will, purposes and ways for us. But we have sufficient evidence in Scripture that our God is always true to His Word and promises towards us, that as a loving Father He always seeks our good.

In fact we were created for His pleasure so that He delights in us, and "*... works in you both to will and to do for His good pleasure (Philippians 2:13).* It is with this understanding that the Psalmist exclaims,

> *Let them shout for joy and be glad, Who favour my righteous cause; And let them say continually, "Let the Lord be magnified, Who has pleasure in the prosperity of His servant." (Psalms 35:27. also see Ps. 149:4)*

Similarly, the prayer and desire of the Apostle John who by the inspiration of the Holy Spirit prays for our all-round prosperity, demonstrates just how God delights in His people doing well in all things at all times: *"Beloved, I pray that you may prosper in all things and be in health, just as your soul prospers (3 John 1:2)."*
But when it comes to the Father's thoughts, as a whole, one of the more direct and bold statement of His thoughts is what He says in Jeremiah 29:11: *For I know the thoughts that I think toward you, says the Lord, thoughts of peace and not of evil, to give you a future and a hope.*

Precisely, these are God's thoughts, ... *of peace and not of evil, to give you a future and a hope.* Now, let someone think otherwise about it or try to contradict His thoughts concerning you, and it will change nothing, because His thoughts are not our thoughts. No one feeling envious can just rise and say, 'well I know what God thoughts are concerning you but I will superimpose my kind of thinking and thought on you!' That would be a *foul* that strictly deserves a red-card of the blood of Jesus. That one acting out of arrogance and ignorance would collide only with powers beyond description for violating the Lord's thoughts toward you according to Psalms 105:15 and 1Chronicles 16:21-23 - *Saying, Do not touch My anointed ones, and do My prophets no harm.* Concerning the purposes of God and the business of carrying out the purposes of God, God's thought will always prevail: *Many are the plans in a man's heart, but it is the Lord's purpose that prevails (Prov19:21).*

The Ways of God

The ways of God are even much more interesting and challenging when you consider how He presents it in Isaiah 55:8. Herein lies the true power and revelation of this verse. Whereas God says His thoughts are not our thoughts, when it comes to His ways, He says, our ways are not His ways. Have you seen it, now? Know that, it is one thing if the Father says, 'My ways are not your ways', but when He says, 'your ways are not My ways', He is making a very subtle point and certainly there is a difference in how His statement reads compared to how we have always quoted Him.

We have always thought He said, '*My ways are not your ways*' but He actually says, '*your ways are not My ways*'. It is okay to say 'His thoughts are not our thoughts', but when it comes to His ways, then our ways are not His ways. God wants to set the record straight. It appears to me that He is taking exception to some assumptions that have already been made regarding His ways. Somehow, He is taking issue with either a misunderstanding or a somewhat popular trend, and the way we look at things and deal with things at our level, assuming He concords and approves a certain way of doing or looking at things. The danger here is the temptation to easily transfer or impose upon divine ways, and on God our human ways of looking at issues and dealing with situations (cf Ps 50:21). That is why I believe more than anything, God in this case, is firm about re-educating us regarding His ways.

By saying 'Your ways are not My ways', He is saying 'please, don't impose your ways on me, and in fact you cannot and will never succeed in imposing your ways on my ways'. His ways are His ways; your ways are your ways, period. It is futile to even begin to attempt to think that I can make my ways His ways. Go into tantrum as kids do, spin on your head, but as Proverbs 19:21 says, only His ways (purpose) will prevail. Have you ever seen a child who thought just because he doesn't like school, he can clasp onto his daddy's trouser leg, scream violently as a way of getting his dad to change his mind?

Well, no good daddy changes his mind about sending his child to school just because he or she displayed some kind of great acrobatic manoeuvre. This is the one thing the children of Israel never grasped in their entire walk with God, right from Egypt through the wilderness and into Canaan, the Promised Land. It cost them an entire generation.

Whenever Israel tried to impose their ways on God, He let them have their way only if they were ready for the consequences, and on all occasions, it was disastrous in the end. Whether it was in asking for a human king to rule them as did other nations or their desire to have bread of their own fancy, the outcome was the same.

And they sinned yet more against him by provoking the most High in the wilderness. [18]And they tempted God in their heart by asking meat for their lust. [19]Yea, they spake against God; they said, Can God furnish a table in the wilderness? [20]Behold, he smote the rock, that the waters gushed out, and the streams over-flowed; can he give bread also? can he provide flesh for his people? [21]Therefore the Lord heard this, and was wroth: so a fire was kindled against Jacob, and anger also came up against Israel; [22]Because they believed not in God, and trusted not in his salvation: [23] Though he had commanded the clouds from above, and opened the doors of heaven, [24]And had rained down manna upon them to eat, and had given them of the corn of heaven. [25]Man did eat angels' food: he sent them meat to the full. [26]He caused an east wind to blow in the heaven: and by his power he brought in the south wind. [27]He rained flesh also upon them as dust, and feathered fowls like as the sand of the sea: [28]And he let it fall in the midst of their camp, round about their habitations. [29]So they did eat, and were well filled: for he gave them their own desire; [30]They were not estranged from their lust. But while their meat was yet in their mouths, [31]The wrath of God came upon them, and slew the fattest of them, and smote down the chosen men of Israel. [32]For all this they sinned still, and believed not for his wondrous works. [33]Therefore their days did he consume in vanity, and their years in trouble. [34]When he slew them, then they sought him: and they returned and enquired early after God. [35]And they remembered that God was their rock, and the high God their redeemer. [36]Nevertheless they did flatter him with their mouth, and they lied unto him with their tongues. [37]For their heart was not right with him, neither were they steadfast in his covenant.
(Psalms 78:17 -37KJV)

When it comes to the thoughts and ways of God, there are a few things we must know. Naturally you cannot think God's thoughts, but you can know His thoughts. For example in Jeremiah 29:11, He makes reference to His thoughts for us, saying, *For I know the thoughts that I think toward you, says the Lord, thoughts of peace and not of evil, to give you a future and a hope.* However, you cannot pick and choose His thoughts, even though it is possible to know His thoughts. It is also one thing knowing His thoughts and is another believing or living out His thoughts for you.

It is hard to think that everyone will always believe and live out God's thoughts for them as they should. But if you need your life to glorify God and to reflect His thoughts concerning you, then you will need to deliberately apply yourself to carefully searching His thoughts, and consistently walk accordingly as He makes you able.

He may delight in us, just as the Psalmist says in Psalm 149:4, however, God will never choose our ways nor make our ways His ways. We must rise to His ways which are always good and perfect. Never expect the Father to do your ways unless your ways are first and foremost His ways for you, and this is so crucial for anyone trying to pursue God's purpose for their life.

For God to choose your ways, we would have a scenario of an irresponsible father relinquishing fatherhood to a child, whereby the child rules in the home. And woe to you if the head of the home is a child (Eccles. 10:16). A scenario of this kind of home would look like scenes from the popular motion pictures, *Home Alone, and Bruce Almighty.* Like in *Bruce Almighty,* the main character soon realizes the limit of what man can do and what only God is capable of doing. It really didn't take too long to recognize that God is the One in absolute control, and only God can do what He does. For human beings to choose to have their ways is to invite chaos without measure.

How bizarre and awfully interesting and dangerous would it be if our ways were God's ways?

Think about a day you were having a bad time and were all moody and mixed-up, that certainly would be the day the bottom of the world would fall off. For a world like that, anyone could just decide, 'well, I don't like the way *John* looks, he is just kind of annoying, so I will simply let today be his last day on earth', and that will be it! Even you would be in trouble because your ex-boy friend or ex-girlfriend, who has just been considering getting rid of you, could have their way granted.

Think about the odd prayers commonly dubbed, *dangerous prayers* asking for the head of someone who dislikes you. Well, thank God that His ways are supreme, sovereign, and superior, far removed from the realm of superstitions, pettiness and bitterness. So that even if you had wished or others had wished and thought that you were weird and stupid, you are not. You are how God sees you and relates with you; one who is 'fearfully and wonderfully made (Ps. 139:14).

There is much more to the thoughts and ways of God concerning us. But, let me attempt to explain what I consider to be the fullness of God's thoughts and ways concerning His people including you. God says *"there is hope in your future... (Jerem. 31:17)*. However, *"there are many plans in a man's heart, nevertheless the Lord's counsel that will stand" (Prov. 19:21)*. God says, *" I am the Lord, Who makes all things, Who stretches out the heavens all alone, Who spreads abroad the earth by Myself; Who frustrates the signs of the babblers, And drives diviners mad; Who turns wise men backward, and makes their knowledge foolishness" (Isa.44:24-25)*.

In His unlimited wisdom, *"He leads counselors away plundered, and makes fools of the judges." (Job 12:17)*. In His love, wisdom, and compassion, God *raises the poor out of the dust, and lifts the needy out of the ash heap, that He may seat him with princes (to inherit the throng of glory)—With the princes of His people. He grants the barren woman a home, like a joyful mother of children. Praise the Lord! (Psalms 113:7-9; 1Samuel 2:8)*.

Through His great power, *"the Lord brings the counsel of the nations to nothing; He makes the plans of the peoples of no effect"* *(Psalms 33:10)*. Because of the vastness of His understanding, He boldly ask;, *"Who has directed the Spirit of the Lord or as His counselor has taught Him?" (Isaiah 40:13)*.

No wonder then the Apostle Paul exclaims, *"Oh, the depth of the riches both of the wisdom and knowledge of God! How unsearchable are His judgments and His ways past finding out! For who has known the mind of the Lord? Or who has become His counselor?" (Romans 11:34)*. In view of God's majestic highness in thoughts, deeds and His ways, we therefore admit, only *"In Him also we have obtained an inheritance, being predestined according to the purpose of Him who works all things according to the counsel of His will," (Ephesians 1:11)*.

It gives great confidence to know and to think that concerning the purposes of God, He alone, not man, not even ourselves, can dictate the terms. God who knew you even before you were born, has called you and ordained you to perform His good purposes about which He has counselled Himself. It's never your thoughts nor your ways, but God's. He will certainly watch over His word to perform it. (see Jeremiah 1:5-10). That's His will for your life!

> *For whom He foreknew, He also predestined to be conformed to the image of His Son, that He might be the firstborn among many brethren. [30] Moreover whom He predestined, these He also called; whom He called, these He also justified; and whom He justified, these He also glorified (Romans 8:29-30).*

Discerning the Mysteries of God's Ways for His Purposes: Don't Be Trapped by What You See

❖❖❖

The Mysteries of His Ways

He made known His ways to Moses, His acts to the children of Israel. (Psalms 103:7)

In reality, what we often consider the ways of God are in fact the acts of God. When it comes to His ways, God normally chooses whom He reveals His ways to (See Matthew 13:11-17; Mark 4:11-12; Acts 28:26). Isaiah declares, *"And I will wait on the Lord, Who hides His face from the house of Jacob; and I will hope in Him"* *(Isaiah 8:17).* Job also says concerning God, *"... and when He hides His face, who then can see Him, whether it is against a nation or a man alone?" (Job 34:29).*

The fact that God "hides His face" implies something very characteristic about the nature of His ways, and to a vast extent the role of His sovereignty in relation to His ways. That means, in reference to God's sovereignty, He is under no obligation to "show

His face" or to reveal His ways over which He alone exercises absolute authority, and would use His liberty within His sovereign rights at anytime, to reveal His ways to whomever He chooses, and to those who also seek His ways and wait on Him (Ps 25:4,9,14).

Matthew 13:10-17 gives us a more concrete reference to how the ways of God work, especially when you look at the response of the Lord Jesus to a burning question from His disciples regarding speaking to others in parables. It is clear that in His answer to the disciples' question, the Lord refers to the prophecies of Isaiah, and leaves no ambiguity about the fact that some people, in spite of what they hear and see, do not understand nor perceive. Their hearts have simply grown dull, to the extent that they no longer understand with their hearts so as to turn or to repent and to be healed. However, when it comes to His own disciples whom He has already chosen to make His ways known to, the Lord says to them, *"But blessed are your eyes for they see, and your ears for they hear; for assuredly, I say to you that many prophets and righteous men desired to see what you see, and did not see it, and to hear what you hear, and did not hear it" (vrs 16-17).*

We also have a similar situation recorded in Luke 24 after the Lord Jesus rose from the dead and appeared to two men walking on the Road to Emmaus. Although He drew near, walked and talked with them for about seven miles the men did not recognise the Lord. Their hearts even 'burned' within them when He opened the Scriptures to them, but they still could not see nor understand that it was the Lord Jesus who was reasoning and conversing with them. Their hearts were dull of understanding, and in fact, the passage says that *"But their eyes were restrained, so that they did not know Him" (Luke 24:16).*

When do the men finally recognise it was the Lord? Once He decided to make Himself known to them at super. Immediately, they perceived it was the Lord, and He then vanished from their sight. Although their hearts had 'burned' all along, it took the Lord opening the eyes of the two men, for them to recognise Him.

Moses the man who spoke with God face-to-face, had to humbly ask and petition the Father to make His ways known to him, saying *"If you are pleased with me, teach me your ways so I may know you and continue to find favour with you..." (Exodus 33:11,13).* David in Psalms 25:4 prayed, *"*S*how me Your ways, O Lord, teach me Your paths".* Both men knew the importance of God's ways, knowing it was impossible to know and to continue to find favour with God without Him first revealing to them His ways.

Secondly, that it was the prerogative of God to make His ways known and to teach His ways only to those He freely chooses and He is pleased with. Thirdly, the fact that Moses and David sought God to show them His ways, and God was willing, is good indication that one can literally seek the ways of God. However, it remains in God's power to choose to reveal His ways. To all who seek Him, God says, "if you shall diligently seek Me with all your heart, then you shall find Me" (Jer. 29:13), and He is also the rewarder of those who wholeheartedly seek Him (Heb. 11:6).

Now, clearly it is no secret that, many believers often stop at knowing the "acts of God," and are happy to have some form of knowledge about the "acts of God". They are, all too often, happy for God to show them His acts alone, and therefore have no urgency in themselves for the greater challenge and privilege of knowing God's ways. Such are those who are ever so pleased just to settle for the 'hand' of God and not the 'heart' of God.

On the other hand, those who delight in God's ways and also find His ways as He makes it known to them; such people have greater advantage over the rest, whose only desire is to see and know God's acts. People who stay at the level of the "acts of God" only follow His acts, and have an experience of God that is limited to the *mere* display of the works and powers of God in the earth. They usually miss out on the fullness of His ways, and the revelation of *'as it is in heaven'* which is God's divine intents and purposes which He carries in His heart for His people and nations.

For example, take the text that says, *surely the Lord God does nothing, unless He reveals His secret to His servants the prophets. (Amos 3:7)*. Implied in this text is the fact that someone is going to gain a privileged foreknowledge, ahead of others, concerning whatever the Lord intends to do on the earth, before it is done. It also means that, the majority will only come to know what the Lord intends to do after it has been done, which I call an *afterward knowledge,* normally pinned to empirical or existential experience. Such knowledge may not necessarily be your own. Someone told you so, or you know or believe because you have now seen it with your physical eyes!

As we will see later, God's ways are established in a true and continuous relationship, and His acts are seen and experienced in His performance of what He does for us, including His miracles. And it is possible to have His acts, see His acts, without really knowing Him in a personal relationship. For example, I can be in one place but my gifts and handy work could be with a perfect stranger somewhere in another place because someone asked on their behalf or because I sent them a gift knowing that they needed it. (*God makes His sun rise on the evil and on the good, and sends rain on the just and on the unjust. Matthew 5:45)*.

How many people on earth today have God's gift of life but still do not know Him personally and have no relationship with Him. Some even deny the existence of the very God who has given them the life and health that they have.

Moses and the Ways of God

*Then Moses said to the Lord, "See, You say to me, 'Bring up this people.' But You have not let me know whom You will send with me. Yet You have said, 'I know you by name, and you have also found grace in My sight.' Now therefore, I pray, if I have found grace in Your sight, **show me now Your way, that I may know You and that I may find grace in Your sight**. And consider that this nation is Your people." And He said, "**My Presence will go with you, and I will give you rest**." Then he said to Him, "If Your Presence does not go with us, do not bring us up from here. For how then will it be known that Your people and I have found grace in Your sight, except You go with us? So we shall be separate, Your people and I, from all the people who are upon the face of the earth." So the Lord said to Moses, "I will also do this thing that you have spoken; for you have found grace in My sight, and I know you by name." (Ex. 33:12-17)*

Moses was a man of purpose, who knew what it required to sustain his walk and relationship with God in pursuing God's purposes. He knew what to ask for in order to have both the 'heart' and 'hands' of God at the same time. He knew their order of priority, knowing that God's 'Heart' came before His 'Hand'. *Moses teaches us to get God's 'heart' and then His 'hand' will also follow.*

To have God on His side always, Moses chose to ask for God to show him His ways, that he would know God. The question is, has Moses not known God all this while? He experienced the 'burning bush', he was on Mount Sinai, and saw many miracles in Pharaoh's Egypt, in the Red Sea and in the wilderness. Well, those were the 'acts of God' and they have their place. But, when it comes to knowing God, it requires Him revealing to you His ways. His ways come by His presence and His presence reveals His ways as we come to know and experience Him in person. For New Testament believers, we have now in person, the very enduring presence of God in His Holy Spirit, just as He was also with Moses.

For He said, "Surely they are My people, Children who will not lie." So He became their Saviour. In all their affliction He was afflicted, And the Angel of His Presence saved them; in His love and in His pity He redeemed them; And He bore them and carried them all the days of old. **But they rebelled and grieved His Holy Spirit;** *So He turned Himself against them as an enemy, And He fought against them. Then he remembered the days of old, Moses and his people, saying: " Where is He who brought them up out of the sea with the shepherd of His flock?* **Where is He who put His Holy Spirit within them, Who led them by the right hand of Moses,** *with His glorious arm, dividing the water before them to make for Himself an everlasting name, who led them through the deep, as a horse in the wilderness, that they might not stumble?" as a beast goes down into the valley, and the Spirit of the Lord causes him to rest, so You lead Your people, to make Yourself a glorious name. (Isaiah 63:8-14)*

King David, 'the man after God's heart' associates the Presence of God with the Spirit of God:

Do not cast me away from Your presence, and do not take Your Holy Spirit from me (Psalms 51:11).

The Lord Jesus Christ tells us that, not only will the Holy Spirit of God help and teach us, but He also is definitely God living with us and in us:

And I will pray the Father, and He will give you another Helper, that He may abide with you forever - the Spirit of truth, whom the world cannot receive, because it neither sees Him nor **knows Him; but you know Him, for He dwells with you and will be in you.** *I will not leave you orphans; I will come to you. But the Helper, the Holy Spirit, whom the Father will send in My name, He will teach you all things, and bring to your remembrance all things that I said to you. "A little while longer and the world will see Me no more, but you will see Me. Because I live, you will live also. At that day you will know that I am in My Father, and you in Me, and I in you. (John 14:16-20,26)*

That promise of God, to be with us, and to live in us is realized in the Lord Jesus Christ breathing on us the Holy Spirit; the breath of life as it was in the beginning, "and God breathed on man and he became a living soul" (Gen. 2:7).

And when He had said this, He breathed on them, and said to them, "Receive the Holy Spirit. (John 20:22)

Who else knows God as intimately and who else is as well positioned to reveal the ways of the Father to us better than the Holy Spirit of God? Who is more capable of revealing the purposes of God to us and helping us to pursue and to elegantly complete God's purposes for our lives than the Holy Spirit? *'For it is God who works in you both to will and to do for His good pleasure' (Philip. 2:13).* Hence, when it comes to the purposes of God we need Him – we need the Holy Spirit of God to reveal the Father and His ways to us fully.

Israel and the Ways of God

Whereas Moses asked to know God's ways which God obliged to do, God chose to make known only *His acts to the children of Israel (Psalms 103:7).* What a difference! No wonder the children of Israel always remained just *'children'* of Israel, never maturing into *'adults'*, but always having great need to limit their feed to the *milk of the Word. For everyone who partakes only of milk is unskilled in the word of righteousness, for he is a babe (Hebrews 5:13). As newborn babes, desire the pure milk of the word, that you may grow thereby (1Peter 2:2).*

The children of Israel murmured, complained and rebelled; then they grieved the Holy Spirit of God (Isaiah 63:10). They always wanted to have and to do things their own ways, instead of God's ways. They resolved that it was always going to be their ways or no other way (Psalm 78:18). No matter how difficult things turned for them when they opted to follow their own devices, they still did not seek God's ways, but rather preferred just His acts over His ways. Obviously, God showed them His acts!

Evidently, most *children* love to think that what really is important in life is their parents 'acting' for them all the time. They work it out in their heads that parents are for 'acts'. So, what they often do is to make interesting requests and demands like – *buy me this, and do for me that, or simply, will you come, or will you go*....

In response to their persistent demands, reinforced by their sheer lack of understanding and appreciation for the ways of God, God showed the children of Israel His acts, which were limited to the display of His works and power. He simply lent them 'His Hands', instead of the revelation of His *Person* (presence) and 'Heart'.

Remember, His ways are 'His Heart', His intent and purposes, His secrets; all of which cumulate into knowing Him, His persons and having His presence. By His acts, He showed the children of Israel many mighty signs, wonders and miracles both in the heavenly realms and on earth. God caused manna and quails to rain down on earth. He split the Red sea and congealed the ground in the midst of the water. God overthrew Pharaoh and his chariots, drove enemy armies from before Israel, caused water to flow out of rocks, and many more miracles.

Yet, the children of Israel rebelled, and still turned to other gods of their own fancy, gods which in fact were really no gods but lifeless forms of their imagination. They rejected the Holy and Living God who delivered them from their captivity, adversities and tribulations and who bore them on eagle's wings (1Samuel 10:19). Jeremiah says that, they actually chose to walk according to their own plans and to follow the evil dictates of their own hearts and ways (Jeremiah 18:12).

Jeremiah's assessment seems to be the most prevalent trouble with believers who remain trapped and strapped to the "acts" of God alone. They tend to be spiritually wishy-washy and irresolute in their walk as believers. And it doesn't really matter how much of God's 'acts' in miracles they see and experience. Like the children of Israel, they still wobble in faith, integrity and character towards God. Hence in a way, the 'acts' of God is never enough to bring such people to true Christian commitment. It only serves to cause them to expect the next signs or miracles.

People going after the 'acts' of God will move land and sea, and hop from one miracle service to another and never get settled or planted properly in the house of God where they should flourish (Psalms 92:13). Their desires for signs are so compulsive and insatiable that no amount of signs they see or have can ever suffice: *But although He had done so many signs before them, they did not believe in Him (John 12:37).* As a pastor, you can simply tell which one in your congregation has come just for the 'acts' – that is the 'Hands' of God and not 'His ways' or His 'Heart'.

Throughout the Gospels, the Lord Jesus encountered many such signs seekers and He never restrained from rebuking them. His response in those instances was almost always predictable. Just as He would not submit to Satan, the tempter's demands for a sign, because it was construed to be *tempting* God (Matt. 4:7); likewise He did not oblige when the Pharisees, Sadducees and the surrounding crowds demanded signs. Is it possible then that the majority of those driven more by the signs and 'acts' of God, who are not equally driven by a true appetite and appreciation for the 'ways' of God, might be vulnerable to the influence of Satan, and could be *tempting* God without even knowing it?

Let's see how the Lord Jesus dealt with blatant signs seeking and sign driven followers:

I. *The Scribes, Pharisees and Sadducees*

We have the Scribes and Pharisees whom He described as an 'evil and adulterous generation' probably because they would go after any other 'lovers' and gods that could temporarily *satisfy* their gullible craving. That's nothing but spiritual adultery!

> *Then some of the scribes and Pharisees answered, saying, "Teacher, we want to see a sign from You." But He answered and said to them, "An evil and adulterous generation seeks after a sign, and no sign will be given to it except the sign of the prophet Jonah. For as Jonah was three days and three nights in the belly of the great fish, so will the Son of Man be three days and three*

nights in the heart of the earth. The men of Nineveh will rise up in the judgment with this generation and condemn it, because they repented at the preaching of Jonah; and indeed a greater than Jonah is here. The queen of the South will rise up in the judgment with this generation and condemn it, for she came from the ends of the earth to hear the wisdom of Solomon; and indeed a greater than Solomon is here. (Matt. 12:38-42)

On another occasion, when they confronted the Lord, He referred to the Pharisees and the Sadducees as wicked and adulterous, because they knew what was right but always chose and sought to do their own pleasure, giving blind eyes to what is right. The modern day *Pharisees and Sadducees* will go every length to deceive a man of God, and if possible, use and abuse him, and then afterwards abandon the cause of God for their selfish ambitions.

Then the Pharisees and Sadducees came, and testing Him asked that He would show them a sign from heaven. ² He answered and said to them, "When it is evening you say, 'It will be fair weather, for the sky is red'; ³ and in the morning, 'It will be foul weather today, for the sky is red and threatening.' Hypocrites! You know how to discern the face of the sky, but you cannot discern the signs of the times. A wicked and adulterous generation seeks after a sign, and no sign shall be given to it except the sign of the prophet Jonah." And He left them and departed. (Matt. 16:1-4)

II. *The Gathering Crowd*

Again, here comes *the thickly gathered crowd*, a real mix of the common people and maybe some elites. They have come seeking signs from the Son of God and He will not give them any except that which has already been given, the sign of Jonah. Jesus calls the crowd an 'evil generation', who cannot be compared to the noble people of Nineveh who simply repented by hearing and gladly receiving the Word of God when preached to them.

And while the crowds were thickly gathered together, He began to say, "This is an evil generation. It seeks a sign, and no sign will be given to it except the sign of Jonah the prophet. ³⁰ For as

Jonah became a sign to the Ninevites, so also the Son of Man will be to this generation. [31] The queen of the South will rise up in the judgment with the men of this generation and condemn them, for she came from the ends of the earth to hear the wisdom of Solomon; and indeed a greater than Solomon is here. [32] The men of Nineveh will rise up in the judgment with this generation and condemn it, for they repented at the preaching of Jonah; and indeed a greater than Jonah is here. (Luke 11:29-31)

Are there any lessons to learn from the Lord's reaction to the Sadducees, Pharisees and the crowd who sought signs for signs sake? I believe the Lord's refusal to give and to show a sign just because people required signs, serves an object and principal lesson for our own generation, which has become so sign dependent. Pastors, unfortunately, are under enormous pressure to *perform* signs just to please and to keep people with ever increasing vain appetite for signs. As a result, there's now blatant avoidance of important matters of teaching and establishing believers, which actually produces the signs when believers get to know and to appreciate the ways of God.

Believers and church leaders continue to put the 'cart before the horse'. Unfortunately, we've deviated from the desire to please God and have succumbed to insatiable searching and longing for just signs; *tempting* God as if signs were all that matter. Without doubt, the old way still is the best way, 'seek ye first the Kingdom of God and His righteousness and all these things (including signs) shall follow you' (Matthew 6:33). 'And these signs shall follow all who believe' (Mark 16:17, 18); not all who don't really believe but seek signs selfishly and solely for signs sake. The latter are those who *tempt* God.

His Acts or His Ways? – A Sign Seeker or A Sign Producer?

It is amazing how on every occasion we have seen so far and throughout the Lord's conversations, He only pointed to the one sign of Jonah and then departed; never standing to argue or to prove a point. There was this one occasion when He seemed to teach and re-educate His hearers about what is really important and what God seeks from His people.

> *And when they found Him on the other side of the sea, they said to Him, "Rabbi, when did You come here?" Jesus answered them and said, "Most assuredly, I say to you, you seek Me, not because you saw the signs, but because you ate of the loaves and were filled. **Do not labour for the food which perishes, but for the food which endures to everlasting life,** which the Son of Man will give you, because God the Father has set His seal on Him." Then they said to Him, "What shall we do, that we may work the works of God?"(John 6:25-28)*

The Lord obviously was telling them signs were great; signs were for the children of the kingdom of God, but there's something wrong with just seeking signs for their own sakes. He wanted to drive a point home that it always pays to go beyond the signs and to reach for the One behind the signs. He was literally saying, *go for the heart behind the hand,* and that there is more to life than that which is temporal and fleeting.

Of course, some seemed to have grasped what the Lord Jesus meant, and were soon asking the most important question of purpose; *"What shall we do, that we may work the works of God?"(John 6:28).* Underneath this question lies a powerful desire, wisdom and conviction to break free from the rat race of being a perpetual sign-seeker, or sign-spectator and to become a practicing sign-producer.

It's like Moses asking God, *please show me your way.* That's always the right question and the right request because in as much as God doesn't mind doing things for us, He very much desires to do things with us as His children. This was true for the disciples:

*And they went out and preached everywhere, the Lord **working with them** and confirming the word through the accompanying signs. Amen (Mark 16:20).*

Our Lord Jesus Christ assured us, *he who believes in Me, the works that I do he will do also; and greater works than these he will do, because I go to My Father (John 14:12).* So, instead of seeking signs, or just being spectators of signs, He said we will do them. And instead of following signs, He says signs will rather follow us:

And these signs will follow those who believe: In My name they will cast out demons; they will speak with new tongues; [18] *they will take up serpents; and if they drink anything deadly, it will by no means hurt them; they will lay hands on the sick, and they will recover" (Mark 16:17,18).*

To ensure that all this will happen without fail, He did not just give us His Word of authority, but also the ever abiding presence and power of the Holy Spirit to execute signs, wonders and miracles all the time.

But you shall receive power when the Holy Spirit has come upon you; and you shall be witnesses to Me in Jerusalem, and in all Judea and Samaria, and to the end of the earth" (Acts 1:8)

But the problem with believers is that many do not have, nor do they really desire, the enduring power and the presence of God and the Holy Spirit. They just want the signs. We simply love to put the cart before the horse when it comes to signs; our focus instead is moved away from what and Who is responsible for producing them.

In order to have God's best we need to discern the difference between the 'ways' of God and the 'acts' of God. We can choose like Moses to know God's 'ways' and to also enjoy His 'acts', or selfishly choose as the children of Israel did.

They chose to have God's 'acts' and neglected His 'ways' through which we get to know Him and also get to have what we desire in accordance with God's purposes.

In His 'ways', we can have essential things like rest, peace, protection (Ps. 27:11) and fulfilment. But to have those, including God's supreme rest and peace, will always be as a result of knowing His 'ways' and following through on His 'ways'. By knowing and appreciating His 'ways', we can have both His 'acts' which are His many miracles and His rest, peace and His presence at the same time.

> *Now therefore, I pray, if I have found grace in Your sight, show me now Your way, **that I may know You and that I may find grace in Your sight**. And consider that this nation is Your people." [14] And He said, "**My Presence will go with you, and I will give you rest.**" (Exodus 33:13,14).*

Signs are always great, and they have their place, but there is nothing like knowing the 'ways' of God. Not trusting the God of signs but preferring to see signs before one believes God, really betrays the very basis of our faith. John records how the Lord scolded Thomas saying, *"Thomas, because you have seen Me, you have believed. Blessed are those who have not seen and yet have believed" (John 20:29)*. Similarly the Book of Hebrews argues for us to seek God before His rewards:

> *But without faith it is impossible to please him: for he that cometh to God must believe that he is, and that he is a rewarder of them that diligently seek Him (Hebrews 11:6).*

It is not uncommon to see throughout the Bible that when our hearts first sincerely seek and meet God, either through divine revelation, through supernatural encounters or even by the hearing of Scriptures, the normal measurable outcome will be for the *fear* of God, prayers, and then signs and wonders to take place. This is even very evident with and within the first church in Acts, when the disciples gathered, whether a few or many in number:

And they continued steadfastly in the apostles' doctrine and fellowship, and in breaking of bread, and in prayers. ⁴³And fear came upon every soul: and many wonders and signs were done by the apostles (Acts 2:42,43) Therefore take no thought, saying, What shall we eat? or, What shall we drink? or, Wherewithal shall we be clothed? ³²(For after all these things do the Gentiles seek:) for your heavenly Father knows that you have need of all these things. ³³But seek ye first the kingdom of God, and his righteousness; and all these things shall be added unto you (Matt. 6:31,32)

Those who fail to see the wisdom for going after God's *heart* more than His *hands* are seriously warned by the Lord Jesus Himself, that in their gullibility they could be easily taken and deceived; becoming servants of the devil instead of being servants of God. As Jesus says, *for false christs and false prophets will rise and show signs and wonders to deceive, if possible, even the elect (Mark 13:22).*

This might throw some light on why the Lord was not so keen about showing and giving signs to those whose sole aims were to see signs, either as a proof of Christ's divine power, and sonship or a proof of the existence of God. It is obvious from Mark 13:22 that even *false christs and false prophets,* who are Satan's messengers can show signs and wonders for the purposes of deceiving their victims. That is why, the Lord Jesus Christ is concerned about His followers keeping away from such subtle, and sometimes very blatant, traps of the devil.

The Lord consistently insisted on His people tempering their desire for signs and wonders with good diligence in knowing and believing God, and His Word. He implored us to spend time first seeking to know God's ways.

If you abide in Me, and My words abide in you, you will ask what you desire, and it shall be done for you. By this My Father is glorified, that you bear much fruit; so you will be My disciples. ⁹ "As the Father loved Me, I also have loved you; abide in My love. (John 15:7-9)

*"Therefore I say to you, do not worry about your life, what you will eat or what you will drink; nor about your body, what you will put on. Is not life more than food and the body more than clothing? Look at the birds of the air, for they neither sow nor reap nor gather into barns; yet your heavenly Father feeds them. Are you not of more value than they? Which of you by worrying can add one cubit to his stature? "So why do you worry about clothing? Consider the lilies of the field, how they grow: they neither toil nor spin; and yet I say to you that even Solomon in all his glory was not arrayed like one of these. Now if God so clothes the grass of the field, which today is, and tomorrow is thrown into the oven, will He not much more clothe you, O you of little faith? "Therefore do not worry, saying, 'What shall we eat?' or 'What shall we drink?' or 'What shall we wear?' For after all these things the Gentiles seek. For your heavenly Father knows that you need all these things. **But seek first the kingdom of God and His righteousness, and all these things shall be added to you.** (Matthew 6:25-33)*

Anyone who desires to carry out the purposes of God for their life, and to remain singularly focused, definitely has an awesome responsibility to decide what in their view is more important, the *Hand* or *Heart* of God; or the *Acts* or *Ways* of God. Prioritising in these areas and getting your priority right are the essential keys for doing the impossible in relation to the purposes of God. It's always His ways over yours, and it is always His ways before His acts. Go for His *Hands* and you lose His *Heart*, but go for His Heart, and you have them both. Avoid the enticement of mere sight, and make up your mind to launch deep beneath the glorious and unlimited spiritual wealth of the *Ways* or the *Heart* of God.

Remember, if we are children of God, the Bible says concerning us that "where our treasure is there will our heart be"(Mtt.6:26). How much more our Father in heaven? Surely, *where His heart is there also will His treasure be*. Hence, the golden key to having His treasures is to first go for His *Heart*. Reach surely for His Heart and He will stretch His Hands to you – signs will follow you!

The Open Door to His Purpose: Your Opportunity and the Opposition

❖❖❖

A Bumpy Start

God shall judge the righteous and the wicked, for there is a time there for every purpose and for every work (Eccles. 3:1, 14, 17).

The Apostle Paul has at this time received a sure and sound word from heaven, delivered to him by the Lord, and it came as a source of great encouragement for Paul in his darkest hours. But moments later, he was told another word from the grapevine. Not surprisingly, before the promise that he received from God about Rome could bear any fruit, Paul's persecutors had already formed a plan to kill him the next morning.

By the way, just because you had an angel or the Lord Himself to deliver a good word to you, does not necessarily suggest that you will have no opposition towards the actual delivery of the promise the word contains. We read in the book of Daniel chapter ten, a strange situation in which the Prince of Persia stiffly opposed God's timely word for Daniel; yet the word was dispatched by no ordinary angel, but archangel Gabriel. It took the help of a second archangel, Michael, the field commander of the army of God, to foil the fight of the prince of Persia intended to seize the answer to Daniel's prayers.

So, no sooner had Apostle Paul received a wonderful word of encouragement, and then emerged a great resistance to his word. The resistance came from no mere amateurs. Their threats could not be ignored nor discounted for a fair speech from mouths of babes. They presented a clear and present danger which required immediate attention. The Bible says that, the men in opposition, who were resisting Paul, were religious Jews, more than forty in number who had conspired, *banded together and bound themselves under an oath, saying that they would neither eat nor drink till they had killed Paul (Acts 23:13).* They had already managed to rope in the chief priests and their elders to lure the authorities by sinister means in order to persuade Paul to appear before the council for further questioning, so that they might ambush Paul and kill him.

Now, Paul was not aware of all that was going on, but the God who promised him was surely watching over Paul and watching over His word to perform it. Regarding his purposes for Paul, He was committed to ordering Paul's steps until His word concerning Paul was duly fulfilled without fail.

> *He will not allow your foot to be moved; He who keeps you will not slumber. [4] Behold, He who keeps Israel shall neither slumber nor sleep. [5] The Lord is your keeper; the Lord is your shade at your right hand. [6] The sun shall not strike you by day, nor the moon by night. [7] The Lord shall preserve you from all evil; He shall preserve your soul. The Lord shall preserve your going out and your coming in from this time forth, and even forevermore (Psalms 121:3-7).*

> *... for I will hasten my word to perform it (Jeremiah 1:12).*

> *The Lord watches over the strangers (the vulnerable); He relieves the fatherless and widow; But the way of the wicked He turns upside down (Psalms 146:9).*

Somehow, Paul's young nephew eavesdropped on the Jewish band who agreed to kill Paul. He quickly warned Paul, and upon Paul's advice, the young man immediately informed the Commander-in-charge. By this small but significant move Paul, by the grace of God, foiled an imminent death sentence cleverly hatched by the enemies against the purposes and will of God. All this while, God had been working behind the scenes and moving people and things in favour of Paul, His Apostle.

Question; have you ever thought about Satan's crafty cunningness, his schemes and wicked devices, and how he sniffs on God's people? Of course, Satan is no better or bigger than his name! He is a thief and a liar, exactly how our Lord Jesus Christ refers to Satan and Satan's *children.*

> *The thief does not come except to steal, and to kill, and to destroy... (John10:10).*

> *You are of your father the devil, and the desires of your father you want to do. He was a murderer from the beginning, and does not stand in the truth, because there is no truth in him. When he speaks a lie, he speaks from his own resources, for he is a liar and the father of it (John 8:44).*

Satan is always alright when things are not working for you, but once he hears and knows that things are beginning to pick up, he immediately comes to obstruct, devour and to destroy. He is not really bothered that you are trapped somewhere in a 'prison' of drug addiction, lack of purpose and self-worth, or even a 'prison' of sickness, molestation, abuse, rejection, despondencies, family breakdown, emotional trauma, and the likes. But, once a good future begins to surface because you are beginning to break free from your 'prison' and to give your life some purpose through God's powerful love and Word, he comes quickly – that old big *liar and thief,* to steal away your joy, happiness, and your resolve to break loose and to become free.

You need to know that Satan's schemes are dirty and deadly, intended to absolutely destroy his victims! And watch out, his schemes and traps are not always the bad stuff, they mostly are the 'good looking', 'great taste' and 'mind blowing' offers that immediately appeal to *our eyes, our flesh and our pride* (1 John 2:16). You need to know that Satan got his last PhD in packaging and marketing, and his schemes are cleverly aimed at taking you all the way down. That is why Apostle James advises us, that the only way out whilst we try to break free and to regain our God ordained purpose and freedom is to, with all our might, ... *submit to God. Resist the devil and he will flee from you (James 4:7).*

Apostle Peter also added, when that *liar and thief* comes round, *"Resist him, steadfast in the faith, knowing that the same sufferings are experienced by your brotherhood in the world" (1 Peter 5:9).* You must resist every temptation trying to take you back to your old deeds which kept you prisoner in the past; no matter how appealing Satan re-presents them to you. Believe God's report, that His eyes are on you to do you good and to give you *abundant life (John 10:10), and a future with good hope (Jeremiah 29:11).* Remember my friend, *no weapon formed against you shall prosper and every tongue which rises against you in judgment you shall condemn... says the Lord (Isaiah 54:17), and when the enemy comes in like a flood, the Spirit of the Lord will lift up a standard against him. (Isaiah 59:19).*

Satan, after accusing Paul falsely, because that's who Satan is, *the accuser of the brethren (Rev. 12:10),* he thought he had Paul truly trapped. But, God had another plan, a plan which was actually a master plan, intended in the wisdom of God to grant Paul his long awaited desire and at the same time to fulfil God's purposes. The good thing was, Paul was going to have all that done at the expense of Satan, to travel on gratis and meet with people he had always desired to see in person. All of that wouldn't have been possible by any other means except through what had already been designed by God. That means, even Satan was, and will always be, too late.

My friend, our God is always miles ahead of Satan concerning how He orders our steps once we keep in obedience to Him. Here is a classic example. Consider Joseph; by turning his own brothers against him, Satan thought he had cheated Joseph out of his dreams, desires and God's purposes for him. He induced Joseph's brothers to sell him as a common slave in Egypt because of hatred that sprung from extreme jealousy. In Egypt, Joseph was falsely accused of attempted rape by Potiphar's wife, and was then locked up in prison. All of this was in a bid to *steal, kill and* to *destroy* Joseph, his dreams and all that God purposed for his life.

But in the end, Joseph's own testimony spoke for itself! He says, *but as for you, you meant evil against me; but God meant it for good, in order to bring it about as it is this day, to save many people alive (Genesis 50:20).* This Joseph became second only to Pharaoh in all of Egypt, the land in which he was sold as a mere slave. Again, all that Satan schemed, which God also in His own wisdom permitted, only furthered God's undisclosed purposes for Joseph, and helped Joseph's childhood dreams to be fulfilled in an exceptional way. Once again, Almighty God was miles ahead of Satan. We also see Job, whom God gave twice as much possession in the end, emerging even more prosperous than before (Job 42:10). During the years of his affliction meted upon him by the wicked works and schemes of Satan, he could have easily died.

Think about our Lord Jesus Christ Himself, whom Satan tried to hinder in many ways, and who suffered many things even to death on the cross *on purpose,* and for our sakes. Through His suffering and death, eternal victory over Satan and hell were wrought for whosoever is willing to come to the Father through Jesus our Lord and Saviour. The Bible declares,

> *However, we speak wisdom among those who are mature, yet not the wisdom of this age, nor of the rulers of this age, who are coming to nothing. [7] But we speak the wisdom of God in a mystery, the hidden wisdom which God ordained before the ages for our glory, [8] which none of the rulers of this age knew; for had they known, they would not have crucified the Lord of glory (I Corinthians 2:6-8).*

And you, being dead in your trespasses and the uncircumcision of your flesh, He has made alive together with Him, having forgiven you all trespasses, having wiped out the handwriting of requirements that was against us, which was contrary to us. And He has taken it out of the way, having nailed it to the cross. [15] Having disarmed principalities and powers, He made a public spectacle of them, triumphing over them in it (Col. 2:13-15).

Christ has redeemed us from the curse of the law, having become a curse for us (for it is written, "Cursed is everyone who hangs on a tree"), [14] that the blessing of Abraham might come upon the Gentiles in Christ Jesus, that we might receive the promise of the Spirit through faith (Galatians 3:13-14).

I intentionally brought up these scriptures to help us appreciate every strand of the immense wisdom of God in the life of Jesus and His ministries on earth. Again, it is demonstrably clear that God Almighty was miles ahead of Satan in every aspect. To think that he was crucifying the Son of God only to realize in the end, that in crucifying Jesus, Satan rather colluded to his own public *disgrace, defeat* and *disarmament,* is a wisdom and mystery beyond Satan's comprehension.

Satan is definitely not as wise as some think! Don't submit to his lies and scams, my friend. You will definitely do and become what the Lord Jesus has purposed for your life. No sickness is permitted to kill you and remember God's best is coming upon you. No matter how difficult it seems at the moment, don't quit, because God has on His mind good plans to set you free from your present 'prison' and to promote you to unusual heights.

Wisdom for Overcoming

The real challenge for many believers and mainline Christianity in our time is that, we have somehow utterly disregarded God's foremost commandment to us about the absolute necessity for Godly wisdom and understanding.

We are commanded especially to get wisdom (Proverbs 4:7), at all times to learn to apply our hearts to wisdom and to walk in wisdom (Deut. 4:6; Col. 4:5; Matt. 10:16; 1Pet 5:8). No doubt, having and walking in wisdom are necessary for our ability to respond appropriately to God's love and commandments. But even more crucially, we need wisdom to know how to deal with Satan on terms which will deny him any possibility of outwitting us, or gaining any advantage over us by any of his devices (1Cor. 12:11). On the same basis of wisdom our Lord Jesus Christ, in Matthew 10:16, enjoins believers to be wise, because He knew the ever-present and persistent effort of Satan to resist and to discredit the purposes of God for His children.

The way therefore to outwit Satan and to be able to overcome his cunning devices and oppositions is simple and straight forward. Do just what your Father God does; deal with Satan in the wisdom God has given you. Satan's greatest fear is of those who walk in Godly wisdom. It was a liberating moment when the Lord, by His Holy Spirit revealed this truth to me. The Lord led me to know that one of the reasons He has given us His Holy Spirit was to help us have wisdom. That's why the Holy Spirit is just not the Spirit of truth but also of wisdom. But, there is a 'double edge' to this, which is Christ Jesus Himself, who is our wisdom as well.

> *The Spirit of the Lord shall rest upon Him, the Spirit of wisdom and understanding, The Spirit of counsel and might, The Spirit of knowledge and of the fear of the Lord. (Isaiah 11:2)*

> *But there is a spirit in man and the breath of the Almighty gives him understanding. (Job 32:8)*

> *It is because of him that you are in Christ Jesus, who has become for us wisdom from God - that is, our righteousness, holiness and redemption (1 Corinthians 1:13).*

The Lord showed me through a process of question and answer, how wisdom has always been the way that the children of God were able to resist Satan and to foil his schemes.

Daniel, by his use of wisdom, survived satanic efforts to destroy him, and he became certainly known for his uncommon wisdom in Babylon (Daniel 5:14). David on the other hand used wisdom continuously to escape relentless satanic attempts to end his life. In his entire encounter with King Saul, whose character and actions in various ways typified the persons and schemes of Satan, David overcame King Saul through wisdom.

In the story, every time Saul came against David because of David's purpose, the Bible says, *and David behaved himself wisely, ... very wisely, ... and even more wisely, and Saul the King became the more afraid of David, and became his enemy continually* (I Samuel 18:5, 14 & 15, 29 & 30). There it is. If you want Satan to be afraid of you, get wisdom and walk in wisdom! Satan is never afraid of you but of the wisdom of God that you operate with.

Our Lord Jesus Christ Himself operated with such wisdom, even during the time of His temptation involving Satan. He gracefully overcame all of Satan's temptation because He went into the wilderness full of the Holy Spirit of wisdom, and through wisdom consistently frustrated Satan (Matthew 4:1-11). Hebrews says, *For we do not have a high priest who is unable to sympathize with our weaknesses, but we have one who has been tempted in every way, just as we are - yet was without sin (4:15).* Why? Because, Satan's temptations always bow to God's wisdom.

We have seen how God's good word of promise, delivered in the night to Paul in prison, infuriated Satan and how Satan finally took action to end Paul before his word ever resulted in anything tangible. Indeed, this is historically Satan's old scheme in trying to hijack God's promises and purposes for His people. Satan will attempt to abort every promise of purpose regarding God's people before their word, and they themselves, ever gain any prominence. He did the same to Adam and Eve, to Job, to Joseph, to Moses as a toddler and as a man in Pharaoh's palace. He repeated the same plot against David who was almost destroyed by King Saul through envy and jealousy, and by setting David up into an adulterous relationship with Bathsheba, the wife of Uriah.

Satan schemed against Sampson offering him Delilah. He tried to intercept the answer to Daniel's prayers, but God's warring angels were released against him, and Daniel finally got His prayer answered. Satan even attempted to murder the baby Jesus by inciting King Herod to kill all children within his jurisdiction, hoping that Jesus would be killed. In all of this, the results were always the same. Ultimately, God and His people triumphantly outwitted Satan and his demonic plots. In the end, it was the wisdom of God that prevailed.

If you have received a prophecy from God, or are at the moment holding unto a word of promise from the Lord which seems to be presently opposed and challenged at various levels, take heart. Your *word* from God or your desire and purpose may be suffering some delays at the moment, but don't give up. God who promised is also able to deliver His promise. God who has brought you this far will even take you farther. Remember no amount of oppositions can abort your God given dream, purpose and future except that which you personally succumb to! Like Paul says,

> *And we know that all things work together for good to those who love God, to those who are the called according to His purpose (Romans 8:28)*

Also remember always that, *weeping may endure for a night, but joy comes in the morning (Psalms 30:5),* and then,

> *To everything there is a season, a time for every purpose under heaven: I know that whatever God does, it shall be forever. Nothing can be added to it, and nothing taken from it. God does it, that men should fear before Him. ... "God shall judge the righteous and the wicked, For there is a time there for every purpose and for every work" (Ecclesiastes 3:1,14,17)*

Apostle Peter knows that there is always light at the end of the tunnel, and thus prays for you, *But may the God of all grace, who called us to His eternal glory by Christ Jesus, after you have suffered a while, perfect, establish, strengthen, and settle you (1Peter 5:10).*

Purpose, Promise and Moments of Anxieties

> *Now I beg you, brethren, through the Lord Jesus Christ, and through the love of the Spirit, that you strive together with me in prayers to God for me (Romans 15:30)*

Remember, Paul's lifelong desire was to see Rome, to be of blessing to God's people and to be encouraged himself by having the opportunity to share in fellowship with believers in Rome. In Romans 15:23, Paul describes his longing to be in Rome as a *great desire of many years*. In verse 19 of the same chapter, Paul says he had extensively covered the important territories of his assignment and purpose; fully preaching the Gospel of Christ with mighty signs, wonders and by the power of the Holy Spirit. He had already done a thorough in job reaching both the Jews and Gentiles, right from Jerusalem to Illyricum, and now he was looking forward to a new opportunity.

But this was not just another opportunity to win souls; it also was a privilege to affirm the faith of other believers who possibly were highly revered for their own contribution to the Faith (Romans 1:8; 16:19). He wanted to have the opportunity, if situations permitted, to meet other giants in the Faith, like Andronicus and Junia, who clearly stood out among the apostles, and who also were in Christ before Paul (Romans 16:7). So, the place to go and to be was indeed Rome, the bustling hub of everything cosmopolitan in Paul's days. Rome was indeed the very centre of civilization, the melting pot of cultures, religions, ideas, science and secularism.

Of course, *every real hero never quits 'fighting'*. They die either still fighting or conquering. They always insist on that one more fight or one more medal to be gained, and Paul was a true hero of faith and the Gospel of Christ. He would not quit as long as there was still that bit more to do, and to finish his course of *preaching the Gospel where Christ has not been named,* Spain and Rome being Paul's top priority (Rom. 15:20, 22-24). Although, he was thinking of Spain, it was Rome that he became obsessed about and driven by.

Paul decided that he must see and be in Rome for a while, and was also counting on the good gesture of the believers in Rome to help him get to Spain, but only after he had enjoyed their company (Romans 15:24). From all indication, the majority of the believers in Rome may have only heard of Paul as a disciple of Jesus and not seen him in person. Similarly, it is most likely that Paul himself had not had real personal contact with most of the believers in Rome, but seemed compellingly aware of their great exploits regarding the Faith.

Being so impressed by the believers, it was only fair that a day would come in which they could all together share their stories and experiences in Christian fellowship. However Paul, the mission minded and purpose driven apostle who had never flinched from taking advantage in every situation to preach the gospel of Christ, knew full well that the purpose of his trip transcended just meeting believers and making his presence felt. He declared,

> *For I long to see you, that I may impart to you some spiritual gift, so that you may be established—* [12] *that is, that I may be encouraged together with you by the mutual faith both of you and me.* [13] *Now I do not want you to be unaware, brethren, that I often planned to come to you (but was hindered until now), that I might have some fruit among you also, just as among the other Gentiles.* [14] *I am a debtor both to Greeks and to barbarians, both to wise and to unwise.* [15] *So, as much as is in me, I am ready to preach the gospel to you who are in Rome also (Romans 1:9-15).*

Think about this. Clearly Paul confessed that there were men and women in Rome whose *faith is spoken of throughout the whole world (Roman 1:8).* That sounds like a good thing for the believers in Rome. However, in the same breath, Paul greatly longed to see those believers that he *may impart to (them) some spiritual gift, so that (they) may be established.* Again, just as he had done in other places and among other gentiles, Paul was eager to have *some fruits among those in Rome* as well. He says to them, that he is *ready to preach the gospel to (them) who are in Rome also.*

By the way, purpose is usually a call to *give* or to *donate*, and a person of purpose always seeks every opportunity to fulfil such a call by giving and donating, obviously what they've received (1Cor. 11:23; 1Cor. 4:7, Gen. 12:1-2). Also, your personal purpose is tied in with and relates directly to serving your generation faithfully with all the gifts and abilities God has given you, in accordance with His plans and purposes. It involves using your gifts and talents in positively influencing your circle of influence and for the betterment of humanity, to the will of God and for His glory. That is why, *'Abraham is blessed to be a blessing'* (Gen. 12:2) and *'David served his own generation faithfully* (Acts 13:36).

Now, from what we have seen so far, it seems there was more to Paul's planned visit to Rome than just causally contacting fellow believers on his way to Spain. He gave us only broad strokes of his intentions, but the specifics, we could glean telescopically from his other visits and letters to other churches in other areas. For example, Paul was very keen to delineate his gospel, which he alluded to in Romans 16:25, and now even in more detail in First Corinthians:

> *Moreover, brethren, I declare to you the gospel which I preached to you, which also you received and in which you stand, ² by which also you are saved, if you hold fast that word which I preached to you— unless you believed in vain. ³ For I delivered to you first of all that which I also received: that Christ died for our sins according to the Scriptures, ⁴ and that He was buried, and that He rose again the third day according to the Scriptures, ⁵ and that He was seen by Cephas, then by the twelve.... ⁸ Then last of all He was seen by me also, as by one born out of due time (I Corinthians 15:1-5,8).*

Still arguing for his gospel in his letter to the church of the Galatians, Paul sternly warned them saying,

> *I marvel that you are turning away so soon from Him who called you in the grace of Christ, to a different gospel, ⁷ which is not another; but there are some who trouble you and want to pervert the gospel of Christ.*

But even if we, or an angel from heaven, preach any other gospel to you than what we have preached to you, let him be accursed. As we have said before, so now I say again, if anyone preaches any other gospel to you than what you have received, let him be accursed (Galatians 1:6-9).

Is it possible that Rome was having its share of the challenges that hastily beguiled the Galatians, and therefore drew Paul's attention to them? Reading from Romans 16:17-19, Paul equally warns,

Now I urge you, brethren, note those who cause divisions and offenses, contrary to the doctrine which you learned, and avoid them. For those who are such do not serve our Lord Jesus Christ, but their own belly, and by smooth words and flattering speech deceive the hearts of the simple.

The Apostles were eager to insure their converts and other believers had the full gospel of Christ, and if there was any need for further establishment in any truth that was otherwise not known or fully explained to their recipients, corrections were quickly made. This was the case with Apollos, a Jew born in Alexandria, who was described to be eloquent, mighty in the Scriptures, and also a good man who taught the ways of Christ accurately. However, Appollos was known to possess and to teach only the baptism of John, and when Aquila and Priscilla heard him they immediately took him aside to explain the way of God more accurately to him (Acts 18:24-28).

Also in the book of Acts 19:1-10, we see a work of impartation and establishment, perhaps similar to what Paul intended to do for the believers in Rome.

And it happened, while Apollos was at Corinth, that Paul, having passed through the upper regions, came to Ephesus. And finding some disciples he said to them, "Did you receive the Holy Spirit when you believed?" So they said to him, "We have not so much as heard whether there is a Holy Spirit." And he said to them, "Into what then were you baptized?" So they said, "Into John's baptism."

Then Paul said, "John indeed baptized with a baptism of repentance, saying to the people that they should believe on Him who would come after him, that is, on Christ Jesus." When they heard this, they were baptized in the name of the Lord Jesus. And when Paul had laid hands on them, the Holy Spirit came upon them, and they spoke with tongues and prophesied. Now the men were about twelve in all. And he went into the synagogue and spoke boldly for three months, reasoning and persuading concerning the things of the kingdom of God (Acts 19:1-8).

Now, from all that we see going on, it is deducible what the true intent of the Apostle Paul was for believers in Rome. Clearly, Paul had equally liked to have fruit among those outside the Faith; a convincing demonstration of the power of the gospel which Paul received and preached.

For I am not ashamed of the gospel of Christ, for it is the power of God to salvation for everyone who believes, for the Jew first and also for the Greek. For in it the righteousness of God is revealed from faith to faith; as it is written, "The just shall live by faith" (Romans 1:16).

Now, with all this flooding Paul's mind, his mind was probably working overtime trying to decipher how he was ever going to get his desire for the gospel and for Rome accomplished. Clearly, he was aware of uncertainties and potential perils and challenges along the way, leaving from where he was to where he wanted to go, Rome and Spain.

Being an experienced missionary, who consistently travelled long distances, Paul did not underestimate the sheer weight and demands his proposed trip held for him. He was definitely going to need physical logistical support from believers in Rome as well as their cooperation and fellowship (Romans 15:24). But, more than that, he mainly required and earnestly requested prayer support (Roman 15:30), that believers in Rome should make every effort and stand with him in prayers to God on his behalf.

Paul was experienced enough to know that *prayer goes deeper than our most meticulous planning.* He knew that some things do not necessarily go the way we purpose and plan them, for *there are many plans in a man's heart, nevertheless the Lord's counsel that will stand (Proverbs 19:21).* Hence, the only way to bring a great degree of certainty to our plans is to wrap them up perfectly in prayers and commit our desires and all that concerns us to the Lord who directs our paths (Proverb 3:5-6; Psalms 37:3-5).

After a series of critical challenges, Paul himself began to despair of his ingenious goal of reaching Rome. Not only had it been many years already of trying without success, he had received true prophecies of what should befall him in Jerusalem. Of course in Jerusalem he found himself in prison after a serious riot which could have easily ended his own life. Even while Paul was in prison, a clever plot was hatched to kill him, the morning after he received a good word from God that he must testify also in Rome.

Anyone else in Paul's dilemma, despite their great faith, would easily battle with trying to keep in high spirit and sound mind. However, Paul knew God and counted on his previous experience to draw comfort and strength, that the very God who delivered him in the past would still make a way for him. It is no secret that whenever the Lord says and promises a thing, it must surely come to pass, and indeed, it must surely stand (Isaiah 14:24).

However, the very form of Paul's deliverance and safe passage from Jerusalem to Rome, and secondly, when that would be possible were probably the most pressing issue to try Paul's mind and faith. If you ever found yourself in a prison of a sort and were told that surely your deliverance was coming, I tell you the truth, that good news itself is enough to add further anxieties to your present worries. Yes, you may look forward to your deliverance, but not knowing how and when it will take place leaves your heart hanging.

Have you ever had some of those *open prophecies* without further directions as to what you should do and when you should expect certain things to happen? Well, I must confess, I personally prefer some more details! But, just because you do not know the detail of the *when and how* of God's promises and purposes, does not mean that God will not do what He says He will do. Remember, *for God cannot lie (Titus 1:2), and blessed is she (he) who believed, for there will be a fulfilment of those things which were told her (him) from the Lord" (Luke 1:45).*

It's Time to Go

To everything there is a season, a time for every purpose under heaven (Ecclesiastes 3:1)

Well, the time finally came, and the door to Rome opened in a rather unusual manner. Who ever thought the *Road to Rome* begins from a prison with death threat over your head. But, for a person like Paul who was so focused and mission minded, it was always difficult to predict how his journey would begin and end.

Throughout the book of Acts, we have common occurrences in which Paul plans to visit either a church or city, and then rather unconventionally, he ends up in another city because of a vision, or a compelling need that forces him to stop, detour and preach (see Acts 16 and 17). Quite often, on his journeys, all that Paul had for assurance was God's word of promise to be with him. These were journeys that could best be described as journeys of faith, similar to Abraham's, the father of faith, who received the command early in his walk with God. He was told,

... "Get out of your country, from your family and from your father's house, to a land that I will show you. I will make you a great nation; I will bless you and make your name great; and you shall be a blessing. I will bless those who bless you, and I will curse him who curses you; and in you all the families of the earth shall be blessed." So Abram departed as the Lord had spoken to him..., (Gen. 12:1-4).

Somehow every person of purpose embarks on such journeys at some point in their life, when they are suddenly told it is time, the moment is at hand, leave or go. Needless to say, this kind of command surely leaves you with more questions than answers. You begin to ask and wonder to yourself, *but Lord, where, when, how do I go, and who do I take with me? How long, how hard or easy will my journey be, and why me this time?*

All of those sound like valid questions to ask, but our best response to God's command in such times is what Abraham did, to get busy on your way. If you insist on explaining your side of the story to the Lord, I promise His response will be something like this, *"My grace is sufficient for you, for My strength is made perfect in weakness" (2 Corinthians 12:9)*. Even if you cry out loud, *Lord I'm not able*, He says to you, *I will be with you*. When you try to excuse yourself saying, *but Lord I am only a child*, He will then say to you, *don't say I am only a child because you shall go to all to whom I send you, and whatever I command you, you shall speak. Do not be afraid of their faces, for I am with you to deliver you (Jeremiah 1:6-8)*.

Persisting into His Purposes: You Can Do It!

❖❖❖

Pursuing Purpose with Passion

Bizarre as it may seem, Paul finally began his journey from Jerusalem to Rome. He was hastily transferred overnight from prison to Caesarea, to stand trial at Caesar's Judgment Seat, before Felix the governor. The entire proceeding was initiated by the directive of Claudius Lysias, the Roman commander in Jerusalem who, for good reasons, initially acted quickly and successfully to save Paul from being brutally lynched to death. During a trial, which was presided over by Felix, Paul's accusers accused him of many things including sedition.

Amid their vilifying accusations, Paul took his stand and gave his defence, consistent with what was always his belief and message ever since he met with Christ on the road to Damascus. He was now on the road to Rome and his message, which he simply referred to as his gospel, was becoming much more compelling; being heard not only by common people but also kings, councils and governors.

In his own defence, Paul said,

> *But this I confess to you, that according to the Way which they call a sect, so I worship the God of my fathers, believing all things which are written in the Law and in the Prophets.* [15] *I have hope in God, which they themselves also accept, that there will be a resurrection of the dead, both of the just and the unjust.* [16] *This being so, I myself always strive to have a conscience without offence toward God and men (Acts24:14-16).*

Let's face it, how could someone be made to stand trial for such an innocent message if it were not for destiny and God's purposes at work in the life of Paul? It is very natural, and always in the interest of people and the circumstances of life, to align with and to adhere obediently to the call of purpose and the destiny of God's people. Otherwise, they will be made to concord (Psalms 110:3; Psalms 148:1-13). This is so true my friend, to the extent that even the terrestrial elements are programmed to revolve around and to work in the interest of our Godly purposes and destinies by helping to fulfil God's words of promise concerning our lives.

> *Praise the Lord! Praise the Lord from the heavens; praise Him in the heights! Praise Him, all His angels; praise Him, all His hosts! Praise Him, sun and moon; Praise Him, all you stars of light! Praise Him, you heavens of heavens, and you waters above the heavens! Let them praise the name of the Lord, for He commanded and they were created. He also established them forever and ever;* **He made a decree which shall not pass away. Praise the Lord from the earth, you great sea creatures and all the depths; Fire and hail, snow and clouds; Stormy wind, fulfilling His word;** *Mountains and all hills; fruitful trees and all cedars; Beasts and all cattle; Creeping things and flying fowl; Kings of the earth and all peoples; Princes and all judges of the earth; both young men and maidens; Old men and children.* [13] *Let them praise the name of the Lord, for His name alone is exalted; His glory is above the earth and heaven. And He has exalted the horn of His people, the praise of all His saints - of the children of Israel, a people near to Him. Praise the Lord! (Ps 149:1-14)*

As a matter of fact, we are told that Felix, the governor *had more accurate knowledge of the Way (Acts 24:22)*; so what prevented him from setting Paul free? Of course, he might have known that the accusation levelled against Paul was totally frivolous and untrue. Otherwise, Felix would not have allowed Paul to enjoy the kind of liberty he had if the case against him was deemed to be severe and incriminating. On the contrary, Paul was allowed to see and to receive friends and visitors at will, and some even cared and provided for Paul.

The text implies that Felix befriended Paul and made it obvious to Paul that if he were bribed with money, then he would release Paul in spite of the accusation brought against him. But, why would Paul not buy into that easy offer and such a *generous* proposal to save his own life? And why did Felix deny Paul his liberty when it was only right to let him go free? The answer and reason are simple; God's purposes and the call of destiny must be fulfilled, and anything coming along the way should only lend help to getting Paul to where God wanted him to go, thereby fulfilling the word of promise.

You see, Paul could not be destroyed until all that was written about him and all his purposes according to the will of God were fulfilled. So, the Lord continued to watch over him even when people denied him what was rightly due him. And I dare say, in some cases God orchestrated the situations to work in favour of His purpose for Paul. But, at all times, His eyes were keenly watching over His servant;

> *Behold, the eye of the Lord is on those who fear Him, on those who hope in His mercy, to deliver their soul from death, and to keep them alive in famine (Psalms 33:18-19).*

> *In Him also we have obtained an inheritance, being predestined according to the purpose of Him who **works all things according to the counsel of His will** (Ephesians 1:11).*

This is true for all of God's people, and was true for Paul. God always had a purpose or a *will* for Paul in his situation.

In His *will*, there were things written about Paul which had to happen. It was absolutely necessary that the tenants of the *will* were not contradicted because, when it comes to God's *will*, He orders all things to work together in concert with the *counsel of His will*. Remember this is, and will always be for the good of the believers, those who love God and are called according to God's purpose (Romans 8:28). These are those for whom in everything and for all things, find themselves giving thanks to God in the Name of Jesus Christ, being fully aware of His power, grace, love, purpose and faithfulness.

> *In everything give thanks; for this is the will of God in Christ Jesus for you (1 Thessalonians 5:18). ...giving thanks always for all things to God the Father in the name of our Lord Jesus Christ (Ephesians 5:20).*

Considering all that Paul endured en route to Rome, which seems like a delay and an unnecessary intervention, things were rather turning in his favour to be great open-doors and blessings before him. Felix's wife Drusilla, who was herself a Jew, by divine providence had the opportunity to hear Paul speak about what faith in Christ meant. Paul literally gave them his best delivery about faith and conversion to Jesus Christ because the occasion and environment was ideal, away from noise, distractions and undue interferences. He did it so well that even Felix, who was just listening, was cut to the heart in such a way that he became afraid. He then responded by asking Paul to go away for a while.

What did Paul talk about? Why was Felix so afraid? It is said that Paul *reasoned* about *righteousness, self-control, and the judgment to come (Acts 24:25)*. See, the text says, he *reasoned;* not just a talk or a lecture. It seems to me that Paul's *reasoning* may have involved intense question and answer sessions, with the opportunity to demonstrate, with clear illustrations, the issues that were under discussion. No one could ignore the gospel of Christ coming directly to them in pictorial language, and the effectiveness with which Paul presented it, through the love and power of the Holy Ghost.

People might not say yes to Christ immediately, but the Word of the gospel will certainly penetrate their hearts and confront them as well, although with grace and in truth.

A man like Felix, who had expected to be bribed by Paul for special favour, certainly might have known and practiced corruption in some forms. And *reasoning* about serious holiness issues involving *righteousness, self-control, and the judgment to come,* may not only have been uncomfortable for the governor and his wife, but also might have been the reason for his great fear. Felix stopped Paul as he continued to reason about the gospel because he could not bear the living and powerful Word of God discerning his thoughts and intents, reaching right down to his bones and marrow (Hebrews 4:12).

I wonder how many *Felixes* of our time, instead of hearing a direct message of the truth of the gospel regarding *righteousness, self-control, and the judgment,* get rather a well-rehearsed roundabout speech of fawning and flattery. Instead of leaving convicted they are rather very relaxed in some churches and their so-called highly *sophisticated* preachers. Instead of stopping us because of the power of the truth, the *Felixes* of our times rather grow so comfortable because we only give them what amuses their itching ears. Their conscience remains unchallenged, and they hardly flinch or twitch an inch at our *reasoning*, or even in our presence.

Something is definitely wrong when a *Felix* freely bluffs his way in and out of church services and, if they remain nonchalant in the presence of a preacher or Christian. The only explanation then will be that, *we hardly talk about righteousness, self-control or sin and the judgement to come, which is really the true message of the Holy Spirit that brings about genuine conviction* (John 16:8). We *motivate,* because it has become fashionable to become *motivators* and *motivational speakers* from pulpits.

As a result we have lost our cutting-edge and our messages have equally lost their power to *cut* to the heart or to *melt* hearts which should be asking "what must I do to be born again?". We have, by our own urge to compromise, effectively dulled the sharpness of the Word, so to speak, by not offering the full counsels of God. We've rather put in its place placid clichés of overworked phrases that literally does nothing but to soothe the symptoms of life's real problem rather than cure the problem. We do love to just motivate our *governors* to continue in their corrupt practices and to gloss over issues of deep seated sins!

Without doubt, Felix's gesture for a bribe was the easiest option for Paul if he had wanted to please man and find favour with Felix. All he had to do was to say to him, *Felix, you know you are great and you have nothing to worry about!* But, Paul was a man of faith and integrity, esteeming the reproaches of Christ of greater eternal value than the temporary favour of Felix and his wife Drusilla.

> *For what will it profit a man if he gains the whole world, and loses his own soul? (Matthew 8:36).*

Paul was definitely not the first to choose a moral high ground for the cause of the gospel and Christ, and certainly he will not be the last. Like Paul, Moses,

> *... when he became of age, refused to be called the son of Pharaoh's daughter, choosing rather to suffer affliction with the people of God than to enjoy the passing pleasures of sin, esteeming the reproach of Christ greater riches than the treasures in Egypt; for he looked to the reward. By faith he forsook Egypt, not fearing the wrath of the king; for he endured as seeing Him who is invisible (Hebrews 11:24-27).*

It is high time, I believe, that God's children *come of age;* not only to discern good and evil, but to also stand for the truth without compromising their faith in the living Lord, Jesus Christ. Saying the truth at all times and standing in great integrity is not about personal preference, but it is the issue of purpose. Following God and pursuing God's purposes with passion will require us to stand in moral authority, avowing to follow Christ and to please God rather than men if we have to choose. We are called not just *to* or *with* purpose, but also to defend purpose as well. The proof of passion in the pursuit of purpose, and also the accomplishment of purpose, is to always choose Christ above our own comfort and convenience, being always ready to speak the truth and to stand by the truth.

Looking at the Bigger Picture

But I want you to know, brethren, that the things which happened to me have actually turned out for the furtherance of the gospel (Philippians 1:12)

After two solid years, a new governor, Porcius Festus, took over from Felix and Paul was still a prisoner for reason that the text gives as Felix's desire to do the Jews a favour. However, there were some things to rejoice about in what seemed to be an unjust and unfair delay in dealing with Paul's case. Knowing the passion of Paul for sharing the gospel, he would have certainly preached to all who came to see him including Felix, the prison guards, and ordinary visitors, over a good part of the two years of Felix's rule and Paul's imprisonment in Caesarea.

There are few things worth noting at this point:

I.   While he was held in prison, the purposes of God for Paul were not bound, but on the contrary his situation served to further the cause of the gospel (2Tim. 2:9; Philip. 1:12).

II.   The plot and ploy of Paul's enemies to kill him have at least not succeeded up to now. Paul continued to enjoy God's generous protection.

III.   With his life still in him, there was hope and good reason to believe that the Word of God concerning Paul testifying in Rome had good prospects of coming to pass.

IV.   And the final thing to rejoice about was, the longer Paul stayed in Caesarea, albeit against his personal wish, opportunity continued to avail for Paul to speak to other people and other governors as well. That means God's people will never lack God created and God given opportunities, for which His people can always rejoice, even in the midst of their troubles. The only thing is that we need to look beyond our own sufferings and consider the bigger picture.

Governor Festus was part of the bigger picture surrounding Paul's life, purpose and ministries. Upon the behest of the priests and the chief men of the Jews for undue favour against Paul, the governor agreed to initially try Paul at Caesarea, and to ascertain for himself the truth of their accusation. With many serious complaints from Paul's accusers, but all far from any real proof (Acts 25:7), Paul in his defence pleaded not guilty.

The text does not give all that he said in his defence at this time, but knowing Paul and how in every previous defence he had seized the opportunity to preach Christ, he may have done the same before Festus and his council. Admittedly, Festus did not find compelling legal reasons to sentence Paul (Acts 25:18), but being well disposed to the luring of Paul's accusers for favour (Acts 25:9), was prepared to offer them a Jerusalem trial. And the motive for a Jerusalem trial was clearly diabolical (Acts 25:16, 17), and was sure to take the form of a *kangaroo court* leading to *kangaroo justice.*

Giving No Place to Naivety

Remember, it was in Jerusalem that devout men schemed and laid in wait to ambush Paul under pretence, so that Lysias had to transfer Paul to Caesarea (Acts 23:13-25). Now, the same people were requesting Paul to be taken back to Jerusalem for a *fairer* hearing. What do you think? Anyone faced with Paul's dilemma might find this wisdom of Scripture extremely helpful,

> *Can the Ethiopian change his skin or the leopard its spots? Then may you also do good who are accustomed to do evil (Jer. 13:23).*

It is so absurd and bizarre for anyone to expect a sudden change of mind from people who are after your neck. Paul's accusers promised him a fair trial, while in the same breath, were doing all in their power to kill him. It is nothing short of day-light robbery, a polite oxymoron of double death sentence to say that they will give Paul a chance for a fair trial in Jerusalem. What they asked of Paul was so incongruous even with conventional wisdom that a child's mind could easily fathom it.

Having said that, I have seen and heard about some Christian brothers and sisters who somehow lend themselves to simple and myopic mindedness and as a result have been taken by easy scams even more bizarre than what Paul's accusers offered. The unfortunate thing is that, many of these brothers and sisters being conned are often people who *use* and *quote* Scriptures in their own defence without knowing the difference. Well, it is one thing to *use* and *quote* Scriptures and it is another to *know* and *apply* Scriptures. The former by their *use* and *quoting* of Scriptures are unwise in their ways, and the latter, by their *knowing* and *applying* of Scriptures are wise in the ways of Christ.

Let me illustrate what I am talking about. There was a time when I attempted a research PhD programme. It turned out to be a very expensive endeavour, leaving me with serious debt incurred through some difficult choices I had to make in the end.

I ended up being sent to court for unpaid fees. But a fellow international student and a Christian brother who was sympathetic to my plight, suggested that I use Colossians 2:14,15 in my prayer, claiming my rights to supernatural payment of fees and the cancellation of any satanic hindrance barring me from successfully finishing my course.

The words of that text read, "(*Jesus*) *having wiped out the handwriting of requirements that was against us, which was contrary to us. And He has taken it out of the way, having nailed it to the cross. Having disarmed principalities and powers, He made a public spectacle of them, triumphing over them in it.*" Without doubt, this was the most appropriate text for my situation, and as my nature is, if someone told me something of a truth that is right and also works, I will try it even if it makes me look stupid. I'll always take it to the next level with all my might.

My Christian brother said to me in the time of his own need, especially when he faced similar financial difficulties which threatened his Master degree in Law, he had a special revelation of the same text. He pulled the text out, read it constantly and prayed through it persistently believing the Lord in faith to help him, not only pay his fees but to also finish his degree successfully. It worked for him, and beyond that, after about a year he returned to the same university and completed his doctorate in Law.

Seriously, I would love to say that the same text worked for me and I finished my course at the time, but that was not the case at all. After taking a lot of trouble writing the words of the same scriptural text right across letters and emails from the university claiming debt payment, debt cancellation, and re-instatement on my course, nothing happened in the physical. Unfortunately, in the end I was dragged to court and told to pay the total amount owed to the university with interest and legal fees. Being human, I left the court troubled. You will understand that, I was disappointed not having any justifiable reasons and explanation why the same text that worked copiously for my friend failed to work in my case.

Until recently, I assigned other reasonable causes why the same text that worked beautifully for my friend did not work in my behalf. Here's how the Lord resolved my dilemma after four long years. It actually came on a Sunday morning just in time as an illustration for a message I was going to preach entitled, *All Things to Enjoy,* taken from *I Timothy 6:17; I Corinthians 3:21,22.*

I pondered these passages of Scriptures and began to question the Lord about the actual meaning and implication of what He was saying and teaching. I thought, well Lord if You have given us all things and all things are ours to enjoy, then how come a lot of us Your children are really not having it easy? He said, 'the passages referenced above do not work for a greater number of people for the same reason Colossians 2:14,15 did not work for you. ' I found His answer initially unsympathetic, harsh and too directed, but it was the truth.

The Lord let me know that what the majority of us do is like a game of chance, only using and quoting scriptures to bring 'religious' tilt to whatever we are doing by way of prayer. We go all lengths to borrow another person's *revelation* and make it ours, and then claim to be trusting and believing God, based on His word for our miracle. The Lord let me know that, His words are only His words to us and for our circumstances if we received it from Him in pursuit of our desires through personal revelations.

By personal revelations, I mean words and revelation not borrowed or thrust on us by other well-meaning people, like it was in my case, but words given or received that resonate with our spirit and confirm God's desire for us in our situation. It is the kind of personal revelation that has come to be known as *rhema* word in Christian circles, and it is a word we truly believe, and are committed to deeply, for their manifestations. This is far from just pulling a scriptural passage and saying I have a word from God. Even if it were delivered to you by another person, for example a Pastor, it has to be person and situation specific; something that churns your 'intestine', excites your spirit, with unquestionable knowing in your inner-person that this is mine, and this is from God. Your mind may doubt it, and even disagree with it, but there is that inescapable witness in your spirit – God's Spirit also bearing witness with your spirit, that God has indeed spoken (cf Romans 8:16). The 'lemon test' in this case is; ask yourself, *'did I hear God's voice behind the word, speaking directly to me?'*

This kind of revelation hardly comes by hastily flipping through the Bible for a *word*. It usually comes from meaningful moments of scriptural meditation and quality time spent with God. It comes because we have *set our love on God and known His Name* (Psalms 91:14), and are found in His will and purposes. If all you do is to hastily turn the pages of the Bible for a *word* in time of your need, then God will react to you no more than He did to the children of Israel in time of their great distress.

There was a time when Israel and their priests had little or no regard for the commandments and presence of the Lord, until they found themselves in trouble with the Philistines. In desperation they suddenly remembered the ark of covenant, and quickly sent for it to be brought from Shiloh, hoping that it might save them from the dreadful power of their enemies. They were excited when the ark of covenant arrived and two backslidden priests took their rightful positions with the ark.

However, God did not move on behalf of Israel that day as He did on other occasions, and unfortunately Israel was defeated, the priests were killed and the ark was captured (See 1 Samuel 2 - 4). The Lord therefore taught Israel and everyone a profound lesson, that no one selfishly *uses* His Presence or His Word on their own terms and succeeds.

Sadly, this is how many of us tend to behave toward God. We remember God or His Word only in times of desperation or great needs. But to hastily hatchet passages of Scriptures only for one's convenience, explains the reason behind some of the bitter failures and painful experiences, many unsuspecting believers suffer.

I guess you might have heard some of the most absurd things people fall for. You may hear something like this; a sincere single Christian, sister X, being told by a married, wife-beating, unfaithful 'church' brother, that he loves sister X and will divorce his already battered wife to marry beautiful single sister X. And then he promises her that he will treat her like a queen. The simple minded Christian sister buys into that kind of farce and all her prayers now become focused on the day of their coming honey moon. Ask her what's the Scriptural basis for her prayer, and she will with great confidence and delight present, Psalms 37:4 - *Delight yourself also in the Lord and He shall give you the desires of your heart.*

Here is good wisdom for the simple minded, just in case you know of anyone that simple minded: Anyone who treats another human being disrespectfully will soon get you if you stay in their path. *A diamond will always be nothing more than a mere stone to those who don't know the difference.* And anyone finding a diamond who does not know the difference will treat it the same old way they've always treated a stone. *Don't flirt with a hungry lion*!

The only reason why Paul was succeeding, and was always going to continue to succeed in the line of his purpose, with God opening bigger doors of opportunities despite stiff oppositions and hardship was, Paul was under purpose and he did get a precise word from the Lord delivered and spoken by an angel. He heard clearly what the Lord told him about having to testify about Him in Rome. As long as that word was true and Paul stayed committed to the purposes of God, the word that God spoke was going to continue to pave and to make way for him in spite of oppositions.

Remember, it was not a 'borrowed' word of God intended for another person, nor was Paul acting presumptuously in the name of faith. He followed God's leading, and as long as he remained faithful to God's instruction, Paul was bound to come into bigger and better opportunities for the furtherance of the purposes of God for his life. The same applies to anyone under instructions according to the purposes of God, doors will always open before you on their own accord as part of God's arrangement for you to finish your course and to fulfil your purpose. Even those who hate you will find themselves eventually helping God's purposes for your life; *for when a man's ways pleases the Lord, He makes even his enemies to be at peace with him (Prov. 16:7).*

I Can't Help it, Mr. Governor

Of course there were occasions when people, including Festus, thought Paul was *beside himself* and that too much studying had driven him mad (Acts 26:24&25). But, we know one thing that was true, that at least Paul was not mad enough to fall for Festus' beguiling suggestion for him to return to Jerusalem to die. Paul was *mad*, but *mad* in a good way in the wisdom of God and for God's purposes (2Corinthians 5:13). He never settled for the woes of the world nor gave into the cunning devices of the governor, Festus.

Come to think of it, who was really mad in the true sense of the word? Was it Paul who saw through the plots of his accusers and Festus' lies, or the accusers and Festus who thought someone like Paul, a man full of the Spirit of God, could fall for their little scheme? Who was mad? Was it Paul who singularly and consistently pursued his defence with a great detail and logic before 'powerful men', or Fetus who lost all his diplomacy and roared with a deafening shout upon hearing Paul? (Acts 26:24&25)

Truly, if anyone was mad, then it was the posh, pretending governor Festus. Paul's only trouble was, he couldn't help but speak the whole truth of the counsel of God, and to remain faithful to God's purposes for him. That's just the way it is with people who are completely sold out to their God given purpose; they appear *mad* but are indeed very sound (1 Corinthians 4:10-13; 2 Corinthians 6:4-10). You are very sound my friend, if you are totally engrossed into God's purpose for your life on earth. Take heart and don't be discouraged by your critics!

Wisdom for Purpose: There are eight powerful truths emerging from all this, which are relevant for people of purpose:

i.   People's perception of you is not always right. So, don't allow people to define who you are, or what you can or cannot do or say. Paul, in response to Festus, said exactly who he was and dismissed their ugly labelling of his person and identity. He did it right in the presence of people who looked to be intimidating.

ii. Only you can really tell others who you really and truly are. Don't let people predefine you or put you in a category just to cancel you out. It is commonly said, *if you don't say I am, nobody will say thou art!*

iii. No matter how hard or harsh it is said, what others say and think about you is only a proposal until you accept what they say or think. So Paul, instead of accepting Festus' proposal about his state of mind, he educated him, saying, *"I am not mad, most noble Festus, but speak the words of truth and reason" (Acts 26:25).*

Paul was never afraid to even correct governors and kings about who he was, a reasonable man who knew and spoke words that were true and reasonable. Now, here is where it gets muddy for the noble Festus. By Paul's statement, he was implying that if there was any who was not reasonable enough at their meeting then it was Festus, because Paul exonerated their guest, King Agrippa, appealing to his knowledge and belief in the things he spoke. He said,

> *For the king, before whom I also speak freely, knows these things; for I am convinced that none of these things escapes his attention, since this thing was not done in a corner. King Agrippa, do you believe the prophets? I know that you do believe" (Acts 26:26,27).*

iv. Never be afraid to point out when ignorant people, acting in blind confidence and pretending to know the truth, discredit the truth in your presence. Festus, by his own admission to Agrippa, did not know the truth that Paul and the Jews were divided over (Acts 25:20). But Festus the governor, trying to seriously show off and to impress the king and his entourage, opened his mouth of course in sheer ignorance, and if Paul were intimidated by Festus, he would have lost his respect before King Agrippa.

v. If you don't have enough knowledge of what is being discussed or debated, it is always good wisdom and humility, to keep your mouth shut, except for asking question to learn. *Even a fool, when he holds his peace, is counted wise: and he that shuts his lips is esteemed a man of understanding (*Proverb 17:28).

vi. Don't ever allow a mad person to call you mad. When you have the opportunity, quickly educate them, otherwise, don't blame anyone when everyone, all of a sudden starts to call you mad. It never works in your interest to be assumed mad, it will stigmatise you for life. (Proverbs 26:4,5*) Do not answer a fool according to his folly, lest you also be like him. Answer a fool according to his folly, lest he be wise in his own eyes.*

vii. People will accord you the treatment they think you deserve. They will never act towards you more than they think you deserve. So, if you know you deserve better, let them know, and don't hesitate to correct their error firmly at the very first instance. When Festus and the accusers thought in their minds that Paul was a mere prisoner, mad and deserving nothing more than death, they suggested to him to return to Jerusalem where he could eventually be killed. But Paul refused!

viii. Appeal to Caesar if you must! No one will seek your interest better than you would. The reason is simple; no one feels your pain, like you do. So, take every step in the direction of healing. After two governor's trials coupled with another hearing before a king, and two years of waiting, Paul appealed to Caesar, the Roman Emperor himself because he knew he deserved better than how he was being treated.

Walking in the Purposes of God: It was Part of the Bigger Picture

❖❖❖

More Scenes from the Bigger Picture: Sharing with the King and Queen

Paul refused to return to Jerusalem and appealed to appear before Caesar, the Roman Emperor. Festus of course granted Paul's petition. However, Paul had yet one more open door in the city of Caesarea as part of the bigger picture to *his* purpose. This was no ordinary door, it was one that was divinely arranged for Paul to testify before King Agrippa and his *sister* Bernice. Unlike the previous, this other door allowed Paul to do what would be the most extensive and most eloquent of all his presentations of the gospel along with his full testimony. It was on this very occasion that Festus himself, having summoned Paul at the behest of King Agrippa, got the opportunity to hear the gospel of Christ in full.

But before we delve into what took place during Paul's hearing, let's have a little background into how King Agrippa and Bernice got involved, and how their personal issues help to enlighten our observation about all that took place during Paul's trial.

The King and His *Sister*, the Queen

The King referred to here is King Agrippa II, the great-grandson of Herod the Great. Herod as you may well know, was the king who ordered children under the age of two to be killed hoping, to destroy Jesus in his infancy (Matthew 2:16-18). Agrippa's own father, King Agrippa I, harassed the church, beheaded Apostle James and arrested and jailed Peter, and also attempted to kill him. God miraculously set Peter free after constant prayers were offered by the believers, and because the Lord grew increasingly unhappy with King Agrippa I, he died violently in Caesarea (see Acts 12).

King Agrippa I, had three children who were Agrippa II and his two sisters, Queen Bernice, and Drusilla who became the wife of Felix. When Agrippa I died his son, Agrippa II was in Rome training as an heir to the throne. He later became king of a small area in the Lebanon Valley, an area previously under his uncle, Herod of Chalcis. The dominion and territories of Agrippa II later extended to include regions of Traconitis, Abilene, Iturea Perea and cities in Galilee.

Apparently, Agrippa II did not have children of his own, and at the time of meeting with Paul, he was having affairs with his junior sister, Bernice, who as a teenager was initially married to their uncle Chalcis. Unfortunately Chalcis died leaving Bernice with two children. She then returned to live with her brother, Agrippa II. That explains why they travelled together to Caesarea.

Bernice seemed to have had real trouble as a widow because apart from living with and practising incest with her brother, Agrippa II, she later had relationship with Titus, the son of Vespasian, the Roman Emperor.

We are not told if Bernice was religious or if she had a good knowledge of the Christian faith. But we know that King Agrippa II, was considered an authority on Jewish culture, religion and the Christian Faith (cf Acts 26:26). He was also a good friend and supporter of Caesar and Rome.

The King's Involvement with Paul

King Agrippa and Bernice's visit to Caesarea was purely political, to call on the newly appointed governor Festus and to pursue bilateral relationship with him. He only heard about Paul's predicament while in Caesarea. Apparently, he may have taken interest in hearing Paul simply because, unlike Festus, the King had good knowledge of the debate and arguments surrounding Paul's accusations vis-à-vis the Christian beliefs.

Or perhaps, Festus was simply inquisitive, and also considered that seeing and hearing Paul could be a politically profitable exercise to impress his guests. Similar instance occurred in the case of the Lord Jesus. We know of the other Herod, Antipas who wanted to see Jesus just to witness a miracle, desiring to prove if what he heard about the miracle working power of Jesus was true (Lk 23:8).

In the Firing line of Purpose: the King, Queen, Governor and Famous Elites Face the Truth

Something very remarkable about Paul was that, he never shied away from any God-given opportunity to deliver the gospel. With Festus and his guests, King Agrippa and *Queen* Bernice, and the eminent citizens including accredited Roman officials of Caesarea, all in place, Paul delivered under the power of the Holy Spirit, what I believe, was well rehearsed for the occasion. His delivery was so crisp, clear and detailed that he left nothing untouched. The strength of Paul's message was in his undeniable historical background set alongside his unassailable transformation and new life, which were self-evident even before his hearers.

It is a fact that historically, many men and women of *high offices* and some belonging to a self-styled corps of so-called *famous* elite and the highly *educated* can hardly stand the truth. They mostly would oppose the truth because they are inclined to think that opposing the truth somehow helps to blot out light, especially when works clearly in darkness have to continue.

Some also oppose the truth in order to maintain the status quo without having to disturb the delicate *balance* in an over-appeased, over-pacified but still guilty conscience. This might be exactly what we see governor Festus doing in the story; a *balancing act*.

Although we are told that he was unlearned in what Paul was educating him about, at least through his testimonies, Festus was bent on opposing the truth because it seemed easy to do so. He seemed to be fooled into thinking that simply shouting, being rude and aggressive would curb the truth (Acts 26:25). Also, Festus' formula for curbing the truth seemed easy because all you have to do is to shout loudly, to bully and to intimidate your opponent.

However, just like Festus, we all come to accept later in life the uncomfortable reality that standing against the truth is a game we cannot win, until we recognize the truth and become subject to it (Acts 26:9-20). You will require some real guts to admit and to allow the truth to prevail, but that is the right way forward, since *we can do nothing against the truth, but for the truth (2 Corinthians 13:8)*.

Our real problem with the truth is that we tend to get very comfortable with the familiar, and anything that places demand on us to reassess what we already accept as the rule, immediately its seems like a threat. But, here is Scriptural wisdom for those who think they can get away with simply opposing the truth because it appears easy to do so: *the truth you ignore today will haunt you tomorrow, and the truth you oppose right now will be the greatest enemy to your free future.* Jesus says, *And you shall know the truth, and the truth shall make you free (John 8:32)*.

Paul took his time to tell Festus, the King and all present about the very secret to his new found life; how he converted from darkness into the wonderful saving light of Jesus Christ. He explained to them the secret of his great hope and new life coupled with his freedom over the power of death and the fear of human beings and authorities. He withheld nothing from all who heard him, showing how everyone could discover their personal purpose, and equally benefit from the great grace and forgiveness of God.

Paul presented his listeners with unparalleled wisdom from God's Word, beginning from the Old Testament, and then related it to the awful human condition of sin and death. After that Paul told them about how anyone could find total freedom and victory in Christ Jesus. Regrettably, those listening to Paul were simply not willing or prepared to receive Paul's testimony. They would not believe that they might be saved, which was similar to the plight of the Pharisees, whom Jesus literally lamented over, when He said they would die in their sins because of their unbelief and deliberate refusal to accept His testimony.

The Pharisees therefore said to Him, "You bear witness of Yourself; Your witness is not true." Jesus answered and said to them, "Even if I bear witness of Myself, My witness is true, for I know where I came from and where I am going; but you do not know where I come from and where I am going. You judge according to the flesh; I judge no one. And yet if I do judge, My judgment is true; for I am not alone, but I am with the Father who sent Me. It is also written in your law that the testimony of two men is true. I am One who bears witness of Myself, and the Father who sent Me bears witness of Me." Then they said to Him, "Where is Your Father?" Jesus answered, "You know neither Me nor My Father. If you had known Me, you would have known My Father also." These words Jesus spoke in the treasury, as He taught in the temple; and no one laid hands on Him, for His hour had not yet come. Then Jesus said to them again, "I am going away, and you will seek Me, and will die in your sin. Where I go you cannot come." So the Jews said, "Will He kill Himself, because He says, 'Where I go you cannot come'?" And He said to them, "You are from beneath; I am from above. You are of this world; I am not of this world. Therefore I said to you that you will die in your sins; for if you do not believe that I am He, you will die in your sins." (John 8:13-24)

Again, why didn't they believe Paul? Probably we can glean some reasons from Paul's own testimony concerning his purpose and commission as found in Acts 26:17-20.

> *I will deliver you from the Jewish people, as well as from the Gentiles, to whom I now send you, to open their eyes, in order to turn them from darkness to light, and from the power of Satan to God, that they may receive forgiveness of sins and an inheritance among those who are sanctified by faith in Me.' "Therefore, King Agrippa, I was not disobedient to the heavenly vision, but declared first to those in Damascus and in Jerusalem, and throughout all the region of Judea, and then to the Gentiles, that they should repent, turn to God, and do works befitting repentance.*

From this passage of Scripture we could assign three points as the main reasons for unbelief among those who hear the gospel:

1. **The Power of Darkness**
   *John 3:19 – And this is the condemnation, that the light has come into the world, and men loved darkness rather than light, because their deeds were evil. **Ephesians 2:2**, in which you once walked according to the course of this world, according to the prince of the power of the air, the spirit who now works in the sons of disobedience. **Ephesians 4:17,18** This I say, therefore, and testify in the Lord, that you should no longer walk as the rest of the Gentiles walk, in the futility of their mind, ^{18} having their understanding darkened, being alienated from the life of God, because of the ignorance that is in them, because of the blindness of their heart. **Ephesians 6:12** For we do not wrestle against flesh and blood, but against principalities, against powers, against the rulers of the darkness of this age, against spiritual hosts of wickedness in the heavenly places.*

2. **The Power of Satan**
   *Whose minds the god of this age has blinded, who do not believe, lest the light of the gospel of the glory of Christ, who is the image of God, should shine on them. **2 Corinthians 4:4. Also John 12:31; 14:30***

3. **The Principle and Proposition of Faith**
    Those in the world don't get it. It is difficult for the carnal mind, which is used to all things material, to grasp the principle of faith. They think they can do it the way they have been accustomed to, by scheming and by personal efforts and a behaviour or worldview that is built on *show me and I will believe. Ephesians 2:8,9* say, *for by grace you have been saved through faith and that not of yourselves; it is the gift of God, not of works, lest anyone should boast.*

These three points, in many ways, explain why people fail to receive the truth of the gospel and fail to become converted. But, how about the *Festus'*, the *Agrippas*, the *Bernices* and the so-called *famous, elites* and *highly educated* today, who have serious sin and guilt issues, and live scandalously, yet are the same people too famous, too elitist, and too educated to their own peril? The three points explanation already mentioned may be why the majority of them do not receive the gospel. However, in addition they may also suffer from further limiting barriers, which often relates to either one or a combination from the list below:

1. **People Pleasing -** *"For do I now persuade men, or God? Or do I seek to please men? For if I still pleased men, I would not be a bondservant of Christ"*, *(Galatians 1:10)*. Our Lord Jesus says, *"woe to you when all men speak well of you, for so did their fathers to the false prophets,"* Luke 6:26. He (Jesus) knew all men and would not commit himself to them. (John 2:24)

2. **Personal Pride -** *Pride goes before destruction, and a haughty spirit before a fall, Proverbs 16:18. For the lack of knowledge My people perish, Hosea 4:6. For all that is in the world - the lust of the flesh, the lust of the eyes, and the pride of life - is not of the Father but is of the world. (I John 2:16)*

3. **Procrastination -** This is a sad symptom of a deadly deception in which one thinks he or she is in control. *There is a way that seems right to a man, but its end is the way of death (Proverbs 14:12).*

> ... *"Today, if you will hear His voice, do not harden your hearts as in the rebellion." For who, having heard, rebelled? Indeed, was it not all who came out of Egypt, led by Moses? Now with whom was He angry forty years? Was it not with those who sinned, whose corpses fell in the wilderness? (Hebrews 3:15-17)*

4. **Pleasure and Pressure** - *So the next day, when Agrippa and Bernice had come **with great pomp**, and had entered the auditorium with the commanders and the prominent men of the city, at Festus' command Paul was brought in Acts 25:23); For all that is in the world - the lust of the flesh, the lust of the eyes, and the pride of life - is not of the Father but is of the world, (I John 2:16).*

5. **Prejudice** - *Is this not the carpenter, the Son of Mary, and brother of James, Joses, Judas, and Simon? And are not His sisters here with us?" So they were offended at Him. [4] But Jesus said to them, "A prophet is not without honour except in his own country, among his own relatives, and in his own house." [5] Now He could do no mighty work there, (Mark 6:3-5).* It is like what is said in sales and marketing, 'people buy people'. We take that too far in real life and relationships and it becomes an excuse to despise others and hinder ourselves from receiving the truth from those God has ordained to help us find our way back to Him.

Missed Opportunity

They met and consulted behind closed doors having listened to Paul. Festus who consented to being a *novice* to the things of God (*Acts 25:20*) was the reigning governor. Agrippa and Bernice were morally bankrupt and corrupt. Altogether, they all had real issues, yet they chose to remain adamant and refused to receive the grace of God for them to be forgiven of all their sins. They had the chance to lift the weight of sins and guilt from their overburdened shoulders but, for reasons I have already mentioned, they refused.

Although Paul explained fully that all people were forgivable in spite of their sins, those trying him still permitted their vain and prideful regard for themselves to prevent them from receiving Jesus as their Lord and Saviour, in order to be saved.

Sadly, the passage even admits that Agrippa, the King was convicted (*Acts 26:28*) but refused to translate his conviction into conversion for Christ Jesus in order to be completely set free from personal guilt, shame and damnation of Satan. The Holy Spirit of God touched his heart, but the King would not let go. However, as their custom was, the King, Festus, Bernice, and all that sat with them rather adamantly aroused to consult behind closed doors.

Their verdict from behind close door only affirmed what Paul already knew, but was of no real consequence in regard to God's purpose for Paul's life. Their verdict only confirmed what the bigger picture of God's purpose for Paul entailed; getting Paul to testify about Him before whosoever, whether in chains or without chains. And ultimately, His purpose was to get Paul to Rome.

Although, they do not tell Paul exactly what the details of their verdict were, they agreed – *this man is doing nothing deserving of death or chains...this man might have been set free if he had not appealed to Caesar (Acts 26:31:32).* They reached the same conclusion as Paul had argued all along.

Now, this is no rocket science, my friend; however, know that just like Paul, some difficulties you must go through will not necessarily be as a result of your personal sin or disobedience. They are basically because of your purpose, and as you walk in the purposes of God, those difficulties no matter how tough and tedious, they will only serve God's purposes for your life. So, once again do not fret, but take heart and be courageous as God told Joshua his servant:

> *Have I not commanded you? Be strong and of good courage; do not be afraid, nor be dismayed, for the Lord your God is with you wherever you go.(Joshua 1:9)*

A Clash of Destinies

But what was all this about? It was about a double-pronged work, but under the control of one important thing: *Divine Destiny*. For Paul, it was his personal purpose taking him through what seemed like an unending circle. However, as a man under heavenly commission, he had to go through whatever, meet whoever and go wherever along the line of his preordained purpose, in this case testifying in Rome.

For his listeners and those purported to be trying Paul, including Festus, Agrippa and Bernice, unbeknown to them they were clashing with their destiny to receive a life-time gift of forgiveness and to get right with their Maker. However, they were so trapped in the performance of their man-given commission that they missed their God given opportunity.

Paul, God's messenger, was right before them, but they saw a mere prisoner. It leaves one to wonder, why didn't they consider, if Paul had done nothing deserving of all that he was accused of, could there have been something more purposeful to their meeting with Paul at that crucial time of their lives?

Wisdom for Purpose*:* There is always more to the people God brings your way than the obvious. Take your time and search God's divine purpose behind the people He brings your way – they could be your ladder to the heights you've always desired and your escape from issues that always haunted you.

Dismissing the Angel

Do not forget to entertain strangers, for by so doing some have unwittingly entertained angels (Hebrews 13:2).

Paul knew, and experienced firsthand, what it entails to be under man's commission, and going all out to please human tradition at the risk of following God's righteous commandment. He had previously been zealous for man's service and served man's order and commandments until he encountered Christ on the Damascus road. In His own testimony, Paul confessed,

"My manner of life from my youth, which was spent from the beginning among my own nation at Jerusalem, all the Jews know. [5] They knew me from the first, if they were willing to testify, that according to the strictest sect of our religion I lived a Pharisee... [9] "Indeed, I myself thought I must do many things contrary to the name of Jesus of Nazareth. [10] This I also did in Jerusalem, and many of the saints I shut up in prison, having received authority from the chief priests; and when they were put to death, I cast my vote against them. [11] And I punished them often in every synagogue and compelled them to blaspheme; and being exceedingly enraged against them, I persecuted them even to foreign cities. [12] "While thus occupied, as I journeyed to Damascus with authority and commission from the chief priests, [13] at midday, O king, along the road I saw a light from heaven, brighter than the sun, shining around me and those who journeyed with me. [14] And when we all had fallen to the ground, I heard a voice speaking to me and saying in the Hebrew language, 'Saul, Saul, why are you persecuting Me? It is hard for you to kick against the goads.' [15] So I said, 'Who are You, Lord?' And He said, 'I am Jesus, whom you are persecuting. [16] But rise and stand on your feet; for I have appeared to you for this purpose, to make you a minister and a witness both of the things which you have seen and of the things which I will yet reveal to you (Acts 26:4-16).

Isn't it amazing the wisdom of God and the calibre of people He chooses to speak to us when He needs to speak to us or deliver us according to His eternal purposes! God couldn't have found any better messenger than Paul to speak to Festus, Bernice and Agrippa about His love and forgiveness. Paul was the most appropriate vessel with a background akin to Festus, Bernice and Agrippa. He was a living witness, the one person with every audacity to speak plainly about the wonderful power of the grace of God to all who have deviated from the path of righteousness to follow vague and empty pleasures contrary to God's purposes. Referring to his past occupation and manner of life, Paul admits,

> *This is a faithful saying and worthy of all acceptance, that Christ Jesus came into the world to save sinners, of whom I am chief.* [16] *However, for this reason I obtained mercy, that in me first Jesus Christ might show all longsuffering, as a pattern to those who are going to believe on Him for everlasting life. Now to the King eternal, immortal, invisible, to God who alone is wise be honour and glory forever and ever. Amen (I Timothy 1:15-17).*

He is a *chief of sinners,* Paul says! But that's not the whole story. He also knew that God saved him as a pattern and example for those who are going to believe on Christ Jesus for eternal life. And what Paul was saying is; if he could be saved, a chief of sinners, then anyone else, regardless of their sins, can be saved. This was the message of hope that came through Paul's brilliant testimony before those who judged him, including Festus, Bernice and Agrippa. But they rejected the testimony of Paul!

What else could God do when sinners so blatantly turned their back on what is the most basic but quintessential thing to do in life for one's soul, happiness and freedom now and forevermore? Festus, Bernice, Agrippa and the rest were literally told, your guilt of a life-time could be wiped away immediately, and instead of living recklessly for yourself and for things that do not bring true joy, you can begin to have a life of purpose with true satisfaction. But they refused.

Although it seemed like an ordinary meeting, one cannot help but begin to wonder, if those trying Paul, especially their leaders did not see the connection and how the plans and purposes of God was unfolding in the wake of their discussion and arrangements.

First, just as Paul *stumbled* into the Kingdom of God on the Damascus' Road, it happened to be the same arrangement for Festus, Bernice and Agrippa. Even though they were having what they thought was a political visit, this was indeed their *Damascus' Road*. It is difficult to discredit the wisdom that Felix, leaving Paul in prison although he had no reason to, was divinely occasioned by God to permit Paul to speak to Festus about the love of Christ. Unfortunately, he dismissed Paul as someone who was mad.

My question to you right now is; who has God sent to you to be of blessing that you are dismissing as *mad* and *crazy?* Can you perceive the wisdom of God in your daily encounters with such people as your help from God? Who and what have you already cancelled out just because they did not fit your particular expectation and description of what or who you think they should have been and looked like? I have seen people dismiss pastors and men of God just because they did not look like *real* pastors, and yet they were God-sent for their deliverance. They've literally missed their God-sent angels because they were too busy being preoccupied with themselves.

> *Do not forget to entertain strangers, for by so doing some have unwittingly entertained angels (Hebrews 13:2).*

> *But the Lord said to Samuel, "Do not look at his appearance- or at his physical stature, because I have refused him. For the Lord does not see as man sees; for man looks at the outward appearance, but the Lord looks at the heart" (1 Samuel 16:7)*

It is not unusual that a great number of people including Christians, have missed their moments with the Lord Jesus just because they were full of prejudice, and probably over familiarity as we see happened in Nazareth. When those who despised Jesus in their hearts saw Him, they began to question,

Is this not the carpenter, the Son of Mary, and brother of James, Joses, Judas, and Simon? And are not His sisters here with us?" *So they were offended at Him.[4] But Jesus said to them, "A prophet is not without honour except in his own country, among his own relatives, and in his own house."[5] Now He could do no mighty work there, except that He laid His hands on a few sick people and healed them.[6] And He marvelled because of their unbelief. Then He went about the villages in a circuit, teaching (Mark 6:3-6).*

How sad, that King Agrippa, Bernice and Festus could not go beyond artificial, self-imposed and self-perpetuated boundaries to become free from sin and to be saved by grace. How odd that many who have eyes don't see. I pray that you can and will see the difference, and when the Master comes passing by, you will seize your moments with Him and be healed and be saved. Paul was definitely the angel sent from God, the most appropriate person to bring God's good news of salvation to King Agrippa, Queen Bernice, governor Festus and the eminent citizens in their company. But unfortunately, they saw a prisoner instead of God's messenger.

I leave you with three stanzas of Fanny Crosby's, 1868 all-time great hymn that has inspired myself and millions of others. It represents the heart of a person truly recognising their need for the Saviour, Jesus Christ, and indeed recognising their need for purpose in life and then translating that desire into taking practical steps to achieve it.

Pass me not, O gentle Saviour,
Hear my humble cry;
While on others Thou art calling,
Do not pass me by.

Trusting only in Thy merit,
Would I seek Thy face;
Heal my wounded, broken spirit,
Save me by Thy grace.[1]

Let me at Thy throne of mercy
Find a sweet relief,
Kneeling there in deep contrition
Help my unbelief.

Refrain
Saviour, Saviour
Hear my humble cry;
While on others Thou art calling
Do not pass me by.

The Unavoidable Challenges to His Purposes: Never Loose Heart

❖❖❖

Many Dangers and Toils

"... and lo, I am with you always, even to the end of the age" Amen (Matt. 28:20). "Now I know for certain that the Lord has sent His angel, and has delivered me from the hand of Herod and from all the expectation of the Jewish people" (Acts 12:11)

Dangerous Decision - the Experts say, Yes

Paul's plea to stand trial in Rome before Caesar's Judgement Seat was granted. Instead of a Jerusalem trial, which was nothing but a secret scam hatched by Paul's accusers to destroy him. Appearing before Caesar's Judgement seat was at least better than returning to Jerusalem. God's grace prevailed, and the wicked expectations of Paul's enemies were thwarted, saving him from having to worry about any immediate threat of death, since the snare of Jerusalem's death sentence was broken (Psalms 124:7). He could now focus on the long journey to Rome as a prisoner.

Julius, a centurion of the Augustan Regiment, was charged with the responsibility of delivering Paul and other prisoners to Rome. Accompanying Paul from Caesarea were his associates in ministry, Luke, the Physician (Col. 4:14) and Aristarchus, a Macedonian of Thessalonica. They were there to provide the much needed support and companionship Paul would require through his time of need. It was only a day into their trip and Paul had already found favour with Julius, who allowed him to freely visit his friends and to receive essential care whenever they had the opportunity to dock, either to change ship or to shelter briefly in places.

Right from the outset, their trip promised to be difficult. The winds and waves of the sea were already posing great difficulties as they blew and thrashed contrary to their direction. As a result sailing became tediously slow and very treacherous (Acts 27:4-9). Conditions at sea presented another situation of its own. Paul, who had escaped the return-to-Jerusalem plots and dangers from his accusers and Festus, was now facing another danger of different calibre against some of the most powerful elements in the universe (cf Galatians 4:3,9; 2 Peter 3:10), the winds and waves of the sea.

It is one thing to face human enemies, but totally another thing to wrestle against ferocious, inanimate forces with monstrous power to destroy life, but with no ability to reason. Where do you start? But Paul, the man of God, saw that it would not be long before all on board including their possessions would be buried at sea if they continued in the way they were heading. He perceived real, looming danger ahead, and advised against setting sail from their present harbour in order to prevent loss of lives and property.

However, the majority on board the ship, including Julius the centurion and the helmsman of the ship, decided differently to Paul's advice, and set sail all the same. Remember, to shrug off Paul and to snub his advice was also to ignore the wisdom of a man of God. We find from the passage two main reasons why the authority on board the ship refused Paul's advice and suggestions: first, *Majority Decision* and second, *Unsuitable Circumstance* not allowing them to winter at their present harbour.

Another reason which is implied by the passage is this; *Expert Advice.* They would not listen to Paul because obviously Julius the Centurion found the *expert* advice of the helmsman and the owner of the ship more persuasive (Acts 26:11).

Note the last reason for not heeding Paul's advice was because of Expert Advice. Does that sound familiar? I'm sure it does. How often we've taken things for granted or done things purely based on what the experts said, only to find out in the end that the expert themselves were terribly wrong. That does not mean you stop listening to experts, it's only that experts are never God, even if some presume to play god.

Unfortunately, that's one of the major problems plaguing most societies today. We have a few arrogant people posing as experts on almost everything conceivable. They force their expert advice on gullible people; telling them everything from climate change to how to live, how to run their homes and raise their children. By their advice, families and what used to be a beautiful oeuvre of communities and life in general, has not only suffered great loss, but as it stands, future generations face even greater threats as a result. Similarly, the men and women with sheer majority power, who act on so-called experts' statistics and advice, backed by unmatched resources don't mind throwing things out of balance by refusing to acknowledge that there is more to life than mere stats.

When it comes to church life the situation is not so different. Believers unfortunately turn to use majority consent as a rule for the way things should be done. As a result you have committees and boards, who are more than half of the time wrong, but because the majority registered a *yes* vote for a wrong decision, the pastor and those who see things a little differently are expected to just follow. Regard for God's leading and spiritual authority under such situations is simply thrown out of the widow for human wisdom instead. Churches and believers also go on to make important choices and to take critical decisions based on what is generally acceptable in majority opinion, instead of what is expedient based on God's Word, and the leadings of His Holy Spirit.

We can't but ask this generation also, like the great Prophet Isaiah in his popular but pointed question saying, *who has believed our report? And to whom has the arm of the Lord been revealed? (Isaiah 53:1)*

***Wisdom for Purpose*:** Few things to note. First, think twice before making a decision about your future. Never allow the pressure of circumstances to rush you into hasty decision of uncalculated consequences.

Second, think twice if you will have to ignore your Man of God's advice and perspective within a potentially volatile situation. Never ignore a reasoning or advice from your true Man of God. It may prove fatally dangerous in the end.

Thirdly, don't think twice if you have to choose between the voice of God and majority opinion. The choice is clear – God wins! You are more than a majority with God on your side, and God's voice and God's perspective will always prevail in the end.

> *The floods have lifted up, O Lord, the floods have lifted up their voice; the floods lift up their waves. The Lord on high is mightier than the noise of many waters, than the mighty waves of the sea (Psalms 93:3-4).*

> *... that your faith should not be in the wisdom of men but in the power of God (1 Corinthians 2:5).*

> *For the wisdom of this world is foolishness with God. For it is written, "He catches the wise in their own craftiness" (1 Cor. 3:19)*

Temporary Relief – the Majority says, Yes

Despite the encompassing danger, together Julius the Centurion, the helmsman, the owner of the ship and the majority on board the ship, agreed to set sail, not willing to winter at the harbour of Fair Haven. Of course, their decision to sail under very dangerous and unfriendly weather condition had no regard for their safety at sea.

The authorities decided to set sail against Paul's advice, motivated by their need to press forward to Phoenix; thinking Phoenix was a more suitable harbour to winter at (Acts 27:11,12). They blatantly ignored Paul's advice that everyone on board the ship might lose their life if they sailed from Fair Haven. They decided to set sail and took things in their own hands because the majority on board the ship merely feared momentary winter cold at Fair Haven, but were ready to risk losing their lives on the sea. In a way, the majority decided to jump from the frying pan to the fire, so to speak, and to strain out the speck but only to swallow the plank! Isn't it ironic that the majority often argues and fights over trivialities but ignores what really matters; in this case, life?

We all do it sometimes, but the majority will keep us doing it often just because we are often told by so-called experts *if we must act and take decisions, it must be now* while the pressure is on. And why do we have to make the decision now? Because the pressure is on, and we think we must do everything to avoid the pressure of what is now, even when we have not actually considered what lies ahead. It is called, *treating the symptoms,* and *having a temporary relief* from our immediate pain and pressure only to realise a more severe one after the effect of whatever *painkiller* we took has worn off.

A Heavy Price to Pay

The way forward is to decide in favour of long term, permanent solutions even if our temporary pain and pressure in the present seem severe. Imagine if the crew on the ship decided to winter at Fair Haven despite the bitter winter cold, it would have meant avoidance of a life-threatening sail over very tempestuous sea for the long term. However, the crew on board decided to sail based on short term benefit of avoiding winter cold at a harbour they thought was unsuitable for wintering in.

In the end, the decision of the majority paid quite a dividend. It was shockingly beyond the majority's expectation and turned out to be exactly what Paul predicted. Instead of having the pleasure of their decision to set sail against the advice of Paul, they were now engaged in serious and desperate fight to hang onto their lives and to save the cargo on board the ship.

Like most bad decision we make, their worst consequences tend to be delayed, and we are fooled into believing in the wisdom of our decision or even patting ourselves on the back initially. And this is where we could even be trapped further into getting complacent, because everything about our decision in the meantime seems to be yielding their desired results. As the passage indicates, all was going well, according to plan and the helmsman and others concerned seemed to be in control. And then came the unexpected. Instead of being in control and driving the ship, they lost control and were being driven by the ship wherever the storm led them.

> *When a gentle south wind began to blow, they thought they had obtained what they wanted; so they weighed anchor and sailed along the shore of Crete. Before very long, a wind of hurricane force, called the "northeaster," swept down from the island. The ship was caught by the storm and could not head into the wind; so we gave way to it and were driven along. As we passed to the lee of a small island called Cauda, we were hardly able to make the lifeboat secure. When the men had hoisted it aboard, they passed ropes under the ship itself to hold it together. Fearing that they would run aground on the sandbars of Syrtis, they lowered the sea anchor and let the ship be driven along (Acts 27:13-17 NIV).*

Have you ever been lashed and driven by your decision or choice? Yes, it can be hard and harsh when you are left to the mercies of your poor decisions and their outcomes. They literally drive you mad and insane. You try to gain control again, but it seems like a wild *Spanish Bull Run* gone out of hand in which the Bull goes about in frenzy heading and mauling everyone in its path. Soon you realize that although you took the decision alone to let the 'Bull' out, others also get adversely affected in the violent wake of things getting out of control as a result of your poor choices.

Running with the Bull: the Price of Poor Choices

If you've witnessed the traditional Spanish Bull Run then you might get a more vivid picture of what I mean by saying that the outcome of our poor choices and decisions literally *drive* and haunt us in the end. The traditional Spanish Bull Run attracts thousands of people from around the world. At their own volition, they descend on Spain every year from the 7th to 14th July at Pamplona to start Spain's famous bull-running festival to honour Navarre capital's patron saint, San Fermin.

After daybreak, on the 7th of July, the runners gather at the starting line and ask San Fermín, as their Patron, to guide them through the Bull Run and to give them what they believe is his blessing. The run begins and the bulls are loosed onto the street. The bulls run along the narrow strait of about half a mile to a bullring. The runners then dash along in front of the bulls, aiming to feel the breath of the bull on their backs, getting as close as possible whilst trying to avoid getting gored by their sharp horns. Before the Run, the bulls are aggressively stirred until they cannot tolerate human beings. They are ready to viciously gore anyone down. In short they are raised and trained purposely to kill out of boiling anger.

It is one of the maddest things to do on earth for no particular trophy, recognition or reward. Men do it simply for the pleasure they derive, and probably also in an attempt to continue to keep an old tradition alive. Some participants get viciously horn-gored or mauled by untamed and ferocious bulls. The rule of the game is, you have to run for your life and run in such a way that you never cross the path of any of the wild bulls which randomly chase everyone. Runners look for a gap in the fence to slip through or jump over, or a space against the wall of the street. When the bulls finally reach the end of the street, they go into pens and are kept until later that day, when they are killed in bullfights.

Originally only a few brave people ran with the bulls but now thousands travel from around the world to run before killer bulls that weigh about 1500lbs each. A number of fatal injuries and deaths by goring and trampling have been reported.

The most recent, as recorded by news reporters, was in July 2009 when a 27 year old was unfortunately pierced in the neck and lung during a run, in which one bull suddenly separated from the pack.

How does all this relate to our discussion about how our decisions and their outcome could *drive* and haunt us in ways that we had not conceived? Again, this is not about moral judgment of decisions or even the morality of participating in a Bull Run. I am using the Bull Run illustration to make a point about the innate power embedded in decisions and decision making, which when care is not taken, might derail God's purposes for us and eventually ruin our lives. It is about the perils and how our unsuspecting desires for immediate pleasure without calculating their inevitable price we have to pay in the long run, could change or ruin our lives forever.

In our Bull Run scenario, the participants are aware of the huge stakes involved, yet for some reason, without being coerced, they voluntarily decide to do the Run. Remember it is their decision to run before the killer bulls. A decision, that was taken probably days or weeks prior to the actual run, soon becomes very real when they finally find themselves before the raging killer bulls as the runners fight to save their lives. Why are they running? Their decision! They are being *driven* as an outcome of their decision to participate in a daring and vicious 'game' with an animal that they cannot control in anyway. If they should lose their lives or escape *by the skin of the teeth* it all hinges on the initial decision to participate in a bull run.

However, losing life or incurring fatal injuries are always the worst consequence of the decision to run before the bull. But, as with most decisions, we initially tend to justify why we settle for one and not the other. And quite often, we tend to have that brief honeymoon period when we think our decisions are paying as expected. That is exactly what happens in the Bull Run. You decide to run; although you have some butterflies in your stomach, it is fun when you initially start the Bull Run. You seem to be in control right from the outset because there are no immediate surprises yet.

The reasons for this are pretty simple. The bull runners initially are allowed a safe distance between themselves and the bulls. Runners start out when a rocket is fired into the air, and then a number of fighting bulls are let out onto the streets. A second rocket is fired to ensure that everyone knows the killer bulls are loosed in the street. Until the bulls really get very close to you, or until you begin to see and feel the crowd of other runners helplessly crushing against you, you don't really fully appreciate the seriousness or madness of your decision to participate.

I suppose Julius the Centurion, the owner of the ship and the majority who had initially decided not to listen to Paul, realized the seriousness of their error, only when they became caught in the storm. They have had their brief honeymoon period, *when the south wind blew softly.* Then suddenly, they could do nothing except allow themselves to be *driven.* Their decision only returned to bite them.

> *When the south wind blew softly, supposing that they had obtained their desire, putting out to sea, they sailed close by Crete. But not long after, a tempestuous head wind arose, called Euroclydon. So when the ship was caught, and could not head into the wind, we let her drive (Acts 27:13-15).*

Storm of Life May Come

It was now a fight for survival more than anything else. They were overwhelmed, having experienced persistent violent battering from the storm. They became terrifyingly left at the mercies of the tempest and, being full of fear for their own safety and that of the ship, they began to do the unthinkable by throwing their cargo overboard (Acts 27:18-20). This was followed by throwing the ship's tackle overboard with their own hands, a sign of great desperation. It might have been quite some job they had to do, trying to brave the storm and at the same time trying to discharge cargo from the ship over a violent sea!

Such is life. It takes only one dangerous turn and you unavoidably find yourself in a thick quagmire of untold proportion. You try everything you know to reverse the circle of mess you find yourself in, but it only leads to another mess. All of a sudden life gets you even busier than you have hands to handle. Just like Paul and those on the ship, while attempting to throw overboard your *cargo* of issues that are weighing you down and trying to ground your *ship* of life, here comes the crashing *tackle* of your ship calling for your attention at the same time. While you're still at it, you soon realise the violent tempestuous storm is never abating, if anything, it only seems to intensify each time you look up.

Often we come across good intentioned people who attempt a great business project in *summer* but all of a sudden because *winter* sets in unexpectedly, they pray if it were possible to breakeven. Instead of profiting, they are forced to fight for recouping only their initial investment, because things went wrong. But, while they are still thinking and hoping that things will change, the bad news comes. Not only can they not save their business, but they have to forfeit their home as well because they cannot keep up with payments to their creditors. And, just when they were trying to negotiate with their creditors to defer some payments, something else happens. Their spouse that could no longer cope with the unbearable weight of their financial burdens on the family decides it was time to quit their marriage, blaming it all on their partner's decision and stupidity. That's called the storms of life, and has many ramifications and applications. But, hold on!

Hope Does not Disappoint

> *Yes, and I will continue to rejoice, for I know that through your prayers and the help given by the Spirit of Jesus Christ, **what has happened to me will turn out for my deliverance. I eagerly expect and hope that I will in no way be ashamed,** but will have sufficient courage so that now as always Christ will be exalted in my body, whether by life or by death. For to me, to live is Christ and to die is gain. If I am to go on living in the body, this will mean fruitful labour for me. Yet what shall I choose? I do not know! I am torn between the two: I desire to depart and be with Christ, which is better by far; but it is more necessary for you that I remain in the body. Convinced of this, I know that I will remain, and I will continue with all of you for your progress and joy in the faith (Philippians 1:19-25).*

The worst was yet to come. It was already three days since they had been tossed up and down continuously on high sea. The ship and all who were in it were headed for a completely unintended destination. However, they had no control whatsoever to navigate into their desired direction. Even natural means of navigation like the stars had hidden their face. The sun would not rise over them, and it had been so for many days. Now, it was tougher than when they first began. So, those on board came to one conclusion which seemed completely logical under the circumstances. They ... *finally gave up all hope of being saved (Acts 27:20).*

But for Paul, who had now known and walked with the Lord for about two decades, he knew hope comes hard under such circumstance but hope does come in the end and hope does not disappoint!

> *And not only that, but we also glory in tribulations, knowing that tribulation produces perseverance; and perseverance, character; and character, hope. Now hope does not disappoint, because the love of God has been poured out in our hearts by the Holy Spirit who was given to us (Roman 5:3-5).*

Paul and the brothers accompanying him probably realised it was time to pray, and they might have been praying through all that mighty turbulence.

The passage admits that they fasted and abstained from food for a long time. Whether this was intentional or not, spiritual or forced upon them because they were disturbed through the much struggle at sea, no one can tell with absolute certainty. But, it is feasible to think that Paul and Luke, and probably other Christians on board, would have had some spiritual basis for abstaining from food to pray and to ask God's help for their deliverance.

It is against good logic to think that while they had bread on board (see vr 35 of chpt 27), people going through such hardship would voluntarily decide not to eat for strength, if it were not for a good reason like fast and prayer. On the other hand in verse 5 of chapter 27, the Fast or Day of Atonement is mentioned. Could they have just carried it through? Whatever the case was, it was normal to fast when seeking God's assistance. In the Book of Daniel chapter ten, Daniel himself similarly waited on the Lord for twenty-one days when he wanted answers from God.

Paul's desire and, I believe, his prayers were answered. Think about that appropriate expletive that has become well known about how our Lord works in answer to prayers: *Divine Delay is not Divine Denial.* Our God is always on time, and He will never leave you nor forsake you. Hope may come not so easily and in the time we desire it, but hope comes eventually. And Hope in God does not disappoint.

> *Whenever I am afraid, I will trust in You. You number my wanderings; Put my tears into Your bottle; are they not in Your book? When I cry out to You, then my enemies will turn back; this I know, because God is for me. In God (I will praise His word), In the Lord (I will praise His word), In God I have put my trust; I will not be afraid. What can man do to me? (Psalms 56:3,8-10)*

The Driving Force Behind His Purpose: You Have What it Takes, Use it

❖❖❖

Belief Beyond Doubts

I love what follows after Paul's time of waiting. For me its very tone and atmosphere radiate utter and great confidence, and refutes any suggestion of uncertainties from Paul about his future, although he was in great difficulties at sea. Have a read and hear Paul for yourself:

But after long abstinence from food, then Paul stood in the midst of them and said, "Men, you should have listened to me, and not have sailed from Crete and incurred this disaster and loss. [22] And now I urge you to take heart, for there will be no loss of life among you, but only of the ship. [23] For there stood by me this night an angel of the God to whom I belong and whom I serve, [24] saying, 'Do not be afraid, Paul; you must be brought before Caesar; and indeed God has granted you all those who sail with you.' [25] Therefore take heart, men, for I believe God that it will be just as it was told me (Acts 27:21-25).

There is no trace of uncertainty, no doubt or sign of a troubled heart with Paul. He is so convinced beyond belief! Can't he see that the waves and sea water intend to destroy them, or has he any clue the depth of threat to their lives? I am of the view that this was the kind of reaction Paul's fellow passengers had when he spoke and acted as though everything was under control. There's no doubt in my mind that some even dismissed him as a lunatic.

But such is our faith in God, and there is no better time to show and stand in faith than when you find yourself in the middle of nowhere, surrounded by the waters of the sea. That is the right time to work your faith, *calling those things that be not as though they were (Romans 4:17).* Right in the middle of the sea, is high time to maintain and sustain a good confession of our faith (1Timothy 6:12,13) in the Great God of the seas, always knowing that *we walk not by sight but by faith* (2 Corinthians 5:7)!

Paul the prisoner has all of a sudden taken charge as a child of the Kingdom of God. He's no longer just a common prisoner on board, he is the one everyone, including the Centurion and the owner of the ship must listen to. You see my friend, the Spirit of God inside us can never be dominated by our external situations. He always loves to take charge and to give us control over our predicaments. He loves to give us the victory no matter where we find ourselves; *now thanks be to God who always leads us in triumph in Christ, and through us diffuses the fragrance of His knowledge in every place (2 Corinthians 2:14).*

The Bible declares that even while our outward man perishes, our inward man is being renewed (2 Corinthians 4:16). Paul, also reckoned that our temporary setbacks and afflictions always work for us a greater measure of glory (2 Corinthians 4:17). Yes, that's exactly what they do, *always working for us!*

With this kind of understanding, we have absolutely no place for doubt. Neither can we allow ourselves to be arrested by the power of doubt, to the extent that we begin to lose heart concerning the promises of God. There's only one way forward, to believe against all odds and to stand on the faithfulness of God even in the very midst of troubling seas of difficulties.

Taking Control: the Power of Purpose

As soon as Paul knew their temporary setback on the ship was beginning to work in his favour, he rose to the occasion and took charge of the situation on board. First, he rebuked all who were responsible for allowing them to set sail in the first place. Remember, it was the majority's decision against Paul's wise advice that got them in trouble when they decided to ignore Paul. He went on to put their minds to rest like a good father saying, *take heart,* none of you will die, except that they might lose the ship. No doubt he got their attention at this point. But, there was one more thing he needed to tell them to complete his good news concerning what was to come.

He told them, *however, we must run aground on a certain island.* What was so significant about Paul's statement? Here it is; do you know that our God is thorough and precise in the details? Yes, He is the Alpha and Omega, knowing and declaring the end from the beginning (Rev. 1:8; Isa. 46:10). How else could they know that God had actually spoken to Paul, and how could they determine that Paul was actually a man of God pursuing God's purposes, unless these things were foretold and happened just as Paul said they would. God speaks most clearly to the doubtful and the unbelieving through the signs He performs (Exodus 4:1-9; I Corinthians 14:22).

Historically, God has always affirmed and honoured His servants in ways quite unlike we are used to today; by signs, wonders, miracles and declaring things that must come to pass shortly afterwards. This is exactly where God wants to get His church and people back to; where signs and wonders, miracles and prophecies are common occurrences in our services.

Take for example, men of God of former times, and you will understand exactly why Paul spoke with such audacity about things that were yet to come, thereby taking over control of the situation on the ship.

God told 'young' Joshua, 'I will be with you, son and will honour you before these people who are noted for being stiff-necked, arrogant and disrespectful'. And of course, Joshua was under no illusion that he had real problems on his hands with the Israelites whom the Lord had charged to Joshua's leadership. These were direct sons and daughters of people who almost drove Moses insane and caused him great distress. They moved Moses to the point of causing him to sidestep God's instructions through anger, which also led to Moses himself being stopped from reaching the Promised Land.

So, the Lord knew, and Joshua was also aware, that unless God did something spectacular for him to win the respect of the Israelites, he was in real trouble. There was nothing Joshua could have done personally to win the hearts and minds of the Israelites. If they had disdained and complained against Moses, the most charismatic leader of their time, how much more a young and inexperienced Joshua? But then, God had a wonderful plan. He told Joshua,

> *I will give you every place where you set your foot, as I promised Moses. ⁴ Your territory will extend from the desert to Lebanon, and from the great river, the Euphrates—all the Hittite country— to the Great Sea on the west. ⁵ No one will be able to stand up against you all the days of your life. As I was with Moses, so I will be with you; I will never leave you nor forsake you. ⁹ Have I not commanded you? Be strong and courageous. Do not be terrified; do not be discouraged, for the Lord your God will be with you wherever you go." (Joshua 1:3-5,9).*

The Lord did exactly as he promised, to be with Joshua. His very first attempt to bring instruction about crossing the Jordan into the Promised Land was well received, but not without exception.

Then they answered Joshua, "Whatever you have commanded us
we will do, and wherever you send us we will go. [17] *Just as we*
fully obeyed Moses, so we will obey you. Only may the Lord your
God be with you as He was with Moses. [18] *Whoever rebels*
against your word and does not obey your words, whatever you
may command them, will be put to death. Only be strong and
courageous!"(Joshua1:16-18)

Still in keeping with His promise to be with Joshua just as He was
with Moses, God parted River Jordan, as if to replicate the great
miracle of crossing the Red Sea. The Israelites crossed the Jordan
on dry ground, and the events and spectacles surrounding the
crossing of the Jordan under Joshua's leadership etched in the
minds of the people a deep respect for Joshua, the man of God.

That day the Lord exalted Joshua in the sight of all Israel; and
they feared him all the days of his life, just as they had feared
Moses (Joshua 4:14).

Thereafter, the Lord showed Joshua great favour in their battles
against their enemies. Even in taking the city of Jericho, the Lord
appeared to Joshua as the *Commander of the army of the Lord*
(Joshua 5:14). And when Jericho fell to Joshua and the Israelites,
the passage brilliantly concludes, so *the Lord was with Joshua, and*
his fame spread throughout the land (Joshua 6:27).

Even in the case of Elijah, the great prophet of God, it took a
special miracle of raising a dead son of the widow of Zarephath for
her to become truly convinced that Elijah was a man of God.

Then the woman said to Elijah, "Now by this I know that you are
a man of God, and that the word of the Lord in your mouth is the
truth" (1 Kings 17:24).

Similarly, the disciples were reckoned as true followers of Christ
through undeniable miracles and their outstanding boldness.

Now when they saw the boldness of Peter and John, and perceived that they were uneducated and untrained men, they marvelled. And they realized that they had been with Jesus. [16] saying, "What shall we do to these men? For, indeed, that a notable miracle has been done through them is evident to all who dwell in Jerusalem, and we cannot deny it. (Acts 4:13,16).

Our God Himself differentiated between those whom He has truly chosen, called, and sent, and those who were false and fake.

(God) Who frustrates the signs of the babblers, and drives diviners mad; Who turns wise men backward, and makes their knowledge foolishness; [26] Who confirms the word of His servant, and performs the counsel of His messengers... (Isaiah 44:25,26)

Now, let me tell you why I have gone all this length, to draw on other passages apart from what we were looking at in Acts 27, especially the purpose of the prophetic declaration that Paul made regarding their lives and situation on the violent sea.

1.   First, God always knows what His people are faced with to the extent that He knows even your tomorrow. It should give you good comfort to know that God who keeps you never sleeps nor slumbers (Psalms 121:3-8). But also, even when the sun will not rise even upon trouble waters as was in the case of Paul and his fellow passengers, our God still sees you, for He is *El Roi* (Genesis 16:13). He can reach you anywhere. He is the *Omnipresent One, and Jehovah Shammah*, the One who is always present with you even in your calamities and captivities (Ezekiel 48:35). He says to you,

> *When you pass through the waters, I will be with you; and through the rivers, they shall not overflow you. When you walk through the fire, you shall not be burned, nor shall the flame scorch you. [3] For I am the Lord your God, the Holy One of Israel, your Saviour... (Isaiah 43:2-3).*

2. The second reason for Paul having to speak openly about what was ahead of them even before it took place, saying that *they must run aground on a certain Island* is this: without argument, the proof of the supernatural is the spectacular, and the spectacular points to the supernatural. This is why Paul does not concern himself so much with good speeches of *persuasive words of human wisdom, but in demonstration of the Spirit and of power (1 Corinthians 2:4).* Pharaoh's magicians resisted Moses and Aaron to a point, but after they saw and experienced the spectacular works of God through them, the magicians confessed, *"This is the finger of God" (Exodus 8:19).*

Only miracles, signs and wonders, not fair speeches, demonstrate that the *Divine* is at work, or that the *Heavenly* is engaged with the earthly for a purpose. It will take a fool to doubt that God is at work in one's life to save it when a medically incurable deformity is healed in the Name of Jesus! Only fools will not pay heed when they are told exactly what the outcome of their life and situations are, and they live to see the same unfold just as they were told.

> *But if all prophesy, and an unbeliever or an uninformed person comes in, he is convinced by all, he is convicted by all. And thus the secrets of his heart are revealed; and so, falling down on his face, he will worship God and report that God is truly among you (1Corinthians 14:24,25).*

This explains why God allowed Paul to even tell the rest of the passengers what was to come as well. Once things began to unfold as Paul had declared beforehand, obviously, the men on the ship were full of deep respect for the man of God, Paul. And don't forget, all of that was intended by God to affirm and to honour His servant, just as we have seen with Joshua and Elijah in other places. You might wonder, can God really honour a man? Yes, He does for those who first honour Him by obeying His commandments and satisfying His will or purpose (Isaiah 48:8; 2Chronicles 20:7; John 14:15-17).

Likewise, God will honour you no matter your circumstances if you first honour Him and satisfy His purposes. He is always willing to help those who serve Him and who are His. Keep your trust firmly in God, do not doubt but believe, and no matter your circumstance your help is on the way.

Taking Over: the Power of Faith and Open Confession

In the book of 1Timothy 6 and verse 6, we are told to *"Fight the good fight of faith, lay hold on eternal life, to which you were also called and have confessed the good confession in the presence of many witnesses"*. This is exactly what we find Paul doing when he stood up and boldly declared to his fellow passengers what he believed the Lord had told him. He said to them,

> *For there stood by me this night an angel of the God to whom I belong and whom I serve, [24] saying, 'Do not be afraid, Paul; you must be brought before Caesar; and indeed God has granted you all those who sail with you.' [25] Therefore take heart, men, for I believe God that it will be just as it was told me (Acts 27:23&24).*

Paul was simply confessing a good confession before many witnesses, thereby subjecting every other thought, *rational* doubt and indeed the whole situation with the ship under absolute control of the word of faith he received and openly confessed. By this, he was acting on a powerful principle of faith that says, *so then, faith comes by hearing and hearing by the word of God (Roman 10:17).*

The fact that Paul had heard the word of God spoken to him by the angel of God means that faith was already in place. But faith is not yet faith until it leaves the realm of the silent heart into the viable realms of open confession, affirming that what was heard is true and must come to pass.

> *And since we have the same spirit of faith, according to what is written, "I believed and therefore I spoke," we also believe and therefore speak, (2Corinthians 4:13).*

O Corinthians! We have spoken openly to you, our heart is wide open (2Corinthians 6:11).

Faith needs to be vocalised if faith must amount to the actual substance of things hoped for. To become the actual evidence of things not seen, faith must be vocalised always, in spite of any contradictory physical sign or symptoms. You need to say what you believe, and it shall be according to your faith and just as you said it (Matthew 9:29).

Our Lord Jesus Himself, taught this principle to His disciples, how to vocalise their faith through open confession. He showed them the importance of translating their faith from just *believing* faith to verbalising and speaking their faith. In the story of the Fig Tree, we are told,

> *Now the next day, when they had come out from Bethany, He was hungry. *[13]* And seeing from afar a fig tree having leaves, He went to see if perhaps He would find something on it. When He came to it, He found nothing but leaves, for it was not the season for figs. *[14]* In response Jesus said to it, "Let no one eat fruit from you ever again." And His disciples heard it (Mark 11:12-14).*

Did you notice the end of the passage? It says, *and his disciples heard it.* Why was it necessary for the Scripture to add that brief note at the end? It is simple. Because, that represented the intended and most important lesson the Lord wanted to teach His disciples when He reacted to the tree in the manner He did. On this occasion, the Lord deliberately did what He did, having to speak in the hearing of his disciples, in order to teach them that when you vocalise your faith it works.

To demonstrate that indeed the Lord intended to teach about speaking our faith aloud when He spoke to the fig tree, let's read what He said to them when His disciples, in shock, came to Him to announce the death of the Fig tree.

Now in the morning, as they passed by, they saw the fig tree dried up from the roots. [21] And Peter, remembering, said to Him, "Rabbi, look! The fig tree which You cursed has withered away." [22] So Jesus answered and said to them, "Have faith in God. [23] For assuredly, I say to you, whoever says to this mountain, 'Be removed and be cast into the sea,' and does not doubt in his heart, but believes that those things he says will be done, he will have whatever he says (Mark 11:20-23).

Note how the Lord made a brilliant connection between 'saying' and what is in the 'heart', and how easy it is to get whatever one says. Do you see how much emphasis He placed on 'saying'? He said to His disciples, it is okay to have faith in God, or to put it more literally, *have the God kind of faith.* And then He goes on to explain how the *God kind of faith* works. That it begins with *saying* and ends with what was said.

My point here is, whatever you believe or have faith to do, needs to be accompanied by vocalising, saying or confessing what you believe in order to have what you believe and say. Our God did it that way right from the beginning of creation, *calling those things that are not as though they were* (Romans 4:17). Every time He was going to create something new, He *said* what He desired or believed, and had what He *said.* For example, when we see God at work in the book of Genesis this very principle of *verbalising or saying* what we believe comes alive. Although you will find this throughout Genesis chapters 1 and 2, I will draw on the first few verses for illustration purposes.

In the beginning God created the heavens and the earth. [2] The earth was without form, and void; and darkness was on the face of the deep. And the Spirit of God was hovering over the face of the waters.[3] Then God said, "Let there be light"; and there was light. [4] And God saw the light, that it was good; and God divided the light from the darkness. [5] God called the light Day, and the darkness He called Night. So the evening and the morning were the first day (Genesis 1:1-5).

The majority of believers today have their faith safely shut and tightly secure in their hearts. Only their hearts know what they believe and are standing in faith for, so the rest of their faculties, especially their minds and inner vision refuse to align or to correspond with that which is securely locked up in their hearts.

Wisdom for Purpose: There are two main advantages of vocalising or saying your faith.

i.   First, by vocalising your faith it helps command everything in you to conform to your faith based expectations. The more you vocalise your faith, the more intense it becomes, and the more the rest of 'you' will begin to catch the vibe of your faith and align with what you are believing for.

ii.   Second, Your doubts subside and your mind succumbs to your heart (spirit), when you vocalise your faith. At this intensity and frequency of faith, every other thing around you will begin to respond because, all of a sudden, you are beginning to hear, see, know, and feel differently. Things literally get centred and your entire being gravitates towards the leading of your spirit; instead of your mind and emotions determining what you should think, feel, hear, see, know, or even taste. You, at this point respond to one thing and one thing only – what faith says by the wisdom of the Word of God and the power His Holy Spirit.

Those who hide and keep their faith silently locked in their hearts usually pride themselves in mere religious sentiments like, *I have faith*. Whereas those who dare have the *God kind of faith*, never mind vocalising their faith, saying exactly what they believe, in order to have what they say. Such people literally control their environment by vocalising what they believe. These are those whose faith is literally seen, and will have what they say (see Mathew 15:21-28; Mark 5:27; Matthew 9:1; and Matthew 8:8, 13).

Are you expecting a miracle from God? Then have faith in God, but also openly speak up and out your expectations boldly by faith. Add some good confessions to your faith, and you will have what you say. Remember, this one truth, *death and life are in the power of the tongue, And those who love it will eat its fruit (Proverbs 18:21).*

Don't Jump – Wait: Conquering the Suggestions of Fear

> *For you have need of endurance, so that after you have done the will of God, you may receive the promise (Hebrews 10:36)*

How often you tell people exactly what God said and they turn immediately afterwards and do just the complete opposite. And this is not only for unbelievers, because faith professing and proclaiming Christians tend to be the worst culprits. It doesn't matter how hard you try or how long you stay with them, fear not faith tends to drive and control their emotions, choices, and actions.

> *Now when the fourteenth night had come, as we were driven up and down in the Adriatic Sea, about midnight the sailors sensed that they were drawing near some land.* [28] *And they took soundings and found it to be twenty fathoms; and when they had gone a little farther, they took soundings again and found it to be fifteen fathoms.* [29] *Then, fearing lest we should run aground on the rocks, they dropped four anchors from the stern, and prayed for day to come.* [30] *And as the sailors were seeking to escape from the ship, when they had let down the skiff into the sea, under pretence of putting out anchors from the prow,* [31] *Paul said to the centurion and the soldiers, "Unless these men stay in the ship, you cannot be saved."* [32] *Then the soldiers cut away the ropes of the skiff and let it fall off (Acts 27:27-32).*

Have you ever heard people say, 'sometimes things get worse before they get better'? I really don't fully sub-scribe to the tenants of that kind of belief, but it is very certain that our faith will be tried, tested and stretched by the things we are allowed to go through. However, on face value, the belief that 'sometimes things get worse before they get better' can sometimes be true taking individual situations on their own merits.

For example, when the Lord Jesus Christ spoke about the end of this age and His imminent return, He intimated that things will get worse before they get better. So, His personal advice to the disciples was that, they should not be troubled, not even by the perilous times of wars and rumours of wars (Matthew 24:6). Instead, He asked them to put their total trust in the Father and in Him, promising a time of bliss when He shall return to receive all His disciples to Himself (John 14:1-4).

In that regard, we must always expect calm after the storm, day to follow the night and deliverance for our captivity. It normally then could get worse before it gets better, so to speak. However, it also means if you find yourself in a dire situation, expect your deliverance, and know that there is always a way out, but only in the Lord.

Unfortunately, many will choose to focus on their present troubles, bow and succumb to the pressure of life instead of totally trusting the Lord in their situation. Jesus the Lord, always desires that we keep our eyes on the end, which unfortunately does not come until the pressures of our present situation have served their purpose and elapsed. The victory is placed in the end, for those that endure to the end, in total trust and confidence in the Lord (Hebrews 10:36).

And you shall hear of wars and rumours of wars: see that you be not troubled: for all these things must come to pass, but the end is not yet. [12]And because iniquity shall abound, the love of many shall grow cold. [13]But he that shall endure unto the end, the same shall be saved (Matthew 24:6)

My brethren, count it all joy when you fall into various trials, [3] knowing that the testing of your faith produces patience. [4] But let patience have its perfect work, that you may be perfect and complete, lacking nothing. [5] If any of you lacks wisdom, let him ask of God, who gives to all liberally and without reproach, and it will be given to him. [6] But let him ask in faith, with no doubting, for he who doubts is like a wave of the sea driven and tossed by the wind. [7] For let not that man suppose that he will receive anything from the Lord; [8] he is a double-minded man, unstable in all his ways (James 1:2-8).

Most of the time, it might not look like our victory or deliverance is near because of how things seem in the physical. The signs might be so contrary to anything that looks like deliverance. And, suddenly tension mounts up, pressure at all levels ensues, and soon our faith and hope begin to suffer if, care is not taken.

Now, returning to the men on the ship with Paul, unfortunately, this was their problem. They had a clear and sure word of comfort and prophecies from God through the Apostle Paul. Yet because things did not seem in the physical to agree immediately with what Paul said, they became very anxious, agitated, and were about to do something stupid. Understandably, after Paul's prophecies, the violent waves did not die down. In fact, it seemed to have grown worse, and it was terribly dark over the sea.

But, as soon as they realised that the ship has reached a point where they could manage to anchor the ship, albeit still in deep sea, the sailors tried to escape under pretence after they lowered the skiff of the ship. What nerve; getting out of relative safety of the ship and right into the whirlpool of a violent sea when it was still dark on a frosty winter night. That indeed was nothing but a release of the spirit of suicide, through satanic suggestion to the men to take their own lives in the name of trying to escape.

Under freezing temperatures with turbulent sea waves, they would have been trapped either way; death by drowning or through hypothermia. It sounds odd, but that's exactly how far over-whelming fear, pressure, anxiety and loss of hope could push people; making them to jump from relative safety into a freezing deep blue sea under dark nights. The men had no intention to endure to the end but a hasty spirit to take things in their own hands. What they failed to realise was that their deliverance, although in their own minds seemed very far away, was actually minutes away not hours. So, in essence, the real battle for their safety was in their minds.

They had waited and endured so far, but for their impatience to hold on a little longer, they were going to drown themselves right before the time of their word of prophecies was fulfilled. If it were not for the darkness on that frosty winter night, and the men on board were able to see clearly ahead of them, the situation might have been different. Instead of trying to jump too soon into the violent sea, they would wait until it was safe enough, seeing now that the shores were approaching.

Have you ever been there; when you tried to jump off in the night instead of waiting for the morning of your deliverance? Most people who have had a whole lot of trouble have, under the burden and weight of their troubles, turned to help themselves, when indeed God was just a second away from lifting them up. Self-help is the one thing that the pressure of fear wants to drive you to in order to negate your faith in waiting on the Hand of the Lord. Likewise, it is so tempting to quit under darkness, thinking that all is lost, when in reality your desired help is in sight and always ready to be revealed when the hindrance of darkness gives way to the break of morning light.

Wisdom for Purpose:

i. Always remember, fear will cause you to jump ahead of time, but faith will sail you to safe shores when over troubled waters.

ii. For every good word of promise and prophecies, the faith required for enduring the times of the manifestation of the promise or prophecies, will always be tested and stretched. The test may take any form, including difficult hindrances and seeming delays in the wake of waiting. But take courage, it's only a test of your faith!

iii. Do not give up hope because your faith, if it is truly anchored in Christ, will definitely overcome and you are coming through victoriously. Don't Jump – Wait!

Important Scriptural Suggestions to help Strengthen Your Faith

Wait on the Lord, be of good courage, and He shall strengthen your heart. Wait, I say, on the Lord! (Psalms 27:14).

Note: the Hebrew term used for wait (qawah) is so powerful. It is more than just waiting for waiting sake. It actually means waiting *expectantly, waiting hopefully, obediently, patiently, and confidently.* It is waiting in faith, believing and trusting God, Who alone is able to do and perform a timely work or deed on your behalf without fail.

Rest in the Lord, and wait patiently for Him, do not fret because of him who prospers in his way, Because of the man who brings wicked schemes to pass (Psalms 37:7).

... weeping may endure for a night, but joy comes in the morning (Psalms 30:5).

For whatever is born of God overcomes the world. And this is the victory that has overcome the world - our faith (1John 5:4).

For God has not given us a spirit of fear, but of power and of love and of a sound mind (2Timothy 1:7).

Go on, Eat Bread! - Walking By Faith

And as day was about to dawn, Paul implored them all to take food, saying, "Today is the fourteenth day you have waited and continued without food, and eaten nothing. ³⁴ Therefore I urge you to take nourishment, for this is for your survival, since not a hair will fall from the head of any of you." ³⁵ And when he had said these things, he took bread and gave thanks to God in the presence of them all; and when he had broken it he began to eat. ³⁶ Then they were all encouraged, and also took food themselves (Acts 27:33-36).

It had been fourteen trying days of uncertainties and just barely managing to hold up under immense pressure and treacherous conditions on the sea. After unsuccessful attempts at trying to help things out, Paul finally rose as the conscience on the 'sinking' ship. Knowing what to do, he advised his fellow passengers that in order to survive their plight, everyone must stay on the ship.

Unlike other times when they ignored Paul and set sail seeing it was dangerous to sail, this time they heeded *pastor* Paul's warning. Instead of jumping overboard, they stayed on the ship, retracting from their fear instilled scheme initially hatched to help them escape under the cover of the dark. Heeding Paul's advice and wisdom came as a big change in their relationship, given that the same people right from the start of their journey had ignored Paul but relied on 'expert advice', 'majority vote', and their personal whims and biases.

Isn't it interesting how people manage to swallow their pride and begin to listen when they hit the rocks? How interesting, that obstinate people allow themselves to suffer some kind of catastrophic failure or setbacks before God gets their attention; when all we need in the first place is to listen the first time.

Having realised their willingness to corporate, Paul took things to the next level. He knew that fourteen days had already passed and the men on the ship have had no food. He encouraged them to take some bread, admonishing that it was good for their survival.

But, there was another good reason for them to eat bread, and this was because *not a hair will fall from the head of any of you (Acts 27:34)*, says Paul. By the way, may this be the same way God speaks for you in the midst of your trials and hardships – that you would lose nothing, not even a strand of your hair!

First, if you believe God and His word, then your action and choices must begin to mimic the faith that you claim to have in Him; that God will perform what He says He will do. Second, if God says He will deliver you, you must begin now to act commensurate with the promise of God by exercising yourself in deliverance. *Act as if, feel as if, and see as if it is already done!*

Don't wait to see clues, and signs of what was promised before you begin to concord, conform or even celebrate. The principle is, God's promises are as good as God's actions, and what God says He will do is as good as already done! It is more about God's integrity than it is about how you feel about what God's says. Hence, to still be held bound by fear, and to still have a million more questions about the possibility of you being delivered is to act contrary to faith, and to doubt God's ability to deliver you.

> *... for whatever is not from faith is sin (Romans 14:23).*

I am reminded of a situation we had in church similar in principle to the advice Paul gave to his fellow passengers. A couple who were at the verge of losing their rights to stay and to work in the United Kingdom were beginning to get very troubled. The man had had his application for permanent residency declined a few times already, and because his wife had joined him as a dependent, she too was directly affected. He could not continue in his existing job because his original work permit belonged to his former employer, who had suffered bankruptcy.

To be able to get another job, the couple needed new work permits. Until then, the wife had managed to stay with her original work place which was now also about to go into administration. Eventually the husband got another job but it was not long before the new company sacked him from work because he could not produce a valid work permit to stay employed.

At the height of what was fast becoming a real crisis for him and his wife, the husband came to see me at church one afternoon. Alarmed, but managing to maintain his composure, he tried to explain the situation about his job and the unfortunate difficulties regarding his failed permit application, monies involved and legal bottlenecks. As I listened to him, *I immediately interrupted him, and demanded him to eat and share my bread with me.* He responded just as I asked, tearing off a piece of my burger I bought earlier from next door. And then I told him that, all was well and that he should not worry; God was in control. That was it. We held hands and prayed briefly afterwards mainly for other things.

But, here was the amazing thing of all. The gentleman was fasting concerning his permit when he came in to see me. I did not know that he was fasting. He only told me about his fast after he had eaten a piece of my bread as I demanded. So, in effect, without knowing I asked him to break his fast, and he did so without protest. I, his pastor, asked him to eat, and he did what his pastor said even though he had not seen any physical sign of possible change in his situation. He believed and agreed when I told him all was well, and that nobody could remove him from the United Kingdom. His countenance brightened up and we went to talk about other unrelated matters.

That's faith! Within about two months, the couple had their permanent UK residence status granted, each on individual merits, instead of one relying on the other as a dependent. Their new status on individual merits surpassed what they had originally requested on their failed dependency applications.

The husband got his original position restored to him with the same employer. As I write, the wife of the man has also gained employment with the same company where her husband works.

My friend, when God says it, you believe it and leave the worry bit with Him. Quit asking how can this be? Quit trying to figure out how God will do it. He will do it, that's His responsibility to decide the *how*, as well as the *why,* especially when you think you don't deserve it. But, you go on and begin to act and talk like it is done. Eat bread! Paul and his friends went ahead to eat and were encouraged afterwards, knowing that not even a hair on their head would be lost and agreeing with God's promise to Paul. So, it was no time to weep and to bemoan their difficult conditions, but it was time to be encouraged and to celebrate in faith, in view of the promise and purposes of God.

I leave you with two great passages of positive examples from two wonderful sisters in the Bible. They had only received words of promise but in faith rejoiced as if in reality they already had what was promised.

Hannah: She began in bitterness of soul but after God's servant brought God's word and blessings, she left encouraged and went and ate and was no more sad.

> *And she was in bitterness of soul, and prayed to the Lord and wept in anguish.* [11] *Then she made a vow and said, "O Lord of hosts, if You will indeed look on the affliction of Your maidservant and remember me, and not forget Your maidservant, but will give Your maidservant a male child, then I will give him to the Lord all the days of his life, and no razor shall come upon his head."* [12] *And it happened, as she continued praying before the Lord, that Eli watched her mouth.* [13] *Now Hannah spoke in her heart; only her lips moved, but her voice was not heard. Therefore Eli thought she was drunk.* [14] *So Eli said to her, "How long will you be drunk? Put your wine away from you!"* [15] *But Hannah answered and said, "No, my lord, I am a woman of sorrowful spirit. I have drunk neither wine nor intoxicating drink, but have*

poured out my soul before the Lord. Do not consider your maidservant a wicked woman, for out of the abundance of my complaint and grief I have spoken until now." Then Eli answered and said, "Go in peace, and the God of Israel grant your petition which you have asked of Him." [18] *And she said, "Let your maidservant find favour in your sight." So the woman went her way and ate, and her face was no longer sad (1Samuel 1:10-19).*

Mary: She was initially troubled, astonished, hesitant and somewhat doubtful in her mind regarding what seemed an impossible proposition from an angel. But in the end, she went away believing, rejoicing and offering up lavish praise to the God who makes the impossible possible.

But when she saw him, she was troubled at his saying, and considered what manner of greeting this was. [30] *Then the angel said to her, "Do not be afraid, Mary, for you have found favour with God.* [31] *And behold, you will conceive in your womb and bring forth a Son, and shall call His name JESUS.* [32] *He will be great, and will be called the Son of the Highest; and the Lord God will give Him the throne of His father David.* [33] *And He will reign over the house of Jacob forever, and of His kingdom there will be no end."* [34] *Then Mary said to the angel, "How can this be, since I do not know a man?"* [35] *And the angel answered and said to her, "The Holy Spirit will come upon you, and the power of the Highest will overshadow you; therefore, also, that Holy One who is to be born will be called the Son of God.* [36] *Now indeed, Elizabeth your relative has also conceived a son in her old age; and this is now the sixth month for her who was called barren.* [37] *For with God nothing will be impossible."* [38] *Then Mary said, "Behold the maidservant of the Lord! Let it be to me according to your word." And the angel departed from her.* [45] *Blessed is she who believed, for there will be a fulfilment of those things which were told her from the Lord."* [46] *And Mary said: " My soul magnifies the Lord,* [47] *And my spirit has rejoiced in God my Saviour (Luke 1:29-38,45-47).*

Wisdom for Purpose:

i.   Never forget this; it is either you believe and have it, or you don't believe and go without it!

ii.   When it comes to the promises of God for your life, always *act as if, feel as if, and see as if it is already done*! Once you have a word from God or one of His trusted servants, *acting as if, feeling as if, and seeing as if* will work as your faith booster and activator for becoming and having what the Lord has promised.

Demonstrating the Power of Purpose: Unless You Step Up, They Can't Believe

❖❖❖

Church on Sinking Ship: Putting Faith into Action

Now I want you to know, brothers, that what has happened to me has really served to advance the gospel (Philippians 1:12).

If you want your faith to profit then do something in line with your faith. If you want your faith to be seen, then show it just like Paul did. After Paul had spoken to his fellow passengers about what his God promised him, *he took bread and gave thanks to God in the presence of them all* and then went right ahead to eat as if they were already safe (Acts 27:35). Guess what impact Paul's bold gesture of faith had on those seeing and listening to him? They were assured, and *then they were all encouraged, and also took food themselves (Acts 27:36).*

Paul's tenacious faith sparked faith in his colleagues, and not only did they believe Paul, but also the God of Paul who promised to deliver them. Remember, *as iron sharpens iron so a man sharpens the countenance of his friends (Proverbs 27:17)*. Faith can be so contagious that if a fearful, faithless person encounters one with a living and tenacious faith, they cannot but respond in faith.

Paul's faith sparked, inspired and excited the faith of two hundred and seventy-five fearful people who were on board the ship. One man's audacity to believe and to act on what he was told blessed and turned a very ominous atmosphere aboard the *sinking* ship into hopeful expectation. With that kind of expectation, anything was possible, including sinking with the ship if they had to, but still having to cling onto life until help came. They could cling to life because every decision to stand in faith and to hope for a better outcome, ignites the spirit of a person to overcome even the most hostile of conditions.

Think of earth quake victims, like it happened unfortunately in Haiti, in which people were still being dug out alive after ten days of going without food, water, and clothes.[2] They were caught in horrifying darkness and exposed to inhumane temperatures under tough, solid rubble of bricks mixed with steel. Most people with broken body parts were trapped under the sheer weight of massive concrete fragments as a result of the quake. Although everything around them literally told them that they could not survive another day, and that they should give up and die, they held on with the hope that they would be rescued sooner or later. Just that hope, coupled with their resilience to hang on to life, kept them until they were finally rescued.

Most of them came out terribly dehydrated, emaciated and exhausted after days of excruciating pain, thirst and hunger, but they came out alive. One of them told her story about how they kept encouraging one another, saying *I promise if I am rescued I will tell the rescuers to come for you as well.* Something in her, she believed, kept telling her not yet, because there was still more for her in this physical life that death could not deny or snatch away.

That shows the attitude of people who have quit worrying about death and got busy clinging onto life despite the odds against them. Of course, they were finally rescued and told their breath-taking stories on international cable news networks around the world.

Quit Worrying and Start Living!

I believe one of the things that our faith offers, over our fear and worries, is this one important thing: not worrying about dying or failing, but getting busy with living and getting on with what's left to do. We see this with Paul's two hundred and seventy-five *captive* church members on the ship.

Until now, they have been trapped with the fear of dying and death on high seas through the tremendous power of crashing wave threatening to break their ship into unidentifiable pieces. Their minds drew and conceived no better pictures for them than seeing themselves being already painfully killed and eaten by big man-eating killer fish. They had their focus fixed on the worst things that could happen to them, instead of the best possible means of escape that could possibly arise for them. Their thoughts were painfully full of fear of the worst possibilities instead of hopeful possibilities. And so, their vital energies were drained and sapped out of them trying to cater for their greatest fears instead of their greatest hope.

They lost the appetite to eat and to sustain life because in their minds eating was no worthy pursuit for a person who was about to die. They would rather worry than eat! Unfortunately, it is an established fact that worrying and fearing consume most of our vital energies, and kill our creative instinct. They never encourage nor give hope with expectations for good things to happen to us.

On the contrary, good hope and keeping positive inspires helpful natural mental juices and creative energies, which easily move our whole body into taking constructive actions.

It carries with it a feel-good effect that looks forward to something good as well. Eventually all of that ultimately converges to our advantage when channelled appropriately. This is when we are at our best, whether for an athlete attempting an unfamiliar acrobatic manoeuvre, or a preacher facing a crowd of a million people for the first time.

So, Paul's admonition to his colleagues and *congregants* to eat was in good faith, to help them to stop focusing on worse scenarios and begin to think more positively. The fact that they agreed to eat meant that, there was a change in their mental attitude, from woe to hope. Paul had to try to break the circle and control of fear and worry aimed at stealing the lives of his colleagues, and then try to instil hope. Instead of worrying about dying, they needed to begin thinking about surviving their unpleasant plight. No degree of melancholy or worry could change anything; on the contrary, it only would render them helpless, passive victims made ready to be devoured by the overpowering sea water.

Often, the best scheme of Satan will be to create vivid photographs of worst scenarios about your sufferings, limitations, weaknesses, or situations. If he can succeed in doing that to you and get you to believe his lies, then he succeeds in breaking your resolve to fight back and to stay on course. Instead of looking unto Christ, you begin to look upon yourself, and instead of counting on the help of God you begin to count on the help of men. Of course, the arm of flesh will always certainly fail you because the battle is never yours but the Lord's (1 Samuel 17:47).

You are called to stop worrying and to cast all your cares upon the Lord because He cares for you (1Peter 5:7). But, by no means should you depend on your personal strength, for God is with you to help you fight your battles (2 Chron. 32:8), as you keep looking unto Jesus who is the author and finisher of your faith (Heb. 12:2).

You will survive all your struggles, my friend!

Walking the Talk of Faith: Defying the Hypocritical Spirit

To turn things around, Paul did something significant, which is what good mentors, role models or pastors do, *walking the talk.* Jesus our Lord, never liked hypocrites. In fact, His finest definition of a hypocrite is found in Matthew 23:3, referring to the Pharisees while addressing His disciples. Hypocrites in our Lord's definition were people who *say and do not do.*

If Paul was to convince his hearers on the ship and change their thinking to begin to expect deliverance, then it was not just enough to say what the angel promised, but to also be seen applying himself to it. He believed the message of the angel, and how does he demonstrate his belief? He kept his cool and went ahead to eat as if the sea were already calm.

He did not join the two hundred and seventy-five in their worries about dying and sinking, but got busy with surviving the storm and completing his purpose and assignment just as the angel promised. The angel promised Paul that God has already given him the lives of all the men on board with him, and that he must appear before Caesar (Acts 27:24). Paul heeded and went on to take charge.

He showed no sign of fear even when others became edgy and jittery. When they tried to jump off the tottering ship, Paul warned them to stay on. Right in their presence, as if totally oblivious to what was happening both inside and outside the ship, Paul got engrossed with worship service to the Lord (Acts 27:35).

Undoubtedly, it was going to take only a fool to ignore Paul's selective but powerful response in the midst of their storms. He chose to control himself rather than allow whatever was happening around him to control him. He chose his response, rather than to allow the external happenings to dictate his response. He became a proactive victor rather than a petulant victim. As soon as his colleagues saw what great strength of will and character Paul showed, despite the foes against them, they decided to yield to his advice to eat bread. Paul, through his actions and choices had abundantly demonstrated to his *church on the ship* that, he believed what he preached and told them. So, it was easy for them to do what he did: relax, be positive and then eat.

My friend, nothing can be so convincing and contagious in times of great uncertainties and hopelessness than a person who *walks the talk!* Historically, people who *walk the talk* have not only galvanised great followership, but have also been able to amass great power to effect and bring about necessary changes to dubious regimes, policies and places.

On a personal level, one man with the right idea, who pursues it with all his might and everything in him, has caused many others to change their directions and to support his cause. This is how the cruel back of apartheid in South Africa was broken in the 1990's. Some guys spearheaded by Mr. Nelson Mandela decided 'enough is enough' and decided to *walk* the hard road to freedom, no matter how stubborn apartheid was and the cost involved.

I have no doubt that *walking the talk* is about taking risks. But I also believe that it is often about being positively 'stubborn', and staying on course, fully convinced about what God has told you in private. It sometimes means you've got something to prove to others, especially those you need to take as partners with you on your 'journey' of purpose. This is because the people you intend to take along were not there when God spoke to you. So, the onus lies on your shoulder to let others see, hear and believe in what you claimed to have heard by amply demonstrating that you yourself believe in what you are talking about.

To make others 'see with you and believe with you', is what Paul was about on their journey which eventually turned out to be now even more perilous than when they first began. He had to literally convince his colleagues on board to entrust their lives to him, on the integrity of the word an angel spoke to him in private. How could he ever get his fellow passengers to trust him with their lives; the one precious thing they were trying with all their might to preserve?

This is often where faith steps in. Paul believed the angel and, as a man of faith, he had to maintain his belief until the end as he announced earlier, *for I believe God that it will be just as it was told me (Acts 27:25).* But, that was just saying what he believed – *talking the talk!* He needed to take things to the next level, because *talk* is only *talk* without some actions, just like faith without works is practically dead.

> *Thus also faith by itself, if it does not have works, is dead. [18] But someone will say, "You have faith, and I have works." Show me your faith without your works, and I will show you my faith by my works. [20] But do you want to know, O foolish man, that faith without works is dead? [21] Was not Abraham our father justified by works when he offered Isaac his son on the altar? [22] Do you see that faith was working together with his works, and by works faith was made perfect? [23] And the Scripture was fulfilled which says, "Abraham believed God, and it was accounted to him for righteousness." And he was called the friend of God. [24] You see then that a man is justified by works, and not by faith only. [26] For as the body without the spirit is dead, so faith without works is dead also (James 2:17-18,20-24,26).*

That 'old rascal', the *hypocritical spirit* that beguiles many well-intentioned people just to talk and talk, without any meaningful corresponding actions, must be conquered by all means!

Living by Every Word of God

> *...that He might make you know that man shall not live by bread alone; but man lives by every word that proceeds from the mouth of the Lord (Deuteronomy 8:3).*

To take his faith or *talk* further and to make it more convincing, Paul stayed put on the ship while others tried to escape (Acts 27:30-33). He frankly discouraged the whole idea of trying to escape and went on to suggest that only by staying on the ship could they be saved.

Furthermore, given their plight, he made what seemed a ridiculous promise to his colleagues, that *no hair will fall from the head of any of you (vr 34)*, urging them to take some food.

As if that was not ridiculous enough, Paul did the more radical thing before all on board. He slipped into thanking and worshiping God Almighty who promised through His angel that none on board the ship will lose their life. With his thanksgiving, he also got the Lord's Supper or Communion prepared and served. All this while, only Paul is worshiping and taking his Communion all by himself. At this time, one could literally hear what some of his colleagues might have been thinking: '*oh, he is just a religious fanatic – Festus, was probably right, he is indeed beside himself!*'

Anyway, their sarcasm would not continue long because Paul would not stop praising and thanking God before their intimidating presence. The more Paul freely thanked his God and began to eat, his colleagues changed their minds. They would not eat before, but now they wanted to eat. But here is what was fascinating about what Paul had going on. Paul's colleagues have not even eaten yet, but as Paul broke his bread and began to eat, *then they were all encouraged, and also took food themselves (Acts 27:36)*.

Why were they encouraged when nothing physical about their situation has changed? The level of threat to their lives had not diminished by any means. If anything, things grew worse, it was still dark over the sea, and they were still very hungry, having not eaten for fourteen days. Why such a sudden change from feeling depressed and preparing to die to now desiring to live? Did the captain of the ship do anything different? No! Then what accounts for the abrupt spring of hope in the passengers?

Here is what happened. They finally were able to see and hear collectively what Paul only heard and saw privately, in line with purpose. The Word of God which inspires faith and rouses positive energies, had finally found a place in the hearts of the passenger by seeing and hearing Paul *talk and walk the talk*.

We know *faith comes by hearing and hearing by the Word (Romans 10:17)*. Hence, Paul did not renege on speaking to his colleagues about what he heard from the angel of God, as the Word of God, to all on board. Instead, he kept saying it and reinforcing the Word in different ways, but still kept the hub, *you shall be saved!*

Once they have received this truth in their spirits or hearts, suddenly they began to see things differently. Their negative postures changed and gave way to hope, and hope left them with no choice but the desire to live again. So, they also took some food and began to eat. Nothing had physically changed about their condition at sea, but you see; when faith arises in people because of the Word they hear, hope naturally comes alive and inspires the will to live and to continue!

Now with their new found hope, also came a good feeling that converted into physical strength even in the absence of physical food. This works mostly similar to receiving good news that gladdens the heart and works like medicine (Proverbs 17:22). For some people, the only time they are able to control their wild appetite for a while is when they receive exceptionally good news. The good news occupies them so much that, for awhile, they are unable to take physical food, until they've fully absorbed and appreciated the good news long expected. That's why the men on the ship, even before they have had anything to eat physically, the word of faith from Paul and how they saw him openly demonstrate his faith, was good enough to wake them up. *Now the just shall live by faith (Hebrews 10:38).*

Complying with Purpose: Moving from Despair to Hope

They all ate enough physical bread afterwards. Suddenly, things changed considerably, and the men on the ship wanted to make something good of what had taken place in their hearts. With their newly found courage coming through the inspiration of their *pastor,* Paul, they could now allow themselves to think more constructively regarding how to manage their crisis at sea. Until now, they had been very random and erratic, making all the wrong moves. But this time things were different, they were now much calmer, to think more clearly about what to do next. Remember, it always helps when major decisions regarding safety are taken under a good degree of mental calmness.

A proof of their positive outlook on their situation, and their faith to live, came soon afterwards. After they have had enough to eat, it occurred to them that they could lighten their ship as a safety measure. The idea was to ensure that whatever happened they would keep trying to minimize damage and to guide the ship to safety if it were possible. From despair, the men on board have regained their positive fighting spirit. Instead of flapping about and over reacting to every hint of crisis, they chose to take some control by engaging their good senses. Instead of succumbing to the *wind,* they decided to win over it by taking appropriate measures to minimise and to curb the effect of the fierce powers of the *wind.*

We can apply the situation on board the ship in many and various ways. But true to the context of the passage, is the responsibility that children of God have to believe and to walk in the promises of God, without necessarily waiting for all the good physical signs. We have to believe to have whatever God promised, or simply disbelieve and go without what God promised.

Equally so, we cannot depend solely on our personal wisdom and strength to face life's challenges. It is either God's ways or ours, but it is a wise choice to lean on God always (Proverbs 3:5-6).

With respect to Christian leadership, the stake is even much more huge and challenging. First Peter admonishes,

> *Shepherd the flock of God which is among you, serving as overseers, not by compulsion but willingly, not for dishonest gain but eagerly;* [3] *nor as being lords over those entrusted to you, but being examples to the flock (1Peter 5:2,3).*

Being a good example to the people we lead is what this is all about. Our faith is definitely contagious and has real and tangible effects on those around us. Depending on how we exercise our faith, we are either inspiring or discouraging more people than we imagine. Just by being good examples, and by applying and directing our faith in wisdom, we can positively influence entire nations towards God and His agenda for them.

However, we have the awesome responsibility of demonstrating that our faith and hope are true and tangible, no faking it. No hypocrisy and no letting down our guard just because people don't necessarily see or hear what we saw or heard. With a little bit of persistence, a man of true faith can and will have the final word over a whole congregation and nations of doubters. Faith will overcome fear and the world anytime, anywhere! Your faith can make you free; exercise it.

> *For whatever is born of God overcomes the world. And this is the victory that has overcome the world—our faith (I John 5:4).*

> *For God has not given us a spirit of fear, but of power and of love and of a sound mind (2 Timothy 1:17).*

The Wisdom of Frustration in His Purposes: It's Part of the Plan, Don't Ignore the Signs

❖❖❖

Frustrations

And we desire that each one of you show the same diligence to the full assurance of hope until the end, that you do not become sluggish, but imitate those who through faith and patience inherit the promises (Hebrews 6:11-12).

Some form of deliverance was certainly in sight, except that none aboard the reeling ship knew how or when that deliverance would finally take place. As the day light began to dawn, they could see where they were likely heading, possibly to shore for safety. But under the circumstances, just seeing what was probable was not the same as having the desired outcome. It could be miles before Paul and those on the ship ever realise their desire to beach the ship or to dock safely.

And here lies the challenge. When someone is anxiously awaiting deliverance, it truly doesn't satisfy that their only chance for help is a word of promise on the one hand, while their struggles fume on the other hand. That in itself is always a cause for further anxieties. Also, if help is in sight, and at the same time inaccessible due to impossible *in-betweens,* which separates where I am now from where I really want to be, then of course it seems in the meantime I have no help at all whilst I desperately stand in need.

This, in most aspects, technically compares with the struggles and frustrations of the children of Israel when they were in the wilderness, with Egypt behind them and the Promised Land before them. From Egypt to the Promised Land they had to go through the wilderness, which was in their case an impossible and problematic *in-between.* The wilderness represented, and quickly became, a source of great frustration and hold-up for most of the children of Israel as they found themselves stagnated away from attaining their goal of a Promised Land.

They had successfully left the worst behind them having escaped Egypt and the Red Sea, and now with the Promised Land right ahead of them, they could wait no longer. They desperately wanted a land of their own and to settle down. But there were potential problems and soon the Israelites in their impatience grew awfully frustrated resulting in self-help measures. They could not wait to get quickly across Jordan and to realise the actual promise. However, the wilderness was also one mountain of an opposition to overcome.

I truthfully cannot think of anything that teases one's patience and endurance more than knowing what you urgently need is right across there, but at the same time you cannot reach it. That's the one thing every person, no matter your endurance and patience level is most likely to do something about. We see Daniel, the man of God having to wrestle with similar situations in which, what was indeed so close was still so far in reality. In the tenth chapter of the book of Daniel, it says,

> *In the third year of Cyrus king of Persia a mes-sage was revealed to Daniel, whose name was called Belteshazzar. The message was true, but the appointed time was long; and he understood the*

message, and had understanding of the vision. In those days I, Daniel, was mourning three full weeks. I ate no pleasant food, no meat or wine came into my mouth, nor did I anoint myself at all, till three whole weeks were fulfilled (Daniel 10:1-3).

So, the actual problem is never that the promises of God are untrue nor is it that the certainty of what God said is in any doubt. It is just that it seems long, and because we can almost smell it, but just can't reach it yet, the whole situation then frustrates us almost to a point of total resignation. It reaches a point when we begin to question if things will truly materialise as God said it would. We have faith but also we cannot help not to do something more, because it is so natural with us to try to work things out anyway.

My question is: what would you do if you knew all that God promised you concerning a long awaited desire were so near but you cannot have it just yet? Do you wait or thrust forward to grab it by all means? Let's say, you have been waiting for a very long time for a significant life-changing promotion at your current job. Indeed, you've prayed and fasted and have all the qualifications for promotion. Suddenly, while at church you received a true word of prophecy from a proven man of God that your promotion is due, and based on the prophecy, you also went to see your boss. Your boss literally confirmed your prophecy. By now you are excited, and the next thing you did was to announce to your family and colleagues your good news regarding your promotion that is due.

You are by this time beginning to see and feel yourself really promoted, even though your promotion letter has not been awarded. But you really trust your boss, so you are imagining all the extra benefits and comfort in many ways your promotion will bring, including financial freedom. You are happy and ecstatic, and in anticipation you went ahead and spent your savings to celebrate and to prepare for your promotion that is due. You've done all that because you literally can see every possibility of your promise being fulfilled. However, time went by, and you heard nothing more from your boss. But, just as you arrived one morning at work, your boss saw you and told you, that surely your promotion was still due, but, few more things needed to be taken care of.

Before you assume your new role a few background-check reports were delayed in coming, and your boss does not say when he expects to finalise the decision about your promotion. He cannot also give anymore assurance pending the delayed report, so he leaves things open-ended. What will you do?

Take another scenario. Sue is a single, forty year old Christian sister who has been very faithful in waiting on God for a husband. She made few mistakes in the past, but that doesn't matter because she prayed for forgiveness. Also, in answer to Sue's prayer Billy a wonderful Christian brother came along. No doubt, Billy is the kind of man Sue desires. But while Sue was preparing for her engagement, God says, *well, Sue I know you love Billy, I have given him to you, but you got to wait because I've got a few more things to do with him!*

Do you think Sue will say, okay Lord that's great? What would you do? Wouldn't, you rise every morning hoping that today was the day, praying even harder that the Lord will do a quick work or else you'll be tempted to move things forward? That's exactly the problem with promises being true, but their time not yet! They can be very unnerving and seriously frustrating and could drive you to the breaking point. At this stage, we often suffer enormous conflict within ourselves as to what to do, and very often we are kept hanging in the balance. What do I do? Go for it or wait? Should I endure to the end or just quit now? Obviously, in Sue's case, because of her age things already feel like there is no time to lose.

While all of that is going through your mind, and you are careful not to offend God, that's when sly old Satan will come along with a "good" suggestion, *it's enough, you can't help it. It is not your fault, you are only human! After all, countless others are doing the same thing, including pastors, are you the only righteous person on earth?* Although this way of reasoning might sound great and convincing, remember that's only the cunning voice of Satan. You have a choice either to keep waiting on God or to go along with Satan's suggestions. If you take things in your own hands and do things in your own strength just because you think you can afford to, then it's still your choice. But always remember that the wisdom and commandments of God require us to follow the 'high road' and *to obey is better than sacrifice* (1Samuel 15:22). It is immensely important for people of purpose to learn how to handle the time of frustration in between the promise and the actual realisation of the promise. Because what you do with that time of frustration, the brief interval of waiting, has enormous bearing on the final outcome of the promise itself.

There are three main things you can do to help whilst waiting in earnest expectation, and when the time of your promise and blessing are still due:

i. Abiding in Him

> *Abide in Me, and I in you. As the branch cannot bear fruit of itself, unless it abides in the vine, neither can you, unless you abide in Me. "I am the vine, you are the branches. He who abides in Me, and I in him, bears much fruit; for without Me you can do nothing. If anyone does not abide in Me, he is cast out as a branch and is withered... (John 15:4-6)*

Using a household metaphor, in my view, "abiding in Him" simply means "moving in with God, living with Him and doing whatever He says to do. It also means like a child to a parent, "getting into His presence and staying there as long as He allows you to".

For any child of God finding themselves in a dilemma situation regarding what to do with the frustration leading to the tangible realisation of the promises of God in their life, it is important that they learn to *abide*. By abiding, I mean maintaining continuous trust and faith in God's love for you, His promises and abilities to overcome the frustrations that lie between what you see and know to be true and what you are yet to experience in reality, as a gift of God to you. It becomes bearable and endurable when we abide in Him who makes the promise and determines the seasons and times (Daniel 2:21) to finish His work, and to perfect His purpose concerning us (Psalm 138:8).

ii. **Crying to Him**

King David had many anxious moments in his own life time. But he had to learn to cry unto God by lifting up passionate prayers to Him. He didn't pray prayers like "all is well". He had to be honest and to converse with His Father God, who knows and thoroughly understands our frustrations in times of need and waiting. In one of his many prayers, David acknowledged the one thing we are all confronted with in time of waiting; our time here on earth which is so short. Does God know that? Yes, but our part is to pray and let Him know that we are standing in expectation in view of His promises and covenant.

> *How long, Lord? Will You hide Yourself forever? Will Your wrath burn like fire? Remember how short my time is; for what futility have You created all the children of men? ... Blessed be the Lord forevermore! Amen and Amen (Psalms 89:46,47,52).*

iii. **Blessing Him**

After we've cried to Him, we still have to in the end bless God, just like David in blessing the Lord forevermore! By blessing Him, we acknowledge that after all is said and done, God is Almighty and He is always sovereign. Not only that, but God knows what's best for us, and blessing Him after we've abided in Him and prayed is the expression of our confidence in His choice for us according to His purposes. Blessing the Lord also means we acknowledge Him as our Source and are eternally grateful for what He is doing, about to do and has done (see Psalms 103).

Very often, what seems like frustration to us is what Apostle James refers to as the test of our faith, and by extension, our obedience (James 1:2). And God will test each one of His children to qualify them for the blessing He intends to bestow and to release upon His children.

Making Sense of Times of Frustration: From Pastoral Point of View

Some time ago, I remember questioning God about why sometimes for some people, and I say this cautiously, it takes too long to receive answers to the prayers we pray regarding their needs. Surely, anyone who has been a pastor or who still pastors will understand just what I am talking about. Understandably, there are various other reasons why God chooses to answer some prayers in certain ways and others in totally different ways.

However, I believe there's nothing more physically, spiritually, and emotionally *frustrating* for a pastor than when they see people in their congregation, whom they considered to be some of the most sincere, dedicated, and helpful, go through difficulties in almost endless fashion. At least, in the physical the brother or sister appears very committed and faithful, that is what we know, even if they have other issues. But, one also knows that at least they seem intentional about their love for God and often they are the people who seem to be attending most regular church services, and helping out very much in most cases. So, how do we explain to these people why things appear not to be working or happening as expected? And just like countless others, I went to the Lord with my concerns. The following are a few things I found out, although I admit that these might not help everyone:

i. **More than Blessings**

As pastors we desire those under our stewardship to be and do well, having every means for abundant life. So, after I asked the Father about what seemed to be real delays regarding answers to some prayers, His answer was quick and terse. That He is interested in *character and building character* so that His blessing and those who receive His blessing will not have to endure it but enjoy it. Please wait, I will explain.

It is a fact that *the Lord's blessings make rich and He adds no sorrow to them (Proverb 10:22)*. So, in the light of this fact, I fully understand! But, how about just blessing Your people Lord because you love them?

We need to understand that because His blessing adds or brings no sorrow, He wants to bestow His blessing upon one with character (cf Romans 5:1-5). The Lord let me know He has no trouble blessing His children especially when I pray. His issue mainly regards those who are not yet ready for the blessing, because after they become blessed, they allow the same blessing to hinder them. Again, as far as knowing a person goes, sometimes we even shock ourselves when we find ourselves doing the very thing we vowed never to do. So really, I cannot argue with God who knows the heart. He knows about my potential or hidden strengths, weaknesses and of course the future. If He says to me 'you are not ready', He is right. Although I may think and feel very ready, by virtue of my human limitations I can't resist the Lord's opinion of me. I know some try to, but the wisest thing to do is to be found in the perfect will of God for your life by allowing Him total control.

Taking the case of the prodigal son in Luke 15, God allows His blessing to come on some people who think they are ready to handle it, only to realise in the end that they cannot manage and keep the blessing of God. Often, because of their true lack of preparedness, the very blessing of God may turn out to be a great *hindrance* to their faith and progress. People in this category usually use the blessing of God already received to explain why they suddenly cannot be regular in church anymore. With the same blessing, suddenly they lose or slack on their initial commitment to the things of God. Today, this unfortunately is some of the hard and harsh realities confronting most local churches and their congregations, when *blessing* all of a sudden becomes a *hindrance* due to lack of character, maturity and preparedness.

So the Lord said to me, '*that is why sometimes I allow time to show you what you don't know and see about people you pray for*'.

In other words, *sometimes the time you think that God is not answering your prayer as quickly as you wish, He is actually using that interval of time to introduce you to yourself,* and for the pastor to see the other side of you, otherwise hidden or covered so well. And this is not to expose the person to shame and reproach, but is done in Godly wisdom as an indirect answer to prayer for the seeker to be helped in view of the blessing the Lord intends to bestow.

ii. God Supplies the Cup before His Water

The way pastors usually pray when they ask for God's blessings on behalf of their people can be likened to asking the Lord to pour water down, when in fact the cup or vessel to catch and to contain the expected water, is not ready or available at all. Certainly, in as much as you asked for water, and in as much as the Lord is willing to give you His water, He will first provide you the cup, so that you can retain and serve the water when He releases it. I insist on serving the received water, because we are blessed to become a blessing (Genesis 12:2).

Depending on how you look at it, whether it is about God in truth *introducing us to ourselves* or revealing things that were otherwise hidden to the pastor, that's still part of the process of building character in the people who intend to have God's blessing without sorrow. In most instances it regards pride, selfishness, bitterness, unforgiveness, or other character issues. It's amazing how things like that, which were hitherto hidden from the pastor, soon become apparent, and others even more apparent! All of this happens during that critical time of frustration or waiting.

All of a sudden, people flip and change, and you quickly realise now why God would prefer to first build character in a person before giving them the desire of their hearts. I learnt as the Lord led me to find out, never to attempt to as it were *'force'* God to do something or answer someone's prayer just because I sympathise and empathise with their situation. You say can you *'force'* God to do something for someone? Well, I am His child, servant, and messenger and I expect Him to honour my word, especially when I am in His will (Isaiah 44:26). The balance here is that, just because God allows or permit a thing does not suggest that we have His perfect will on it (cf Romans 12:1-2). Or, just because something is good, does not necessarily means it is the right choice or the right thing!

iii. **Don't interfere with the Process**

Through my encounter, the Lord then spoke to me about allowing people to have and to benefit from their training in character building; a process that precedes and qualifies His children for sustainable blessings without sorrow. As hard as it might be, especially for the *heart* of a true pastor to take, I am learning to do it God's way. As subjective as it may sound, I have proven it. And I know whatever God does, He does it out of love and He does not intend to hinder anyone from coming into the fullness of His blessings. But, He has the loving responsibility of proving and refining our real motives for what we ask or seek from Him.

I also now understand that if I love my people enough, then I should not interfere with their training towards attaining their blessing by rushing them through the process of blessing, whether by my prayers or some material hand-out, intending to make it *easy* for them. I cannot make it any easier than the Father has already made it. I need to decide my role only by doing what the Lord leads me to, whether in teaching, encouragement or any form of help the Lord prefers including appropriate hand-outs in cash or goods that are necessary from time to time. But I must be equally discerning and spiritually sensitive to the needs of the person *in training* and respond appropriately as we trust God together for the best outcome at all times.

Making Sense of Times of Frustration: a Biblical Point of View

Isaac's Wife Rebekah

When we read Scriptures, we realise that there was always a time between what God promised to do and when He did them. Whether it was Abraham, Israel, Gideon, Rebekah, Joseph or Mary and Paul, the story was always the same. They had times when they had to wait; a period we have already described as the *time of frustration,* when in most cases all you have to do is to do nothing but wait faithfully on God.

This period usually seems dry and barren, and nothing seems to happen except that you know what you want, can *see* and imagine what you want, but you just can't have it yet. It is a period of intense frustration that tries your patience and level of endurance. Sometimes you find yourself under pressure to do something more about the situation during this period, and in some instances it is because you feel like all of hell has broken lose against you. This is the time you are tempted to ask, like Rebekah the wife of Isaac during her own period of frustration, *if all is well, why am I like this?*

> *Now Isaac pleaded with the Lord for his wife, because she was barren; and the Lord granted his plea, and Rebekah his wife conceived. [22] But the children struggled together within her; and she said, "If all is well, why am I like this?|" So she went to inquire of the Lord (Genesis 25:21-22).*

Gideon the Man of Valour

Even with Gideon, because their frustration was extremely intense, he seriously doubted if God was actually still with him and his people. During his time of frustration he lost hope, felt lost and indeed succumbed to resignation from all worthy purpose and future pursuit. His whole concern was reduced to survival tactics, hiding in strange places, totally unable to face up to the daily realities of what they had to go through.

In today's parlance, we may say he became manically depressed.

> *Now the Angel of the Lord came and sat under the terebinth tree which was in Ophrah, which belonged to Joash the Abiezrite, while his son Gideon threshed wheat in the winepress, in order to hide it from the Midianites. And the Angel of the Lord appeared to him, and said to him, "The Lord is with you, you mighty man of valor!" Gideon said to Him, "O my lord, if the Lord is with us, why then has all this happened to us? And where are all His miracles which our fathers told us about, saying, 'Did not the Lord bring us up from Egypt?' But now the Lord has forsaken us and delivered us into the hands of the Midianites."(Judges 6:11-13)*

Hagar the Bondwoman

The Lord had to ask Hagar a strange, and what appears to be an awful question in the time of her frustration when, all she could see was a vast dry and empty wilderness, a dying child, hopelessness and complete dejection. She was sat all by herself bemoaning her plight, sobbing about how unjustly Abraham and Sarah had treated her and her son, and probably cursing the day she was born.

When the Lord met her in the wilderness, obviously now disinterested in the whole of life, He asked simply, *"What ails you, Hagar?"*, as if He did not already know. In other words the Lord was telling Hagar, *what's your problem? I was there when Abraham and Sarah decided to send you away. And if this will help, listen, I told Abraham to let you and the boy to go! (1 Samuel 21:12-21my paraphrase)*. What Hagar didn't know was that through all her frustration, the Hand of God was working out His divine purpose, which was right at hand.

The Lord finally opened her eyes, and instead of a bottle of water, she and her son got a well; she became a free woman delivered from been a bondwoman, now a mother with a son unlike when she was in the house of Sarah where all she actually had belonged to Sarah (Genesis 16:2-6). Finally, God made out of Hagar's son, Ishmael, a great nation with many generations (1 Samuel 21:18).

Apostle James - Count it all Joy

Understandably, the time of frustration can be tough. No one should downplay its weight and burdens. However, in a way, our frustrations are to us like the weight is to the athlete. Used wisely, they help build up strength, resilience and the discipline required to win our race and our fights in life, and to gain our "well deserved" trophies.

The Apostle James makes brilliant sense of it all. According to him, the period of frustration is not intended to kill anyone, nor is it intended to be a punishment for your sins. It is just a qualifier, a character builder and a faith builder, which the Apostle James simply refers to as *the test of your faith*. In the end, it is meant to give you mastery over stuff God delivers into your hand, as His gifts as well as responsibilities. It is never God's intension for stuff to gain mystery over His people. Therefore, by and through your frustration, when handled gracefully, you will turn out to become a good and wise steward. So, when Apostle James speaks about frustration, he even makes light of the weight of the burden of our frustrations, and commands us to take it in our stride, counting it all joy! He says,

> *My brethren, count it all joy when you fall into various trials, knowing that the testing of your faith produces patience. ⁴ But let patience have its perfect work, that you may be perfect and complete, lacking nothing (James 1:2-4).*

Prophet Moses – All for Good

Similarly, Moses told the children of Israel, as he recounted both their ordeals and triumph from Egypt through the wilderness, that their prolonged period of frustrations in the wilderness was only a *qualifier,* intended to qualify them for the Promised Land. All that time when they hoped and strove for Canaan, the promise land, and had to endure the daily rationing of manna and quails, it was only a test before the promise was fully delivered into their hands.

God had to somehow ensure that they gained mastery over things, and looked beyond things to the One who provided the things. He had to be sure that the children of Israel would appreciate whatever He gave them or did for and through them by allowing them to develop the necessary character and integrity.

Moses, who benefited immensely from the wisdom of hindsight, brings great insight to the matters of frustration. His contribution documented as his last instruction to the children of Israel, is incredibly helpful that I can't help but quote in full what He actually said in his own words:

> *And you shall remember that the Lord your God led you all the way these forty years in the wilderness, to humble you and test you, to know what was in your heart, whether you would keep His commandments or not.* ^{3} *So He humbled you, allowed you to hunger, and fed you with manna which you did not know nor did your fathers know, that He might make you know that man shall not live by bread alone; but man lives by every word that proceeds from the mouth of the Lord.* ^{4} *Your garments did not wear out on you, nor did your foot swell these forty years.* ^{5} *You should know in your heart that as a man chastens his son, so the Lord your God chastens you.* ^{6} *"Therefore you shall keep the commandments of the Lord your God, to walk in His ways and to fear Him.* ^{7} *For the Lord your God is bringing you into a good land, a land of brooks of water, of fountains and springs, that flow out of valleys and hills;* ^{8} *a land of wheat and barley, of vines and fig trees and pomegranates, a land of olive oil and honey;* ^{9} *a land in which you will eat bread without scarcity, in which you will lack nothing; a land whose stones are iron and out of whose hills you can dig copper.* ^{10} *When you have eaten and are full, then you shall bless the Lord your God for the good land which He has given you.* ^{11} *"Beware that you do not forget the Lord your God by not keeping His commandments,*

His judgments, and His statutes which I command you today, [12] *lest when you have eaten and are full, and have built beautiful houses and dwell in them;* [13] *and when your herds and your flocks multiply, and your silver and your gold are multiplied, and all that you have is multiplied;* [14] *when your heart is lifted up, and you forget the Lord your God who brought you out of the land of Egypt, from the house of bondage;* [15] *who led you through that great and terrible wilderness, in which were fiery serpents and scorpions and thirsty land where there was no water; who brought water for you out of the flinty rock;* [16] *who fed you in the wilderness with manna, which your fathers did not know, that He might humble you and that He might test you, to do you good in the end—* [17] *then you say in your heart, 'My power and the might of my hand have gained me this wealth.'* [18] *"And you shall remember the Lord your God, for it is He who gives you power to get wealth, that He may establish His covenant which He swore to your fathers, as it is this day (Deuteronomy 8:2-18).*

Notice the 16th verse, that the conclusion of all our frustrations regarding God's promises, great character building and qualifying works in us, is so that He will do us good in the end. It involves all things working together for our own good (Romans 8:28), and not against us. Like Moses admits, God knows all our trudging, and how long it has taken us going through the great wilderness of our frustrations, but the good thing is, He has always been there through it with us (Deuteronomy 2:7). The good thing is, we do not lack what is required of us to get through our times of frustrations, and God of course ensures that our *garment does not wear out on us, nor our foot to swell (Deuteronomy 8:4).*

Apostle Paul – You're Being Trained

Apostle Paul, also speaking about our time of frustrations in relation to the promises of God, expands on what Moses in Deuteronomy 8:5 only hinted at briefly, *the chastisement of the Lord*. Paul affirms that the chastisement of the Lord is actually a good thing and it is hugely profitable for anyone having to go through it.

As strange as it may seem and sound, Paul, the man who himself experienced chastening from the Lord firsthand, is convinced and would like all of us to know that the chastisement of the Lord is not to be dismissed, but welcomed as an act of God's love and grace.

Furthermore, it is something that also affirms our legitimacy as children of God. Although sometimes it may seem painful and uncomfortable, chastisement is never to be deemed as *punishment*. It is correction with the aim of making us better and bigger, and *partakers of God's holiness*, blessings and good purposes:

> *For consider Him who endured such hostility from sinners against Himself, lest you become weary and discouraged in your souls. ⁴ You have not yet resisted to bloodshed, striving against sin. ⁵ And you have for- gotten the exhortation which speaks to you as to sons: " My son, do not despise the chastening of the Lord, Nor be discouraged when you are rebuked by Him; ⁶ For whom the Lord loves He chastens, And scourges every son whom He receives." If you endure chastening, God deals with you as with sons; for what son is there whom a father does not chasten? ⁸ But if you are without chastening, of which all have become partakers, then you are illegitimate and not sons. ⁹ Furthermore, we have had human fathers who corrected us, and we paid them respect. Shall we not much more readily be in subjection to the Father of spirits and live? ¹⁰ For they indeed for a few days chastened us as seemed best to them, but He for our profit, that we may be partakers of His holiness. ¹¹Now no chastening seems to be joyful for the present, but painful; nevertheless, afterward it yields the peaceable fruit of righteousness to those who have been trained by it (Hebrews 12:3-11).*

Every legitimate and wise child of God should expect, and in fact always make place for the chastisement of the Lord in their dealings, knowing that he or she stands to be corrected as part of their character building and qualifying process in relation to God's promises and purposes. This has always been the nature of God's dealings with His true children. Take for example Habakkuk, the prophet of God. He knew as a child of God, that correction was certainly one of the things God would do when it was necessary. So, he expected correction, as we see here in Habakkuk 2:1, *"I will stand my watch and set myself on the rampart, and watch to see what He will say to me, and what I will answer when I am corrected."*

While we stand to be corrected in the form of chastening from the Lord, which often brings about frustrations, Apostle Paul desires us to be positive about the whole thing. Our frustrations are good and they literally *work* for us. And if there are any consolations, then it is this; our frustrations are light and not permanent compared to the immense benefit they accord. Our frustrations are temporary but the benefits they accrue, some of which we do not see with our naked eyes, are wonderful and eternal.

> *Therefore we do not lose heart. Even though our outward man is perishing, yet the inward man is being renewed day by day. [17] For our light affliction, which is but for a moment, is working for us a far more exceeding and eternal weight of glory, [18] while we do not look at the things which are seen, but at the things which are not seen. For the things which are seen are temporary, but the things which are not seen are eternal (2 Corinthians 4:16-18).*

Final Words on Frustration: the Soldiers on Your Ship

We now return to our original passage, Acts 27:39 to 44 for our final thoughts on frustration with respect to the imminent promises of God; the period between what we are told, believed and see but cannot yet have, and all that takes place while we wait.

In the passage we find men who, at the break of day, were beginning to realise that truly they could beach safely after all their terrible and titanic-styled ordeal at sea. They saw a bay with a beach a manageable distance away. But they were not quite there yet, and all the anxieties and uncertainties surrounding their safety still remained. Although they saw the bay, and planned to manoeuvre the ship towards the bay hoping to beach it, they seriously were not in control. However, they have had a word through Apostle Paul from the angel from God promising that none would lose their life.

Although they came to believe Paul, under the circumstance it was almost impossible to just lie low. Ever since Paul spoke, the only thing that had physically changed, was the fact that the night was making way for the daylight. The sea, its waves and the wind were still very ferocious. The ship and its passengers were still being tempest tossed and the stern of the ship eventually broke, as they helplessly tried with all their might to have some control of the ship.

Now what else was left to do? Do they stay on board or jump over board and hopefully swim to safety if they might? Some of them had already previously tried to escape from the ship under the cover of darkness, when the wind and waves were still heavily hammering against their ship (vr 30). Obviously, that was nothing but an overt expression of their frustrations. Had they not been sternly warned by Paul to stay on board the ship, they would have, under pretence, jumped and most likely died.

But, think about the conflict and the frustration, when you want to but cannot do, what you think is good for your safety. When it seems you've been told to stay on board for a final death wish. Most people will kick off in a childlike tantrum, supposedly itching to save their lives and to avoid cataclysmic damage. You will think it is more reasonable to help yourself than to listen to some *religious fanatic* like Paul.

Meanwhile, something else was happening behind the scenes which probably most people on board the ship did not know. As if battling the wind and waves for survival were not hard enough, there were men on board with authority to shoot anyone trying to escape. By the way, have you ever found yourself between the proverbial *devil and deep blue sea* or *the rock and the hard place?* The people on board were faced with one such situation! The description sounds comical but the issues very serious.

Up to now, everyone had been feverishly fighting just to survive and to keep their life, but now that the margin for possible survival looks predictably good, it was the turn of the soldiers to threaten the life of determined escapees. The passage says, *the soldiers' plan was to kill the prisoners, lest any of them should swim away and escape (vr42).* Well, that meant Apostle Paul was included because he was a prisoner as well.

The intentions and actions of the soldiers were massively informed by the demonic side of the *law of self-preservation*, a law far removed from a more generous divine law of *love your neighbour as yourself.* The soldiers were selfish, and the only reason why the prisoner must be killed before they escaped was that, if the prisoner escaped alive, the soldiers themselves could eventually be killed for not killing the prisoners (cf Acts 16:27; Matt. 28:11-15).

Let me rush to the final two verses of the passage and thereafter draw out some relevant principles for handling and safeguarding your God given purposes when you find yourself in situations of frustrations.

But the centurion, wanting to save Paul, kept them from their purpose, and commanded that those who could swim should jump overboard first and get to land, [44] and the rest, some on boards and some on parts of the ship. And so it was that they all escaped safely to land (Acts 27:43,44).

***Wisdom for Purpose*:** Four things to ponder;

(1)   Paul's life was preserved with the rest of the prisoners hence thwarting the diabolical plans of the soldiers to destroy the lives of the prisoners who have already survived the storm at sea. How was this possible? Ultimately God intervened, however, it is a fact that *when a man's ways please the Lord, he makes even his enemies to be at peace with him (Proverbs 16:7).* Your unwavering commitment to God's purposes is your guarantee for life amid the camp of your enemy. Always ensure that you are about God's purposes and He will cause your enemy to help you instead of harming you.

(2)   Everyone aboard the ship escaped safely to land, some swimming, others on board, and some using parts of the ship as floats. All of what happened in the end cumulated into the big picture of the initial word of the Lord delivered by the angel ...*take heart, for there will be no loss of life among you, but only of the ship. ... 'Do not be afraid, Paul; you must be brought before Caesar; and indeed God has granted you all those who sail with you.' ... take heart, men, for I believe God that it will be just as it was told me. "However, we must run aground on a certain island" (Acts 27:21-23).* Never forget that even in your time of frustration: *The grass withers, the flower fades, but the word of our God stands forever" (Isaiah 40:8).*

(3)   If you have God's assurance, never let the pressure of your frustrations cause you to jump before it is time. For what seemed like a window of escape for the prisoners before the ship ran aground, and before the centurion's intervention, was in fact an occasion for the soldiers to kill them.

God uses time and opportunity to resolve our moments of frustrations. There is an enemy we know which is more obvious, and we are prepare to face, but there's one nearby even more sly and vicious that we unsuspectingly count as a friend. The latter we normally don't prepare for and takes us unawares. Those are the *soldiers* on your ship who are governed by principles other than those you know – *the law of self-preservation.*

(4)   In all, depending on how you see them or handle them, your frustrations are working for you (Romans 8:28). God, Who began a good work in you and with you, will doubtless bring you to the expected end (Philippians 1:6).

Some powerful Scriptural Encouragement for you:

He who continually goes forth weeping, bearing seed for sowing, Shall doubtless come again with rejoicing, bringing his sheaves with him (Psalms 126:6).

You therefore must endure hardship as a good soldier of Jesus Christ (1Timothy 2:3).

The end of a thing is better than its beginning; The patient in spirit is better than the proud in spirit (Ecclesiastes 7:8).

You will keep him in perfect peace, whose mind is stayed on You, because he trusts in You (Isaiah 26:3).

Be anxious for nothing, but in everything by prayer and supplication, with thanksgiving, let your requests be made known to God; [7] and the peace of God, which surpasses all understanding, will guard your hearts and minds through Christ Jesus (Philippians 4:8-7).

"Therefore I say to you, do not worry about your life, what you will eat or what you will drink; nor about your body, what you will put on. Is not life more than food and the body more than clothing? [26] Look at the birds of the air, for they neither sow nor reap nor gather into barns; yet your heavenly Father feeds them. Are you not of more value than they? [27] Which of you by worrying can add one cubit to his stature? [28] "So why do you worry about clothing? Consider the lilies of the field, how they grow: they neither toil nor spin; [29] and yet I say to you that even Solomon in all his glory was not arrayed like one of these. [30] Now if God so clothes the grass of the field, which today is, and tomorrow is thrown into the oven, will He not much more clothe you, O you of little faith? [31] "Therefore do not worry, saying, 'What shall we eat?' or 'What shall we drink?' or 'What shall we wear?' [32] For after all these things the Gentiles seek. For your heavenly Father knows that you need all these things. [33] But seek first the kingdom of God and His righteousness, and all these things shall be added to you. [34] Therefore do not worry about tomorrow, for tomorrow will worry about its own things. Sufficient for the day is its own trouble (Matthew 6:25-34).

God's Supernatural Strategies for His Purposes: Lean Not On Your Own Understanding

❖❖❖

We know in Part: Purpose Versus Knowledge

For now we see in a mirror, dimly, but then face to face. Now I know in part, but then I shall know just as I also am known. And now abide faith, hope, love, these three; but the greatest of these is love (1 Corinthians 13:12,13).

It happened just as the angel from God had told Paul. They suffered shipwreck on a certain island and everyone on board made it safely to shore. Once on shore, Paul and the others found out that the place was called Malta. This Island was not named in the original message from the angel to Paul. The angel simply referred to an island.

Obviously, there's nothing spiritual or spooky about the name of the Island, but in this case, it is important to stress how God attaches significance to the *main thing* and what matters most.

Some people just love the emotions and sensations of insignificant details, so much so that they lose sight of what God is really saying or doing in a given situation. If the name of the Island was so crucial to the fulfilment of the prophecies or the word of the Lord, God would have mentioned it.

I found out that an awful number of people get stuck on forms and lose the actual meaning of that form. They become so obsessed and particular about petite details, that while focusing on getting all the detail together, they lose sight of the God behind the detail. Can you imagine Paul and his colleagues at sea, already having no control over the ship, but stupidly trying to find a particular Island called Malta? That would have been very interesting!

When it comes to things of faith, we sometimes stand in danger of being hindered by the very things we know. This is the one place where knowledge becomes a bit tricky if care is not taken. Just consider how many genuine people might have unfortunately missed great opportunities or potential spouses because their knowledge of an ideal spouse informed by studies, conferences, or a *word of prophecy* seemingly contradicts what ideally was God's purpose and design for their true spouse.

For example, I knew a long time ago that I would and must marry a God fearing woman, someone with whom, together, we could faithfully fulfil our God given purposes and ministries. Now, with that knowledge, I made up my mind that any woman I intended to marry must have all the right pedigree of a pastor's wife. Also, she had to be a woman preferably preparing for some form of Christian ministries in a church setting with a wonderful 'singing voice'.

Almost every *Pentecostal* pastor you meet in Bible school will have something similar to my own desire for a wife back then, especially for a woman with 'singing voice'! It's funny but single pastors in bible schools have strange prayer points for a future wife. But, when I met my wife, there was no indication or propensity of any possibility of her becoming a pastor's wife. In fact, for a girl or a lady, some would have considered her hobbies, including playing soccer, running and boxing, rather unusual and culturally unacceptable. She could have easily passed as a tomboy for most people meeting her for the first time. Instead of skirts and blouses my wife loved to wear sweat suits with trainers (sneakers), and her entire wardrobe was full of mainly track suits. Instead of theology, she trained as a health and fitness instructor, just for the love of physical exercise.

She was not a regular church goer either, nor did she have any depth of Christian understanding. She did not have a 'singing voice' then. I lean toward Pentecostal style of worship, and I doubt if she even knew the difference between Baptists, Presbyterians, Methodists or Pentecostals. Saying that, I am so glad now that none of that meant anything to her, because her innocence about things of denomination, I believe, contributed to how we met and still is today one reason why she has no barrier problem with reaching out to diverse people with the good news of Christ.

Did God promise He was going to turn her to the wonderful Godly woman she is today? No. I did not have all that confirmation others look for, but I had no choice except to obey God's leading. I knew almost nothing about my wife's background, and it did not bother me. But, in the physical, I knew that she was respectful, kind and generous. By the way; that was what I saw initially, not her face, although she's a princess to behold! I was in the position where I had no option but to obey, despite my bible-school description and prescription for what a pastor's wife should look like. My preconceived knowledge of a pastor's wife, mostly sourced from a list of do's and don'ts derived from *prophecies*, books, and 'good' suggestions from pastor friends in Bible school, stood in my way like brick walls, but I also knew there was more to choosing a wife.

Apart from all that I have said, there were other hurdles to overcome especially from *well-meaning* people who tried to read our motives. They were not only proven wrong, but in the end, turned out to be very helpful seeing that God was with us.

Thank God, had I heeded to the counterproductive signs and challenges leading to our marriage, I would have easily caved in and missed God's best for me. Now, there are times when I wonder, what if I had remained adamant concerning my 'knowledge' based fleece for an ideal wife, waiting until I had at least the majority of them fulfilled before proposing marriage to my wife? Today, this is no less a frightening thought for me, looking back and knowing that because of my personal bias or in some cases naivety, I could have lost the love of my life and God's ordained wife for me according to His purposes.

Let me add that the reason why many Christians are still looking for the miracle God has already provided, is that they are waiting for the specifics of what God has already provided to fit exactly into the specifics of what they thought they heard from God or a man of God, about what God was going to do or provide. And this is often aggravated by servants of God, who most times are genuinely or for other reasons, trying to feed their listeners with unnecessary details which clearly were only good enough for their personal use as men of God.

Without doubt, some specifics of prophetic revelations or words of knowledge and wisdom must be only for the consumption of the servants of God, but some will never decipher what is what. As a result, some try to describe the undesirable, the indescribable and name the unnameable, hence the real message becomes shrouded in mystery or complicated details. As men of God, we do not need to prove anything in anyway, by being unnecessarily and overbearingly detailed, to the extent that we overshadow the main message God wants to communicate to His people.

Surely, for now we only know in part and prophesy in part (1 Corinthians 13:9). Let's not fall for the easy temptation of being caught in a swing of giving, or looking hard for details and specifics; waiting to ensure that all the *signs* are in place before we step out in faith. It is no gift and compliment being a generation that is bent on seeking after signs (Mark 8:12).

But again, even with all the other signs already in place, we still don't believe (John 12:37). Probably that's why the Lord Jesus Christ didn't make it His primary concern to dwell on signs for signs sake. It could be for the same reason that the name of the Island was not initially disclosed, so that the men on the ship including Paul, only found out it was called Malta after they arrived. We need to believe God, and take Him by His Word even in the absence of names of things and places!

Like Abraham, usually all that we will have might be a word from God without specific details. Hence, we need to attempt our journeys of purpose in obedience, being certain of one thing; that God is not the author of confusion (I Corinthians 14:33), and that it will not be difficult to fathom when we finally arrive at His chosen destination for our lives.

Clearly, even in the absence of specifics, we will know when we get there; that indeed this is what the Lord spoke about. Don't wait for the signs and names of your healings. Know that God has said He heals your disease; expect it and go for it. Walk towards your blessings, and when you are there, the Lord will name it! Start heading toward your blessing and purpose, and when you get it, the details will emerge. Don't let the knowledge of what you think you know to be true obstruct or stand in the way of what God, through the power and wisdom of purpose has set before you.

> *Now the Lord had said to Abram: "Get out of your country, from your family and from your father's house, to a land that I will show you. ² I will make you a great nation; I will bless you and make your name great; and you shall be a blessing. ³ I will bless those who bless you, and I will curse him who curses you; and in you all the families of the earth shall be blessed." ⁴ So Abram departed as the Lord had spoken to him, and Lot went with him. And Abram was seventy-five years old when he departed from Haran. ⁵ Then Abram took Sarai his wife and Lot his brother's son, and all their possessions that they had gathered, and the people whom they had acquired in Haran, and they departed to go to the land of Canaan. So they came to the land of Canaan.*

Abram passed through the land to the place of Shechem, as far as the terebinth tree of Moreh. And the Canaanites were then in the land. [7] Then the Lord appeared to Abram and said, "To your descendants I will give this land." And there he built an altar to the Lord, who had appeared to him. (Genesis 12:1-7).

Think about what our original passage in Acts 28 says about the men on the ship after they arrived on the Island. It says, *now when they had escaped, they then found out that the island was called Malta (Acts 28:1).* That means some things are more important than others. It is about priority and prioritising. They escaped alive, and then they found out that the Island was called Malta. Frivolous people and those caught in triviality will be more concerned about what the Island is called than escaping to safety. But, that's another discussion.

The point I want to leave you with is that, focusing on doing the will and purposes of God precede naming your blessings. *Keeping the main thing the main thing* is what God is about. God always has more in stock for us than we see and know now. And truly God is full of surprises. It is so easy to become trapped into details based on what you think is true, only to miss out on God's opportunities and purposes.

But as it is written: "Eye has not seen, nor ear heard, nor have entered into the heart of man the things which God has prepared for those who love Him"(1 Corinthians 2:9).

Purpose and the Love of God

to the intent that now the manifold wisdom of God might be made known by the church to the principalities and powers in the heavenly places, [11] according to the eternal purpose which He accomplished in Christ Jesus our Lord (Ephesians 3:10-11).

Was there more to landing safely on the Island? Was God honouring His servant Paul before the rest of the passengers by ensuring that things happened the way Paul said they would?

Definitely, there might have been some amongst the passengers who may have said, *yea, Paul said it!* But behind all this was a higher, but hidden, purpose of God to reach a little Island of obviously lovely people. They were good people, very hospitable but needed to hear and to know about the saving grace of the Lord Jesus Christ.

How else could they have been reached and evangelised? Thank God for the *wind* and *wave* that drove the ship in their direction. At last they had the opportunity to hear the eternal gospel and they could make a choice for Christ or not for Him. God used the most peculiar way to transport the evangelist to Malta just to preach the gospel, but it was more than that. It was the purpose and the love of God in action.

> *For if we are beside ourselves, it is for God; or if we are of sound mind, it is for you.* [14] *For the love of Christ compels us, because we judge thus: that if One died for all, then all died (2 Corinthians 5:13,14).*

All-in-all, we have in this story the mystery of the workings of God, but also the sure work of His love, power, purpose and wisdom coming together. God will use anyone and anything to get His job done. When He wanted to reach the wicked Ninevites, a people caught in damnable sins, he used again what seemed a bizarre means of transportation.

God transported an unwilling prophet and evangelist, using the combination of waves, wind, a ship and an awkward '*submarine*'. Jonah, the prophet and evangelist, completed the last leg of his journey in the belly of a big fish and as soon as he reached the shores of Nineveh, he knew God was serious. And God has always been serious about the plight of humanity. *But God demonstrates His own love toward us, in that while we were still sinners, Christ died for us (Romans 5:8).*

Purpose and the Favour of God

There are three main things happening in this half of the passage. First, Paul and his fellow passengers are being blessed and favoured greatly while the purposes of God are being fulfilled. Secondly, the unlimited grace and love of God are demonstrated in their most practical forms as God showed no small kindness to an obscure Island, deeply steeped into superstition. Thirdly, God is glorified.

Let's remember that Paul's journey was not one that he purposefully chose and planned in detail. Originally, he had had a desire to visit Rome but nothing close to what we have so far seen unfolded in the story. Incidentally, we see so far in the story; Paul's own desires coinciding with God's purposes throughout his journey which began unpromisingly with his Jerusalem arrest and subsequent imprisonment. Because he was following through on God's assignment in all obedience, he had His protection and provision. God's abiding presence was supernaturally bestowed upon him, giving him the assurance and comfort necessary to complete His purposes. And Paul, even in the midst of adversities, had known that God was using him as a vessel to carry out His ultimate purpose in the lives of people in the places He took him.

So, in every place, at all times, and with whatever people, Paul went directly for the opportunity to fulfil the purpose of God. Thus Paul was a passionate, mission minded servant of God, solely given to God's purposes for him. Describing his ultimate goal regarding the purposes of God, he proclaims;

> *Not as though I had already attained, either were already perfect: but I follow after, if that I may apprehend that for which also I am apprehended of Christ Jesus. [13]Brethren, I count not myself to have apprehended: but this one thing I do, forgetting those things which are behind, and reaching forth unto those things which are before, [14]I press toward the mark for the prize of the high calling of God in Christ Jesus (Philippians 3:12-14).*

Even when Paul suffered persecution or had sleepless nights, it was for the sake of the gospel of Jesus Christ, the one assignment he was sold out to. No amount of suffering and persecution was enough to stop him because of his special conviction saying, *for to me to live is Christ, and to die is gain (Philippians 1:21)*. Such was the zeal, love, and hope of the great Apostle Paul.

Now as soon as he landed on the Island, God immediately caused Paul to receive unusual favour with the natives of the Island. He and his colleagues were made very welcome, despite the fact that they were deemed criminals and prisoners. The natives were not bothered about who the men were until a poisonous snake wrapped itself around Paul's hand. Obviously this was a rude intervention intended to derail the purposes of God for the natives of the Island, who until now had greatly admired Paul and his colleagues. But God had His own plans and strategies for reaching out, lovingly but powerfully, to the wonderful people of Malta through His servant Paul. How did God execute His mission for the people of Malta?

Strategy #1: Binding the Strong Man, Taking It by Force

No one can enter a strong man's house and plunder his goods, unless he first binds the strong man. And then he will plunder his house (Mark 3:27).

The reason the viper fastened itself to Paul's hand is said to be because of the heat of the fire that Paul was kindling by adding a buddle of sticks to it. But as soon as the viper fastened itself to Paul's hand, immediately, the natives concluded;

"No doubt this man is a murderer, whom, though he has escaped the sea, yet justice does not allow to live." [6] *However, they were expecting that he would swell up or suddenly fall down dead (Acts 28:4,6).*

Obviously, this viper attack was nothing but a satanic device, a cunning working of the *strong man* over that city. This was the likeness of *the Prince of Persia* in Daniel chapter 10 and verse 13, which opposes God's people because of his goal to take complete control over cities and its inhabitants. If any significant inroads were to be made in Malta, that viper, the *strong man* clinging to Paul had to be bound just as the Lord Jesus said (Mark 3:27).

What did Paul do with the snake? He vehemently …

> *shook off the creature into the fire and suffered no harm. …But after they had looked for a long time and saw no harm come to him, they changed their minds and said that he was a god (Acts 28:5,6).*

Wisdom for Purpose

From Paul's encounter, we derive seven all-time great spiritual truths about your favour, and the purposes of God for your life:

(1)   Every favour has an enemy. It is the *strong man* to your favour! Once your favour shows up, *the strong man* will also show up. For every favour that God brings into your life, Satan fights to abort it. Expect favour, but also expect persecution because of those who can't stand you being blessed. It is not strange to find persecution where favour is.

> *For a great and effective door has opened to me, and there are many adversaries (1 Corinthians 16:9).*
>
> *So Jesus answered and said, "Assuredly, I say to you, there is no one who has left house or brothers or sisters or father or mother or wife or children or lands, for My sake and the gospel's, who shall not receive a hundredfold now in this time—houses and brothers and sisters and mothers and children and lands, with persecutions—and in the age to come, eternal life (Mark 10:29-30)*

> *Yes, and all who desire to live godly in Christ Jesus will suffer persecution (2 Timothy 3:12).*

(2)   Those sitting with you may not always stand with you. Paul suffered isolation and was called a murderer immediately after the viper fastened itself to him. They did it to Jesus and they can do it to you. As long as you sit around the fire (Paul and the Natives of Malta) or around the table (Jesus and His disciples), it's okay. But stand to kindle the fire or face your Gethsemane and those with you disassociate. It is normal!

(3)   Play it safe like everyone else and you avoid being smeared. But turn the heat on, and Satan is right at you. The metaphor for Satan in Scripture is the snake or serpent. Paul's presence on the Island obviously upset Satan. Three things Satan can do according to John 10:10; – to steal, kill, and destroy. So, his intension was clearly seen, to stop Paul from carrying out God's present and future assignments by fastening himself to Paul. Ultimately he intended to unleash his venom right into the heart of Paul, but he only succeeded in bringing him into disfavour with his host for a while.

Remember, whether it regards an assignment of God on a very small scale, like in your home, community or the local church, or even on a large scale involving a nationwide campaign, Satan will show up when you turn on the heat of prayer, revival, holiness or the fire of the Holy Spirit.

(4)   People who adhere to God and are on assignment will encounter an enemy whenever they turn up on assignment and where the heat is turned on. But, you can shake the demon (snake) right into the heat! On the basis of your assignment hidden *things* will be forcefully driven to the surface and you must contend for your assignment.

The good news is that you will overcome and, like Paul, suffer no harm. Where the enemy tried to discredit you, people will soon begin to change their minds.

> *You shall tread upon the lion and the cobra, the young lion and the serpent you shall trample underfoot (Psalms 91:13). For the weapons of our warfare are not carnal but mighty in God for pulling down strongholds, casting down arguments and every high thing that exalts itself against the knowledge of God, bringing every thought into captivity to the obedience of Christ (2 Cor. 10:4-5).*

Furthermore, your life is preserved by God and your assignment keeps you alive. While you are on assignment, and are focused on completing your God-given mission you cannot die and can literally negotiate your death.

> *The Lord is on my side; I will not fear. What can man do to me? [7] The Lord is for me among those who help me; therefore I shall see my desire on those who hate me. [8] It is better to trust in the Lord than to put confidence in man. [9] It is better to trust in the Lord than to put confidence in princes. [10] All nations surrounded me, but in the name of the Lord I will destroy them. [11] They surrounded me, yes, they surrounded me; but in the name of the Lord I will destroy them. [12] They surrounded me like bees; They were quenched like a fire of thorns; for in the name of the Lord I will destroy them. [13] You pushed me violently, that I might fall, but the Lord helped me. [14] The Lord is my strength and song, and He has become my salvation. [15] The voice of rejoicing and salvation is in the tents of the righteous; the right hand of the Lord does valiantly. [16] The right hand of the Lord is exalted; the right hand of the Lord does valiantly. [17] I shall not die, but live, and declare the works of the Lord (Psalms 118:6-17).*

> *Therefore submit to God. Resist the devil and he will flee from you (James 4:7). Resist him, steadfast in the faith, ... (1 Pet 5:9).*

(5)   The expectation of the wicked will not stand. God delivers His own but frustrates and thwarts the plans of the wicked. The people of Malta expected Paul to swell up and to die but instead he shook off the viper and disappointed the determined expectation of the people. This is a good indication that God's people never live up to the evil expectation of the wicked.

> *And when Peter had come to himself, he said, "Now I know for certain that the Lord has sent His angel, and has delivered me from the hand of Herod and from all the expectation of the Jewish people." (Acts 12:11).*

> *The hope of the righteous will be gladness, But the expectation of the wicked will perish (Proverbs 10:28).*

> *No weapon formed against you shall prosper, And every tongue which rises against you in judgment You shall condemn. This is the heritage of the servants of the Lord, and their righteousness is from Me," Says the Lord (Isaiah 54:17).*

> *Who (God) frustrates the signs of the babblers, And drives diviners mad; Who turns wise men back-ward, And makes their knowledge foolishness- (Isaiah 44:25).*

(6)   What the enemy meant for evil God will turn for your good.

> *But as for you, you meant evil against me; but God meant it for good, in order to bring it about as it is this day, to save many people alive (Genesis 50:20).*

> *And we know that all things work together for good to those who love God, to those who are the called according to His purpose (Romans 8:28).*

(7)   Is it possible that there's a *strong man* in your life? Bind it! Your *strong man* could be the last decision you took without conferring with God. It could be the bad habit you are protecting – deal with it! Could it be that your *strong man* is not out in far places but where you are? – Change!

Strategy #2: Breaking Wicked Spell, Setting Captives Free

After Paul shook the venomous viper into the very fire he was kindling, something tremendous happened. The viper lost the spell and snare it had cast over the people of the Island. One can see from the passage, and the reactions of the natives of the Island, that they were held bound by extraordinary superstitions assigned to the powers of the viper to dispense and mete out vengeance.

They had believed the viper was quite powerful, until Paul made nothing of its supposed and assigned power by casting it into the fire. What followed after that is exactly what happens when territorial controls, witchcrafts and spells which hold people and communities in bondage are suddenly broken. The passage says, *the people changed their minds,* hence they were now ready to listen to Paul. All of a sudden, there arose great open doors for the gospel to be preached and received.

To change one's mind speaks of repentance and a complete about-turn. It is a change in view, position, perspective or belief. It also suggests a renewal of the mind in view of new information or light, piercing in the midst of darkness.

Historically, when the gospel is preached, or the power of God is clearly demonstrated by the power of the Holy Spirit, evidently it has always resulted in spells being broken and minds being changed toward Christ. The Demoniac of Gadarenes, wielded great sway over the entire region of Decapolis (*ten cities*).

Once the controlling powers of the Legion (demons), who ruled over the region through a demon-possessed man, were broken by the Lord Jesus, the cities and their people became free from wicked spells which had bound them for years (Mark 5:1-30).

Likewise, Simon, the sorcerer and the girl described only as 'slave girl', both of whom benefited from the powers of divination by which they astonished whole cities, had to have their negative powers broken. Obviously, they were being used by Satan to cast wicked spells, to exert control over their cities and to hold people bound from receiving the truth of God.

But there was a certain man called Simon, who previously practiced sorcery in the city and astonished the people of Samaria, claiming that he was someone great, [10] *to whom they all gave heed, from the least to the greatest, saying, "This man is the great power of God."* [11] *And they heeded him because he had astonished them with his sorceries for a long time.* [12] *But when they believed Philip as he preached the things concerning the kingdom of God and the name of Jesus Christ, both men and women were baptized.* [13] *Then Simon himself also believed; and when he was baptized he continued with Philip, and was amazed, seeing the miracles and signs which were done (Acts 8:9-13).*

Now it happened, as we went to prayer, that a certain slave girl possessed with a spirit of divination met us, who brought her masters much profit by for-tune-telling. [17] *... But Paul, greatly annoyed, turned and said to the spirit, "I command you in the name of Jesus Christ to come out of her." And he came out that very hour.* [19] *But when her masters saw that their hope of profit was gone, they seized Paul and Silas and dragged them into the marketplace to the authorities.* [25] *But at midnight Paul and Silas were praying and singing hymns to God, and the prisoners were listening to them.* [26] *Suddenly there was a great earthquake, so that the foundations of the prison were shaken; and immediately all the doors were opened and everyone's chains were loosed.* [27] *And the keeper of the prison, awaking from sleep and seeing the prison doors open, supposing the prisoners had fled, drew his sword and was about to kill himself.*

But Paul called with a loud voice, saying, "Do yourself no harm, for we are all here." [29] *Then he called for a light, ran in, and fell down trembling before Paul and Silas.* [30] *And he brought them out and said, "Sirs, what must I do to be saved?"* [31] *So they said, "Believe on the Lord Jesus Christ, and you will be saved, you and your household."* [32] *Then they spoke the word of the Lord to him and to all who were in his house.* [33] *And he took them the same hour of the night and washed their stripes. And immediately he and all his family were baptized.* [34] *Now when he had brought them into his house, he set food before them; and he rejoiced, having believed in God with all his household (Acts 16:16-19, 25-34).*

Strategy #3: The Bridge to Harvest

Once the back of the devil that held the people of Malta was broken, symbolised by the *roasting* of the viper with subsequent change of minds in the people, God began to make way for the entire region to be evangelised. None of this required any man's strategy, but God's. He chose to open the door for the harvest in a great fashion.

Obviously, He is the *Lord of the Harvest* who knows His harvest and how to enter each field (Matthew 9:38). For this particular harvest, the link God chose was the *leading citizen and magistrate* of the Island *(Acts 28:7)*. He was the prominent Publius, whom by divine arrangement and connection, gladly received and treated Paul and his colleagues with much courtesy for three days.

What does all this mean? God always has a means of appointing a man or a woman beforehand for what He intends to do in every nation. There is always that special key to the heart of localities and geographical areas that the Lord must connect us with for His particular assignment. For the Samaritan village, it was the Samaritan woman the Lord Jesus met at the well (John 4:7-26). Clearly, she must have been influential in some way to have the entire village run after her to meet the Man whom she claimed told her all about her life. What seemed to have been a casual meeting between her and the Lord at the well, cumulated into Samaria experiencing great miracles and great joy, after been fully evangelised by Phillip the Evangelist later in Acts 8:4-13.

It took the demon-possessed man of the Gardarenes to evangelise the cities of the Decapolis (*ten cities*) (Mark 5:1-30). This demoniac carrying legion was Jesus' link for harvesting souls in *ten cities*. His influence in his region was unusual compared to others we have seen so far, but his healing incredibly affected all who saw, knew, and heard about his original state.

Similarly, Cornelius, the man from Caesarea, a centurion of what was called the Italian Regiment, was also positioned as a bridge to bring the gospel of Christ to the gentile nations in Acts 10. That Cornelius was influential in his territory was not in question. His servants and the devout soldiers, who waited on him continually, even referred to Cornelius as a just man having good reputation among the nation of the Jews (Acts 28:22). In verse 2 of Acts 28, Cornelius is described as generous!

On a broad level, people on assignments or who carry out God's purposes in nations and cities, or in their communities should ask God to connect them to the person or persons He has assigned as keys to the heart of their cities, communities or nations. On a personal level, there's that particular person God has also assigned as a necessary pillar for the fulfilment of our God-given destinies.

We need to prayerfully locate and connect to those connections of favour, which God specifically puts along the way, for access to the successful completion of our present assignments. There's a Publius, or an 'unassuming' woman at the well, or a Cornelius with whom our destinies are inextricably linked. We need them, and connecting with them means our job is almost done. They represent strategic leads, and are *necessary* for accessing further doors we require in fulfilling our assignment after the *snake*; the devil that cast spells over our destiny, has been shook into the fire.

Strategy #4: The Occasion for Harvest

The special link to the harvest of souls in Malta became Publius, the leading citizen of the Island. However, the harvest required an occasion or a situation. This in a sense provides the spark which ignites the flame for total takeover. The *occasion* brings the evangelist into contact with the actual populace and serves as an invite and attraction for curiosity. It is the one thing that brings in the inquisitive inquirer or even alerts the inattentive to what's going on around them. In a way, the *occasion is the attractive bait that draws the fish to the fisherman's hook.*

Again, God knows how to instigate the *occasion* for His harvest. This is nothing we do or engineer. In every place and with everyone this may take a different form purely based on God's wisdom and the prevailing situation of the people He intends to reach. He is still the Lord of the Harvest and the Harvest is His. So, the evangelist or the one on assignment may not even know what the occasion for the harvest is or might be.

But, again when the occasion is granted, he recognises it as such and makes the appropriate move, all things begin to fall in place as if he planned it. The best way to describe the *occasion* that leads to the actual harvest or the fulfilment of our assignment and purposes would be what I call the *Divine Moment*. At this crucial point, the door suddenly opens and you just somehow happen to be there and happen to go right through it.

In the case of Malta, that *Divine Moment* came when no other person but Publius' father lay sick of fever and dysentery. What did Paul do? He went straightaway to pray for Publius' father and healed him as God granted by His mercies (Acts 28:8).

There is a spiritual law at work here. It is the law of sowing and reaping. This of course is a law that the adherer directly benefits from. It works on the premise that we directly benefit from the good we do for others, and that it is always in our own interest to do good to others. That *what you make happen for others God make happen for you* (Ephesians 6:8).

We sow kindness and we reap kindness. Sow love and you will reap love. But sow hatred and you definitely reap hatred.

Every person of purpose on God's assignment should look out for their *Divine Moment*, the *occasion* of God for supernatural harvest. In doing so, pay particular attention to someone whom the Lord has already linked you with through their care for you as a man of God. In many instances, because of their generosity and particular care for you, God is most likely going to reward them by addressing their own needs, in order to provide for Himself a *Divine Moment* (cf 2 Kings 4:8-37; Matthew 10:40 - 42).

Some Powerful Scriptures to Remember While in Search of your Divine Moments:

Do not be deceived, God is not mocked; for whatever a man sows, that he will also reap (Galatians 6:7).

The generous soul will be made rich, and he who waters will also be watered himself (Proverbs 11:25).

He who has pity on the poor lends to the Lord, and He will pay back what he has given (Proverbs 19:17).

He who gives to the poor will not lack, but he who hides his eyes to them receives many curses (Proverb 28:27).

And whoever gives one of these little ones only a cup of cold water in the name of a disciple, assuredly, I say to you, he shall by no means lose his reward" (Matthew 10:42).

But love your enemies, do good, and lend, hoping for nothing in return; and your reward will be great, and you will be sons of the Most High. For He is kind to the unthankful and evil (Luke 6:35).

Strategy #5: The Birth of Revival and the Harvest

The ultimate goal here is the harvest. None of all that has already been discussed has any real significance on their own unless they culminate into meaningful harvest. Just like the athlete prepares for years leading to an Olympic championship competition, so we see with things and activities that precede the attainment of our assignments and purposes.

At this point, all is set and we are ready for what has taken place mostly in private to become public. Private influence spills over into public attractions, and private connections become public benefits. Without anticipating it, what began as a family affair in Publius' household moved swiftly into the public domain of Malta, and everyone participated and greatly benefited from what God in His wisdom began on a very small scale, around the fireside when some natives initially welcomed men involved in a shipwreck.

> *Oh, the depth of the riches both of the wisdom and knowledge of God! How unsearchable are His judgments and His ways past finding out (Romans 11:33)!*

Indeed, what God had in mind, which was until now unknown to the Islanders and even to Paul in greater aspects, was beginning to unfold wonderfully. So, we read that after Paul had healed the father of Publius the magistrate, then *the rest of those on the island who had diseases also came and were healed (Acts 28:9).*

Watch, the text says that, *they came.* It wasn't Paul that went from house to house begging them or dropping gospel tracts through their doors. No disrespect intended to knocking on doors or gospel tract distribution which I also personally do. They have their place. However, the Islanders simply saw the need to come and they came at their own accord, having heard and seen what God was doing through Paul on their Island. Not even through many men, but just what God was evidently doing through one man, Paul, and the Island gathered to him.

As God showed mighty signs and miracles through His servant Paul, the Island was revived. Revival broke out, and the signs were visible because people came at their own accord to receive from the Lord through His servant. Ultimately, there were great harvests of souls into the Kingdom of God.

Wisdom for Purpose

What does all this mean for people of purpose in expectation of God's visitation, revival and harvest?

(1)   What God begins He will always complete. Whenever God begins a thing, no matter how insignificant the beginnings might seem, He has a great end in mind. From a small fireside welcome and conversation, the entire Island and its leading citizen were gloriously reached with the power and love of Christ.

> *being confident of this very thing, that He who has begun a good work in you will complete it until the day of Jesus Christ (Philippians 1:6).*
>
> *Though your beginning was small, yet your latter end would increase abundantly (Job 8:7).*
>
> *A little one shall become a thousand, and a small one a strong nation. I, the Lord, will hasten it in its time."* *(Isaiah 60:22)*

(2)   It doesn't take all to win all – God needs just a willing vessel! With a willing vessel, God can do more than with a multitude of unwilling people. Great revival has always taken place not with the many but the right people in God's hand. Paul brought revival to the entire Island, and Philip to Samaria. God wanted the whole world and sent one Man, Jesus. For this very reason God cut down Gideon's 32000 men to 300. He knew with 300 committed soldiers, Gideon would have easy victory without being hindered by 31,700 fearful and uncommitted soldiers.

Concerning your purposes in life, don't empower your weaknesses by allowing them to hinder you – no not once! God who purposed from the beginning, will do with and through you what seems impossible. The greatest weakness of men is the weakness they empower by paying them undue attention. God is the One who will complete what He began in, with, and through you.

> *The Lord will perfect that which concerns me; Your mercy, O Lord, endures forever; Do not forsake the works of Your hands (Psalms 138:8).*

> *'Not by might nor by power, but by My Spirit,' Says the Lord of hosts (Zechariah 4:6).*

> *I can do all things through Christ who strengthens me (Philippians 4:13).*

(3) Whatever God says do, means you can! It is not the process, but the God who is with you in the process, that makes all the difference. With total dependence on Him alone, you can do the impossible. Why are you waiting?

> *But Jesus looked at them and said to them, "With men this is impossible, but with God all things are possible" (Mark 10:27)*

> *Jesus said to him "If you can believe, all things are possible to him who believes" (Mark 9:23).*

(4) It is so easy to succeed! The easiest thing to do on earth is to do what God has given you to do. Succeeding without God will be your worst failure. And the hardest thing you could do would be doing what you want to do in your own way without God.

(5)   The worst failure to experience would be doing Godly assignments without God. But your best success will be doing what He asked you to do, no matter how big or small. From achieving our personal purpose to the revival of nations, the formula is the same; hear God, and do His commandments. Those standing with God, or partnering with God, always have divine backing to pull down "strong cities" and to build "God's desired nations".

> *... for I am ready to perform My word (Jeremiah 1:12)*

> *See, I have this day set you over the nations and over the kingdoms, to root out and to pull down, to destroy and to throw down, to build and to plant." [18] For behold, I have made you this day a fortified city and an iron pillar, and bronze walls against the whole land— Against the kings of Judah, against its princes, against its priests, and against the people of the land. [19] They will fight against you, but they shall not prevail against you. For I am with you," says the Lord, "to deliver you" (Jeremiah 1:10,18-19).*

(6)   The *prisons* of life are not always a bad thing. Just one seemingly weak instruction from our *prison* is worth a lifetime dream! God will do much more than we expect when we obey and step out in faith on His promises. Little did Apostle Paul know that yielding to a simple word of promise from the Lord to him in a little Jerusalem prison would derive extraordinary result on land, sea and island.

> *Now to Him who is able to do exceedingly abundantly above all that we ask or think, according to the power that works in us, to Him be glory, honour... (Ephesians 3:20)*

> *I can do all things through Christ who strengthens me (Philippians 4:13).*

213

God's Unlimited Surplus in His Purposes: Because You Said Yes, You Shall Lack Nothing

❖❖❖

Purpose and Provision: A New Perspective

... "When I sent you without money bag, knapsack, and sandals, did you lack anything?" So they said, "Nothing." (Luke 22:35)

When I finally decided to go into full-time pastoral ministry the challenges were many. I was leaving a paid job with a bank to answer 'yes' to God's leading. There were many nights of real anxieties especially not knowing how our mortgage and other bills would be paid just in case I was wrong about quitting my job. Even greater uncertainties ensued regarding whether the church would be able to pay me or even sustain itself financially.

The reasons for some of my anxieties were simply that we were a relatively new church, less than thirty-five committed members. I believed then that I needed to work to help the church financially. My wife was not sure what to say about my decision to go full time because of the same reasons and concerns I had. She therefore chose to remain discretionally silent. Probably, she didn't want to be responsible if things went wrong. I understood her position, but I still really wanted her '*no*' or '*yes*'. I waited in vain.

Furthermore, I did not know how the church was going to receive the news of my desire for full time ministry. A few of them who appeared to be dependable tithers had problems of their own. Some were in and out of church at will and as long as they wanted to. Others did the usual thing that is commonly done in many churches in which members try to reward their pastors for *good behaviour*. If he preached a message of their preference then, all was well. But, if he preached a truth that did not resonate with their *personal tastes* and *preferences*, then they would ensure that their pastor *suffered* for preaching the truth, either by them staying away from church or by not committing to anything, including tithe and offering. It really is a strange trend but it is worryingly true throughout churches. So, the more you are committed to preaching biblical truths, some people want you to begin to think twice! 'Unfortunately', I decided a long time ago not to be intimidated by things like that.

All-in-all, I had to be sure I was actually in God's will for the move I was about to make. Resigning my position became much more difficult, knowing we had no real personal savings, and were right in the middle of what came to be known as the deepest global economic recession for decades. Many, including some church members, had their jobs on the line because their companies were either down-sizing or going into administration. With all this going on, I became so tense and had so many questions and '*what ifs*' flooding my mind all the time.

It is amazing how God chooses the most challenging times of your life for His most demanding instructions and commandments. He does not make it easy! As I considered quitting my Job, going to work began to frustrate and to stress me out.

I could literally enter the doors at my work place and then immediately begin to check the time. I wanted to be home again. It was during one of those times at work when I felt in my spirit that the Lord was literally asking me, *what are you doing here?* I almost felt like Elijah running from Jezebel and away from his purpose to hide in the wilderness.

Days later, I thought hard about trusting God or allowing situations to determine my destiny. I could go on suffering and feeling unfulfilled, or quit my job and trust God. Despite all the odds and uncertainties, I had to decide. Without further consultation with anyone, not even with my wife, I came home from work one night determined to hand over my notice of resignation. This time, I did not ask for any second opinions from anyone, including church members. I only informed them about my decision after it was made.

I went to work and my line manager, who was totally unaware of my decision to resign, had just had the heat turned up on him to demand the impossible from us. With banks struggling, they had decided to adopt drastic and desperate sales tactics to break even in the midst of the recession. Obviously, things like that just don't settle down well with me. But, that to me was the final straw, and at the end of our meeting, I knew I had to hand in my resignation letter the next day.

Was God aware of all that was going on? Did He know my stress and anxieties about leaving a paid job without any guarantee of having sufficient money for our home, and even church? I can tell you now, that God knew everything about me in detail. He even knew that my fears had no basis if I chose to trust Him completely. How do I know that?

Well, after I returned home that night from work, the Lord gave me this passage, Luke 22:35 - *"When I sent you without money bag, knapsack, and sandals, did you lack anything?" So they said, "Nothing."* This was the moment I was waiting for, but it did not come until I had decided, *yes, Lord I will go!*

Expecting God to say more than that was going to be a waste of time, so I went into full time ministry. And while I write, my wife now works with me in full time ministry as well.

This is what I learned about saying '*yes*' to God when He sends you. Within God's assignment and purposes are His glorious provisions. No one, faithfully and diligently pursuing a God-given assignment, lacks the things that are necessary. If you will focus on elegantly fulfilling God's purpose and assignments, He will arrange provision in forms and ways unimaginable (Proverbs 18:16). However, His provision normally comes while in His assignment, or as you do His assignment.

> *And as you go, preach, saying, 'The kingdom of heaven is at hand.'* [8] *Heal the sick, cleanse the lepers, raise the dead, cast out demons. Freely you have received, freely give.* [9] *Provide neither gold nor silver nor copper in your money belts,* [10] *nor bag for your journey, nor two tunics, nor sandals, nor staffs; for a worker is worthy of his food.* [11] *"Now whatever city or town you enter, inquire who in it is worthy, and stay there till you go out (Matthew 10:11).*

It is a grave error to think that God must provide before you adhere to or pursue God's assignment for you. And never gauge and measure God's assignment by His provision. The reason being that there's the temptation to think that just because one has abundant supply to carry out an idea, vision, or assignment, it means the assignment is from God. Similarly, lacking the necessary provision at the beginning of your assignment, or anytime during your assignment is no indication that the assignment is not from God. We need to know the difference and strike a good balance. What is certain is that, if God calls you, He will provide. When God sends you, get going because He will definitely take care of you.

I quit my job to pursue God's call and purpose fully. Although I had initial misgivings, and some people even passed discouraging comments, today, I can testify like the disciples whom Christ sent without money bag, knapsack, and sandals, but still lacked nothing (Lk 22:35). I have lacked nothing, and still trust Him for each day!

Immediately I decided on full time ministry, it became welcomed news throughout the church. They decided to pay me the equivalent of what I earned when I worked for the bank. Sounds like a lot, no it wasn't! Bankers, especially those below none-senior managers' positions, are some of the lowest earners in the financial services. But even paying me my existing salary clearly was going to be a major challenge for a church of our size then.

Agreeing to pay me was only the initial step but there was a greater question; how was the church going to do that month after month? Only the Lord knew how. But we have been able to see and experience God's miracles in providing enough to pay my salary and to consistently carry out more church outreach activities, to improve our sound equipment and to even desirably honour guest preachers. We've had favour with our landlord in giving us additional space totally rent free for a pastor's office. And most importantly, I have seen God's anointing over my life increased to be able to minister fully to His people. As a result, our church is growing numerically and spiritually.

Now to Him who is able to do exceedingly abundantly above all that we ask or think, according to the power that works in us, to Him be glory in the church by Christ Jesus to all generations, forever and ever. Amen. (Ephesians 3:20-21).

I know this is only my testimony, but I am not alone. It worked for the disciples Jesus sent out without money bags, knapsacks, and sandals. Hence, you don't need to wait to have all you need before embarking on your God-given assignment. Many who have sincerely waited for God to provide, using God's provision as a fleece to indicate God's willingness and confirmation of their assignments and purposes, have often had to wait in vain. Many have terribly missed Godly moments to do great things with God. You are either going to attempt God's assignment and purposes in faith, or in the flesh. The latter ends in disaster or never really begins.

Now the just shall live by faith; but if anyone draws back, My soul has no pleasure in him" (Hebrews 10:38).

But He answered and said, "It is written, 'Man shall not live by bread alone, but by every word that proceeds from the mouth of God'" (Matthew 4:4)

But without faith it is impossible to please Him, for he who comes to God must believe that He is, and that He is a rewarder of those who diligently seek Him (Hebrews 11:6).

The Mistake of Gehazi

We have a rather sad example with a man of God, with great potential for ministry who attempted God's assignment and purpose in the flesh. He unfortunately aborted his assignment in its embryonic state. The reason being, he failed to discern the difference between a time for assignment and a time to receive provisions. He failed to prioritise his purpose over the enticing temptation of taking provision. Gehazi allowed his flesh to dictate how to go about God's assignment. Hence, his flesh and greed overtook his faith and then led him to believe contrary to Elisha, his master's selfless attitude that God will always provide faithfully and appropriately for all those He calls and sends.

But Gehazi, the servant of Elisha the man of God, said, "Look, my master has spared Naaman this Syrian, while not receiving from his hands what he brought; but as the Lord lives, I will run after him and take something from him." So Gehazi pursued Naaman. ... Now he went in and stood before his master. Elisha said to him, "Where did you go, Gehazi?" And he said, "Your servant did not go anywhere." Then he said to him, "Did not my heart go with you when the man turned back from his chariot to meet you? Is it time to receive money and to receive clothing, olive groves and vineyards, sheep and oxen, male and female servants? Therefore the leprosy of Naaman shall cling to you and your descendants forever." And he went out from his presence leprous, as white as snow (2 Kings 5:20,21; 25-27).

Although Gehazi was sincere in his approach and even ran after Naaman in the Name of the Lord, he was totally wrong. Gehazi failed to recognize that God's assignments, in themselves, carry embedded provision – they literally provide for themselves, and we do not have to make it happen in our own ways. The assignments themselves bear seeds that provide for the one on assignment. Hence, it is when the assigned person willingly and diligently plants those seeds of provision that he then harvests the provision accorded to their assignments, according to God's purposes and plans. It is always important to know that God will always designate the right people, places, and times for His provision as well. He determines how your needs will be met as long as He sent you and you also do His will. Take for examples:

- Elijah the prophet, God prepared the widow of Zarephath:

  "Arise, go to Zarephath, which belongs to Sidon, and dwell there. See, I have commanded a widow there to provide for you." (1King 17:9)

- Elisha the prophet, the Lord arranged for a shunammite woman to show him unusual kindness:

  Now it happened one day that Elisha went to Shunem, where there was a notable woman, and she persuaded him to eat some food. So it was, as often as he passed by, he would turn in there to eat some food. ⁹ And she said to her husband, "Look now, I know that this is a holy man of God, who passes by us regularly. ¹⁰ Please, let us make a small upper room on the wall; and let us put a bed for him there, and a table and a chair and a lampstand; so it will be, whenever he comes to us, he can turn in there." (2 Kings 4:8-10)

- Paul the Apostle – Individuals, and not a few churches were appointed by God to supply the needs of His servants. They included the churches of Macedonia:

  that in a great trial of affliction the abundance of their joy and their deep poverty abounded in the riches of their liberality.

For I bear witness that according to their ability, yes, and beyond their ability, they were freely willing, imploring us with much urgency that we would receive the gift and the fellowship of the ministering to the saints (2 Corinthians 8:2-4).

Paul also greatly benefited from the generosities of the churches of the Philippians. God designated the Philippians to provide such things that were necessary while Paul was on assignment in Thessalonica:

Now you Philippians know also that in the beginning of the gospel, when I departed from Macedonia, no church shared with me concerning giving and receiving but you only. [16] *For even in Thessalonica you sent aid once and again for my necessities (Philippians 4:15-16).*

God is Always Able to Provide

That God is always ready to provide for His assignment is clearly what we see happening in the case of Paul and his colleagues in Acts 28:10. God ensured that Paul and his colleagues had all things necessary, without lacking anything needed, for the fulfilment of their God-given assignments. In the same passage, they admit benefiting immensely from the generosity of the people of the Island of Malta. But beyond that, they were supplied with enough to get them to their next place of assignment and purpose. The text says,

They honored us in many ways and when we departed, they provided such things as were necessary (Acts 28:10).

If there was ever one thing that Apostle Paul was certain about, it was the fact that God never takes you where His grace will not reach you *(see 2 Corinthians. 12:9).* Regarding God's provision for His assignments and purposes, Paul knew very well to trust God to always provide for Him such things as were necessary. He knew that, God's assignments carry with them embedded means for supernatural provision. So that, if the man on God-given assignments remains fully committed to the task of his assignment, he would lack nothing required for the fulfilment of his assignment.

No doubt, Paul continually enjoyed sufficient grace and provision from God, through various means, in different situations, and he was content (Philip. 4:10-20). Publius, the renowned Magistrate and the healing of his father, was one means by which God provided for Paul and his colleagues in Malta. By virtue of his assignment, God miraculously opened a door, and Paul had what was required to access the same door through which provision and other opportunities were to follow. Every assignment and purpose of God definitely contains what is needed to provide for that same assignment.

Some Helpful Scriptures for Your Attention:

A man's gift makes room for him, and brings him before great men (Proverbs 18:16).

Provide neither gold nor silver nor copper in your money belts, [10] nor bag for your journey, nor two tunics, nor sandals, nor staffs; for a worker is worthy of his food. (Matthew 10:9-10).

And remain in the same house, eating and drinking such things as they give, for the labourer is worthy of his wages. Do not go from house to house (Luke 10:7).

For the Scripture says, "You shall not muzzle an ox while it treads out the grain," and, "The labourer is worthy of his wages." (1Timothy 5:18)

And He said to them, "When I sent you without money bag, knapsack, and sandals, did you lack anything?" So they said, "Nothing." (Luke 22:35)

Now to Him who is able to do exceedingly abundantly above all that we ask or think, according to the power that works in us, to Him be glory in the church by Christ Jesus to all generations, forever and ever. Amen. (Ephesians 3:20-21).

But He answered and said, "It is written, 'Man shall not live by bread alone, but by every word that proceeds from the mouth of God'" (Matthew 4:4)

Now the just shall live by faith; but if anyone draws back, My soul has no pleasure in him" (Hebrews 10:38).

Obtaining the Purposes of God: You Have Come Too Far to Turn Back

❖❖❖

Nearing the Fulfilment of Purpose

To everything there is a season, a time for every purpose under heaven (Ecclesiastes 3:1)

We began by pursuing a specific promise to Paul from God Himself, saying *"be of good cheer, Paul; for as you have testified for me in Jerusalem, so you must also bear witness at Rome" (Roman 28:11)*. Although it has taken us quite a while in following Paul's amazing journey to Rome, it has also been an intriguing and rewarding experience.

Just like Paul, we can't wait to get to where Paul finally settled down in Rome in fulfilment of the prophetic word of promise from God. With all that has already happened, it's tempting to think, well more than half of the journey has been covered, and hence we can relax. But, in real life and in many cases the closer you are to realising your dreams, the more anxious one becomes, because we cannot entirely rule out eventual surprises that might spring up here and there. It has nothing to do with your level of faith. That's just the way things are. Some degree of anxiety that might spring up in your heart and occasional *butterflies* that may arise in the pit of your belly, are totally legitimate when you have almost reached your long awaited goal.

Especially for Paul, given the strains of long perilous journey, one can understand that by this time he might be looking forward to some peace at his age. He had already endured very unfriendly winter weather, violent sea wind, torrential rain, hunger, and had been away from familiar home territories, all of which might have taken their toll on Paul's already overworked body. By this time, he would have been anxiously expecting, if it were possible, to speed up the process of arriving in Rome. Understandably, along with his expectation would also be Paul's trepidation for the unexpected.

A three months stopover at Malta was a welcomed break for Paul. But it was time to go forward, and there was a ship already ready to board. Of course the nature of their journey required some more essential, brief stopovers in about five different places. Altogether, they still had a length of about twelve days' journey in total before Rome. Their longest stop was in Puteoli and lasted for seven days. Here, Paul and his colleagues, probably Luke and Aristarchus, the Macedonian of Thessalonica, (Acts 27:2) who decided to accompany Paul right from the beginning, now had further opportunity for a good time of open fellowship and to share with some others their challenging stories and Christian experience.

One can only imagine how utterly honoured and well pleased the Christians at Puteoli might have been to host, and to physically set eyes on, the great apostle of faith they had only previously heard about. Some would have already reached their conclusions; that whatever the case was, Paul was not what his accusers had alleged he was. Hence they hosted him for seven whole days, and probably could have kept him longer if it were possible.

The Moments Just Before

Appi Forum and Three Inns were their very last stops before entering Rome. They were now so close to Rome, and knowing the human nature, Paul by this time may be full of mixed emotions. First, this was his dream of visiting Rome coming true, but it has not happened the way he planned it. Second, he was coming to Rome as a prisoner, and would he be permitted to 'impart some spiritual gifts' to the church in Rome as he has originally desired (Rom. 1:11-12)? Third, how will his court hearing turn out?

Rome was nothing like other places the Apostle had visited on all his missionary journeys. Rome was the height of all things extreme, intellectually and socially. By this time, it was possible there was a certain level of expectation from those in Rome regarding Paul, hence placing an uneasy burden on Paul. Many wanted to hear his version of the Christ story for which he was in chains. So, it delighted him when the Christians dwelling closer to Rome, including those from Appi Forum, Three Inns, and probably some from Rome itself decided to come along to meet Paul beforehand.

Some of the Christians coming to meet Paul before his imminent arrival at Rome, probably were seizing their opportunity, thinking that perhaps they may not have the chance to see Paul once he got to Rome. Possibilities were, as soon as he got to Rome as a prisoner, he might be locked away in prison. Yet, Paul was thankful to God and was encouraged when he saw those who came to see him (Acts 28:15).

Let me add that during a time and moment of anxiety comparable to what Paul was experiencing, any word of encouragement, or just having the company of good friends, makes a whole world of difference. This is no time for debate, judgement or offering the *counsel of Job's three* friends, but an opportunity for offering and receiving good words of encouragement from caring hearts.

A word fitly spoken is like apples of gold in settings of silver (Proverbs 25:11).

Anxiety in the heart of man causes depression, But a good word makes it glad (Proverbs 12:25).

The Lord Jesus Had His Moments

We see in Scriptures many such intense moments of anxiety. The Lord Jesus Christ Himself experienced similar moments of anxiety when He needed His friends around Him. First when He celebrated with them on the last Passover before His betrayal and arrest. The Lord Jesus gathered His disciples around the table and the Scriptures say;

> *When the hour had come, He sat down, and the twelve apostles with Him. [15] Then He said to them, "With fervent desire I have desired to eat this Passover with you before I suffer (Luke 22:14-15).*

That *hour* was an extreme moment of anxiety for the Lord. In fact, it was in the same hour, just before the *breaking of bread* but while still eating with His disciples, that He identified His betrayal. Matthew then says;

> *Now as they were eating, He said, "Assuredly, I say to you, one of you will betray Me." [22] And they were exceedingly sorrowful, and each of them began to say to Him, "Lord, is it I?"(Matthew 26:21-22).*

Think about having your enemy as your friend, and knowing who is on their way to betray you in the same hour that you're eating with them. What would you do if you knew that the one with whom you've entrusted your secrets is the very one who would sell you out?

Wouldn't it be quite a moment in your lifetime, to know that it is your best friend on the run with your spouse? Sounds extreme, but moments like these are full of terrific anxieties. I pray God will spare you!

The second time our Lord Jesus Christ faced another moment of serious anxiety was in the Garden of Gethsemane. Faced with the vivid reality of gruesome torture and violent death, He needed His friends. So, among His twelve closest friends He chose three, Peter, James and John, to watch with Him while He prayed. Right there before them, '... *He began to be sorrowful and deeply distressed' (Matthew 26:37).*

During this time of great agony, right after the Lord Jesus Himself confessed to His friends about how *exceedingly sorrowful His soul was even unto death,* guess what they did? He returned from the first hour of prayer to find them fast asleep. Then, He asked Peter, *"What! Could you not watch with Me one hour? (Matthew 26:46).* It is amazing how He picked on Peter alone, having come and seen them all asleep. Could it be that He was saying, '*Peter, stand with me; I am counting on you most in this hour?* '

Again, the second hour, and then the third, this time they were dreaming and snoring. When the Lord woke them up which was actually in their interest, it is said that they couldn't even say a thing for they were all very heavily sleepy. The Lord didn't have many words after that to speak to them, except to say *it is enough!*

> *Again He went away and prayed, and spoke the same words. And when He returned, He found them asleep again, for their eyes were heavy; and they did not know what to answer Him. Then He came the third time and said to them, "Are you still sleeping and resting? It is enough! The hour has come; behold, the Son of Man is being betrayed into the hands of sinners. Rise, let us be going. See, My betrayer is at hand"(Mark 14:39-42).*

If you haven't yet, somehow, we all come to such moments of anxieties in some ways in our lifetime. Moments when sometimes you turn and ask like Job, *Lord where are you?* I pray when your moment comes the Lord will faithfully raise some trusted friends who will surround you in good support to encourage you, just as He did for Paul.

And who can be more trustworthy than the Holy Spirit of comfort and Peace, who brings and gives peace that far surpasses our understanding (Philippians 4:7)? The Lord be with you always!

If you are presently going through one of those intense moments of anxiety, I pray God's mighty hands will move on your behalf to bring you into His perfect rest (Isa. 26:3)! Remember you are not alone. God cares and He is with you as you do His will (Isa. 43:2) .

> *When you pass through the waters, I will be with you; And through the rivers, they shall not overflow you. When you walk through the fire, you shall not be burned, Nor shall the flame scorch you (Isa. 43:2). God is able to do exceedingly abundantly above all that we ask or think, according to the power that works in us (Ephesians 3:20).*

The Moment when it Happened

In fulfilment of the word of prophecies that was given and received in his Jerusalem prison, the Lord had preserved Paul's life from destruction up to now. The Lord had miraculously provided for Paul and linked him with the right people and right places to ensure His purposes were done. But also, Paul was beginning to relish and to enjoy the experience overall, including the process and the outcome of each encounter along his journey. He had lived through all that had happened, he had learned, and his spiritual experience was also greatly enriched. His faith was affirmed and his confidence in the God who cannot lie was boosted. What's more, his lifelong desire to visit Rome finally materialized, without any burden of bills and trustportation costs to pay.

Paul arrived in Rome safely. Instead of being treated like a criminal, he was allowed to "live large", dwelling by himself with "personal bodyguards" (Acts 28:16). Exactly what Paul wanted, because as many bodyguards he was permitted to have throughout his time in Rome, that was how many potentially new converts for the Lord, that were indirectly coming his way.

Testifying to the Jews

Paul wasted no time but got on with business, the purpose for which he was divinely transferred to Rome. His assignment and purpose was defined, *to testify and to bear witness at Rome (Acts 23:11)*. Only three days in Rome, and he summoned the leaders of the Jews together and, after initial conversation, they set a date to hear him out. When the day came, notice the Jews brought themselves – Paul did not go after them! And they were also not a few but *many*.

> *So when they had appointed him a day, many came to him at his lodging, to whom he explained and solemnly testified of the kingdom of God, persuading them concerning Jesus from both the Law of Moses and the Prophets, from morning till evening (Acts 28:23).*

What an elegant way to go about testifying of the Kingdom of God. What was impossible for him in Jerusalem was happening in Rome. He couldn't have had that many Jews, especially their leaders in one place in Jerusalem to hear him freely without massive confrontation. And note that it was not the common Jews, but their leaders. One leader converted means potentially the leader and his followers under his direct influence converted for Christ.

Testifying to All in Rome

After Paul had testified to the Jewish leaders and possibly other Jews as well, he turned his focus on *all who came to him.*

> *Then Paul dwelt two whole years in his own rented house, and received all who came to him, [31] preaching the kingdom of God and teaching the things which concern the Lord Jesus Christ with all confidence, no one forbidding him. (Acts 28:30-31)*

Notice that, he was in his own rented house, with no one forbidding him. So God continued to provide for him and to make way for him to testify.

Again, he moved from just testifying and witnessing to Jewish leaders to *all who came to him.* Paul's audience increased significantly. But the message was the same good old gospel for both the Jews and *all* who came to him. He preached the Kingdom of God, testifying about the Lord Jesus Christ with all confidence.

Purpose Under Review: Assessing the Terms of Purpose

Has God fulfilled His promise which He spelled out for Paul? Why weren't there converts mentioned under the ministry of Paul in Rome? Well, you need to read the tenants of the word of prophecies again. There were only two mean parts to the prophecy:

(i) That Paul will bear witness for the Lord just as he did for Him in Jerusalem.

(ii) He must bear this witness in Rome. Therefore, if he were thinking that his imprisonment in Jerusalem was the end of his ministry, he needed to wake up.

The next logical question then would be; how then did he testify and how was his testimony received in Jerusalem? God simply told Paul he must testify or witness about Him as he did in Jerusalem. So then, what was Paul message? It was the same as in Jerusalem! How was it received; mixed response – some were convinced and probably *converted* but others disbelieved. In the end they were left arguing amongst themselves!

This bares great insight for anyone of purpose pursuing God's purposes. Expect a mixed response to every powerful witness concerning the Kingdom and the Lord Jesus Christ. Know that people of purpose under God's mandate, and bearing God's eternal truth, are not by their own making innately 'controversial'. It's just the way it is. Whatever the responses of people are, God's call and purposes are being fulfilled in all things and through all things.

What then? Only that in every way, whether in pretence or in truth, Christ is preached and in this I rejoice, yes, and will rejoice (Philippians 1:18).

On a brighter note, scholars and biblical historians think that Paul wrote the book of Philippians while he was a prisoner in Rome, because he mentioned saints including Caesar's household and the praetorian guard in this letter (Philip. 4:22). It appears that in this same verse in which Paul refers to the saints, he might also be referring to some converts in Rome in fulfilment of prophecies, even as the Lord told him, that he must bear witness in Rome as well. This is a good testimony, that as always, the purposes of God continue to be worked through the manifold wisdom of God (cf. Ephesians 3:9-11).

That means that, you too can always wholeheartedly count on the promises of God for your life, no matter the constraints and challenges, and God will see you through and cause your desire to come to pass. Remember, He shall never leave you nor forsake you!

Beyond Purpose: Power for You to Do the Will of God

❖❖❖

The Spirit of Boldness

And you shall know the truth, and the truth shall make you free (John 8:32)

Acts chapter four introduces us to a powerful account of two great apostles, Peter and John, who like the apostle Paul were totally consumed with carrying out the purposes of God for their lives. We are told that they were arrested for doing a good thing. By the anointing of the Holy Spirit, they healed a lame man who had suffered severely for over forty years, and sat before the temple gate to beg alms. Through the same healing miracle, the man was completely restored and his hope was rekindled. No sooner had the lame man been healed, that a great door was opened for the mighty Word of God to be preached. They preached so well, declaring the wonderful truth of the Word of God and confirming the Lordship of the Saviour, Jesus Christ.

Just by their good deeds in administering healing and for preaching in the Name of Jesus, they stirred the people and got the attention of a dominant, but dormant religious order. This religious order was unfortunately jealously guarded by priests, temple captain, and Sadducees. The first four verses of Acts chapter four declares,

> *Now as they spoke to the people, the priests, the captain of the temple, and the Sadducees came upon them, ² being greatly disturbed that they taught the people and preached in Jesus the resurrection from the dead. ³ And they laid hands on them, and put them in custody until the next day, for it was already evening. ⁴ However, many of those who heard the word believed; and the number of the men came to be about five thousand (Acts 4:1-4).*

Did you notice that many of those who heard the Word believed, and the number of the men came to be about five thousand? Five thousand men, probably not counting the women and children, who believed the word of truth that was preached in the Name of Jesus. With five thousand or more converts right before a *sleeping* temple, it was a good recipe for opposition.

No wonder the priests, the captain of the temple, and Sadducees came strongly against Peter and John for teaching and for demonstrating the truth of the Gospel of Christ. Their episode gives us a good picture of what might happen to a man or woman who decides to stir up any *sleeping* church or denomination of our time. You will definitely be met with stiff opposition; powerfully induced by mere jealousy, insecurity, and a lack of real conviction concerning truth and righteousness.

So, the priests, the temple captain and the Sadducees fired back, obviously not to affirm what the disciples preached but to prevent them from preaching the Gospel of salvation in the Name of Jesus. Now, you must understand that they had been around long enough to have a lot of influence with the authorities and politicians of their day. It was therefore easy to use their unfair influence on the authorities to carry out whatever they desired. Hence, at their request, Peter and John were thrown into prison.

For the apostles, this was the first time they were physically having a small taste of what their Master and Lord suffered while on earth. Peter and John were seeing and experiencing the cruelty of betrayal, jealousy, anger, deception, hypocrisy, and an attempt to subvert and to suppress the truth by those who claim to be championing the cause of God. Come to think of it, similar aggressions often perpetuated, unfortunately in the name of God, are increasingly becoming common place even in our own time. Extreme persons with violet motives don't mind taking advantage in order to destroy innocent victims and properties.

The only difference here is that, in our time, most people carrying out vile acts including terrorism in the Name of God are suicidal. Whereas those who planted Peter and John into prison lived to continue their resistance against the truth of the Gospel. These are the kind of people who, because of their huge influence and powers, make laws and rules that everyone, including those standing for the truth, must adhere to, otherwise they face possible imprisonment. The *priests, the temple captain and Sadducees* of our own time also enjoy considerable powers with governments of nations. They are the '*bi-shops*' of selected religious orders, who also walk political corridors, and are clearly committed to seeking personal agenda instead of God's purposes.

In Acts 4 verses 5 to 12, there is an interesting scenario. We see the rulers seated with additional high ranking officials, including the high priest's family members. Peter and John are asked to defend themselves and to explain by what means, power and authority was the lame man healed. Then suddenly something swells and wells up in the inside of Peter as he stood to defend himself. Not surprisingly, the passage refers to the stirring on the inside of Peter as the *filling of the Holy Spirit!*

Now, that's dynamic and that's powerful! Peter did not have to utter a word throughout his defence. The Holy Spirit of God took over, in confirmation of the Lord's promise to His disciples while He was still with them saying, *"You will be brought before governors and kings for My sake, as a testimony to them and to the Gentiles. But when they deliver you up, do not worry about how or what you should speak. For it will be given to you in that hour what you should speak; for it is not you who speak, but the Spirit of your Father who speaks in you" (Matthew 10:18-20).*

What followed speaks for itself. Once again an opportunity availed itself for a bold declaration of the truth, this time not just before a select few but before their *rulers, elders, and scribes, as well as Annas the high priest, Caiaphas, John, and Alexander, and as many as were of the family of the high priest, were gathered together at Jerusalem (Acts 4:5-7).* Every one of them heard the Name of Jesus Christ of Nazareth been exalted and glorified.

They heard exactly what they feared and dreaded:

let it be known to you all, and to all the people of Israel, that by the name of Jesus Christ of Nazareth, whom you crucified, whom God raised from the dead, by Him this man stands here before you whole. This is the 'stone which was rejected by you builders, which has become the chief cornerstone.' Nor is there salvation in any other, for there is no other name under heaven given among men by which we must be saved" (Acts 4:1-12).

Such a bold and direct presentation of the whole truth of the Gospel might have come as a great shock to those listening to Peter. They were utterly astonished, and indications are that Peter's testimony was far from what the high Priest and his colleagues had desired to hear. What they had hoped to hear was that *Jesus was dead* so as to stop any further advancement of the Gospel, but Peter declared in truth that Jesus is alive!

They had wished to hear that the authorities and religious leaders had nothing to do with the death of Jesus Christ thereby acquitting themselves of blame and responsibility before their people. But, Peter put the blame squarely on them. He put it to them that, they denied the holy and just Jesus, who went about doing good and healing all that were sick (*see Acts 10:38*).

He put it to them that, they denied, opposed, mocked, scourged and beat the Lord Jesus, and then crucified Him. However, He rose from the dead because it was impossible for death to hold Him captive (Acts 2:24), He lives, reigns and rules victoriously today, and He still heals the sick.

A defence like this must have gone like a red-hot, rude bullet released right into the hearts of the rulers, elders, scribes, Annas, Caiaphas, John, Alexander, and also the family of the high priest, who were probably sitting as members of the jury. Already skilled in trying to kill and dismiss viable evidence (see Matt. 28:1115), they were now trying again to disguise and to dismiss another important truth; the Name of Jesus heals, and He is alive!

The Spirit of Truth

Contrary to the expectations of the Sanhedrin, those investigating Peter and John, the Holy Spirit did not allow Peter to adjust the truth of the Gospel. Rather, the Holy Spirit inspired great boldness for Peter to speak and to defend every iota of the truth of the Gospel of the Lord Jesus Christ. There's an object lesson to learn from this; that anyone who bears the truth of the Word of God in teaching or preaching situations must know that the Holy Spirit only inspires the truth. He is the Spirit of truth and never stands with anyone who takes pleasure in compromising the truth (John 14:17).

Peter remained faithful to the truth of the Word of God because all who presents and hears the Word must have it as it is, and we cannot begin to cherry-pick with the Word. For Peter's audience, the Sanhedrin, this might have come as a great disappointment, given their exalted status in society as the Authorities and Rulers! Thank God that Peter was not so *diplomatic;* a nicer description for injurious compromise and political correctness in this generation, which argues for people who know the truth to become timid and accepting of travesty before the rulers and authorities of the day.

Nowadays in popular circles, you are told to give the rulers and authorities room to be able to keep face, and we have effectively lost that bold and uncompromising spirit displayed by the apostles in speaking and defending the truth of God.

Probably what we need is to get back to that place in which the Holy Spirit is allowed to do what He does. Did you realise the secret behind the boldness and the truth speaking abilities of the apostles was never of themselves? Yes, Peter spoke when he became *filled* by the Holy Spirit. That means, it was the Holy Spirit, the *Spirit of Truth* (John 16:13) who spoke through Peter before the Sanhedrin. Exactly what we need today. Instead of us speaking, we can learn to literally step aside and allow the Holy Spirit to speak through us. At least then we might be able to speak the truth with some boldness. Our preaching and messages would be with such power and authority, and of course the impact on ourselves and our churches and community would be just what God desires for His people.

When we allow the Holy Spirit to actually work in and through us, then healing, holiness, righteousness, justice, mercies, goodness, love, and all the nice things that we normally preach but don't see nor know, might become so manifest and prevalent that God's will, *will be done on earth as it is in heaven, and His Kingdom shall come.* These are not things we can conjure by any means other than the power and witness of the Holy Spirit. We need the Holy Spirit taking over, invading our own lives first, and then allowing Him to speak through us as He did through Peter, the once timid fisherman from Galilee.

The wisdom and power of allowing the Holy Spirit to speak through us is enormous. Let's take for example what John 16:13 says, *"However, when He, the Spirit of truth, has come, He will guide you into all truth; for He will not speak on His own authority, but whatever He hears He will speak; and He will tell you things to come."* Here we have the Holy Spirit of God described as the *Spirit of truth who guides into all truth,* and hears, speaks, and tells even things that are yet to come.

Obviously, the Spirit of God here is all-knowing (Omniscient) and He is definitely, the Spirit of prophecy, because He will tell us of things to come. But for our purpose let's focus on the fact that He is the *Spirit of truth.*

What is Truth?

The question then arises, what really is truth? In John 17:17, the Lord Jesus gives us the meaning of truth like no one does. When He prayed for His disciples, the Lord Jesus asked the Father to *sanctify them by His truth.* And then He added, *Your word is truth.* In Daniel 10:21, the Word of God is referred to as the *Scripture of truth.* Now, if truth is nothing but the Word of God, then who else is best positioned to unveil, interpret and to speak it truthfully except the Holy Spirit of truth, who hears, speaks, and guides believers into all truths including the truth about what is to come?

Who else can really describe our lives and challenges in truth, as God sees them, apart from the Holy Spirit of truth? Who is able to speak concerning our future and God's purposes for us except the Holy Spirit, the Spirit of prophecies, who tells us things to come? Or who else will be able to guide us into the truth of how we need to form and fashion a life that is pleasing to God other than the Holy Spirit of truth who guides believers into all truth? That means I cannot even begin to understand the very words of the Scripture of truth until the Holy Spirit begins to open them up.

Similarly, I cannot even begin to access my purpose, or to speak intelligently about my future and my potential, until I connect with and submit to the Holy Spirit of God. And a great but subtle truth arising from all this understanding is that, anything contrary to the truth of the Word of God, whether it relates to our personal circumstances or our purpose, is a lie and comes from the devil. *"... believe in the Lord your God, and you shall be established; believe His prophets, and you shall prosper" (2 Chronicles 20:20).* Never take the suggestions of the devil and his agents to be true!

The Holy Spirit Protects Purpose

Clearly, if we will allow the Holy Spirit of truth to guide us into God's purposes and to speak through us, a whole lot of things will be different about us and the way we see things, and view our own lives. The Holy Spirit of truth speaking through us means, we can only speak what God says about us, not what others or ourselves and our problems or backgrounds forced on us. There is no way we could lie about the truth of God since the Spirit of truth cannot lie.

And if you didn't already know, I dare say many Christians on earth today are *liars* and this is not a judgment of personality or character. And before you drop this book, let me explain. Do you know that the moment you begin to contradict the truth of the Word of God and His promises for you, you lie? That's right, the moment you speak the opposite of what God says concerning your situation, you simply lie. Why? The reason is this; truth as we saw before is not what you think, feel, smell, or taste; not even what you heard from others, or what they want you to believe about who you are. Truth is really what the Word of God is and says. Secondly, S*atan is not mainly a liar just because he peddles 'untruths' or falsehood, he is a liar and a father of lies because he says to you the opposite of what God actually says and what God's Word declares as truths.* As with the temptation of Christ in the wilderness, Satan might even present to you a convoluted and twisted *truth*, which is in essence a lie.

Remember what Jesus says, *"Your Word is truth" (John 17:17)*, that is why only God's Word can sanctify, and that is why only God's Word has the power and ability to set you free, because !*you shall know the truth, and the truth shall make you free" (John 8:32),* and the Word of God is truth (John 17:17).

I believe that one of the reasons why God the Father gives us His Holy Spirit is to help protect His purposes for our lives. Indeed, the Holy Spirit protects purpose. Otherwise the lies and oppositions of Satan, the challenges of life themselves will cause us to despise God's purposes and also cause us to abandon our future (Acts 13:2; Luke 2:26; John 14:26; Acts 20:28).

The Holy Spirit given to us, living in us, and being with us has a very practical side to Him; saving us from the lies others would tell us, thereby saving us from the lies we tell ourselves that might greatly hinder our potential to live out God's purposes fully.

With the Holy Spirit of truth in us, and speaking through us, we cannot continue to speak defeat, failure, sickness, fear, hatred, or blasphemy, because the Spirit of God in us is the Spirit of faith, love, power, courage, boldness, sound mind, wisdom, health and possibilities. He is never negative but always positive, and He is the Spirit of peace, joy, rest, comfort and compassion. The Holy Spirit mends broken hearts and brings healings to God's people always. He is very reliable and dependable, and He is our Helper in all situations and at all times.

For God has not given us a spirit of fear, but of power and of love and of a sound mind (2 Timothy 1:7).

for the kingdom of God is not eating and drinking, but righteousness and peace and joy in the Holy Spirit (Romans 14:17).

And you became followers of us and of the Lord, having received the word in much affliction, with joy of the Holy Spirit (1 Thessalonians 1:6)

Then the churches throughout all Judea, Galilee, and Samaria had peace and were edified. And walking in the fear of the Lord and in the comfort of the Holy Spirit, they were multiplied (Acts 9:31).

Even the Spirit of truth; whom the world cannot receive, because it sees Him not, neither knows Him: but you know Him; for he dwells with you, and shall be in you. I will not leave you comfortless: I will come to you. Yet a little while, and the world sees me no more; but you will see me: because I live, you shall live also. At that day you shall know that I am in my Father, and you in me, and I in you. He that has my commandments, and keeps them, he it is that loves me: and he that loves me shall be loved of my Father, and I will love him, and will manifest myself to him (John 14:17-21).

The Holy Spirit Trains the Tongue of Purpose

The great apostle of the Lord, James, who is most candid in his approach to spirituality and everyday living has this to say about the human tongue,

> *Even so the tongue is a little member and boasts great things. See how great a forest a little fire kindles!* [6] *And the tongue is a fire, a world of iniquity. The tongue is so set among our members that it defiles the whole body, and sets on fire the course of nature; and it is set on fire by hell.* [7] *For every kind of beast and bird, of reptile and creature of the sea, is tamed and has been tamed by mankind.* [8] *But no man can tame the tongue. It is an unruly evil, full of deadly poison (James 3:5-8).*

Although our tongues are unruly and hard to tame, a real benefit for allowing the Holy Spirit to speak through us is that our tongue becomes perfectly trained and aligned with words of the truth of the Holy Spirit. We will economise on words, meaning our words will be very few but very effective and efficient in saying and for doing the things we want to be done. Instead of being too verbose and aimless about speaking into or against situations, or even too talkative in taking authority over demon spirits, we become very discrete, very precise and apt with specific terms and words that we need in their right combination and quantity to get the job done. All of this is possible when we allow the Holy Spirit of truth, who reveals and searches all things, even the deep things of God, to speak through us (1 Corinthians 2:9-11). This is when our words and speaking become as the *oracles and utterances of God.*

> *If anyone speaks, let him speak as the oracles (utterances) of God. If anyone ministers, let him do it as with the ability which God supplies, that in all things God may be glorified through Jesus Christ, to whom belong the glory and the dominion forever and ever. Amen (1 Peter 4:11).*

The Wisdom of Purpose Revealed: You Can Do All Things through Christ

❖❖❖

All Things Work Together

The incident involving Peter and John shows in many ways that the riches of God's wisdom and judgements as always are unsearchable in matters of God's purposes and the situations He allows us to go through *(Romans 11:33)*. Who could have ever thought that through the arrest of common men like Peter and John, there would arise special opportunity for them to boldly speak the truth about Jesus and to be able to evangelise great rulers and leaders, who were otherwise inaccessible to the disciples.

Their encounter was somewhat similar to how Apostle Paul also got his own opportunity to preach in unusual places and to various high ranking people within diverse communities. Paul was often beaten and dragged into prisons, however in testifying to the Philippians' church, he concluded rather thoughtfully about his situation saying;

> *But I would that you should understand, brethren, that the things which happened unto me have fallen out rather unto the furtherance of the gospel; So that my bonds in Christ are manifest in all the palace, and in all other places; And many of the brethren in the Lord, waxing confident by my bonds, are much more bold to speak the word without fear (Philippians 1:12-15).*

All of this is extremely exciting and once again validates the credibility and power of the Word of God. I am reminded of that glorious declaration in Romans 8:28 that says, "*and we know that all things work together for good to those who love God, to those who are the called according to His purpose.*" Isn't that exactly the case with Peter and John? Wasn't it the same for Paul?

My friend, the Word of God says that our *God cannot lie (Titus 1:2),* and again, *God is not a man, that He should lie; neither the son of man, that He should repent: has He said, and shall He not do it? Or hath He spoken, and shall He not make it good (Numbers 23:19)?* Know this; that whatever your circumstances are right now, God who cannot lie and who is not a man to change His mind concerning you is bringing you His great deliverance.

He will not change His mind concerning His love and promises for you and your future, but He will turn and change for good that bad thing coming against your life and purpose. Never forget, that as a child of God, all things can and must only work together for good for you.

Like Peter and John, whatever happens to you, is only your servant and messenger to cause you to come before greatness and to realize your God given purpose on earth. And when God causes you to locate your purpose, again like Peter and John, God will give you the awesome power of His Holy Spirit to cause you to execute your purpose. You shall have the greatest Helper providing you the greatest help on earth in order to live and to fulfil your purpose.

From Zero to Hero

You can call it anything, *from zero to hero* or *from nobody to somebody!* That was the kind of grace and anointing Peter and John encountered and enjoyed. All of a sudden, men of no name and no reputation of any magnitude found themselves before the great rulers and authorities of their day, speaking boldly with them. They were sharing the same platform, and incidentally their crowd did not just increase in number, but the quality of their crowd simultaneously improved to include *rulers, elders, and scribes, Annas the high priest, Caiaphas, John, and Alexander, and as many as were of the family of the high priest, (Acts 4:5-7).* And the passage also added that where they were gathered together was no small town, but Jerusalem, the capital city. These were Galilean fishermen with a strange accent, which even betrayed Peter when he was questioned about Jesus while he tried to conceal his identity on a bitterly cold night of his Lord's arrest (Mark 14:70; Matthew 26:73).

But you see, when God decides to promote you, prosper you and bring you into great prominence, your accent and your speech really do not matter. Even where you come from, your background and limitations do not count any more, all that matters is God has chosen you to bless you. The Bible says, *for the gifts and the calling of God are irrevocable (Romans 11:29),* and *a man's gift makes room for him, and brings him before great men (Proverbs 18:16).*

Peter and John were called and gifted of God, which is why notable miracles like the healing of a man after forty years of being lame, could be done instantly at their command. With their gifts attested by the power of the Holy Spirit at work in them, they had only one way out, which was the way up. They had to appear before great men because their gifts made room for them and distinguished them. May the Lord bless you and quickly cause your gift to honourably set you apart. May you be repositioned from the bottom to the top; from last to first. As part of God's blessings, may you come before the great men of your generation!

God can use any person to show forth His glory, and it doesn't matter your personal limitations and disabilities. That is why you cannot depend on your own strength but the strength of God. Your confession should be, *I can do all things through Christ who strengthens me (Philippians 4:13)*. And God tells us *"My grace is sufficient for you, for My strength is made perfect in weakness" (2 Corinthians 12:9)*. If that is not convincing enough, then hear this:

> *For you see your calling, brethren, that not many wise according to the flesh, not many mighty, not many noble, are called.* [27] *But God has chosen the foolish things of the world to put to shame the wise, and God has chosen the weak things of the world to put to shame the things which are mighty;* [28] *and the base things of the world and the things which are despised God has chosen, and the things which are not, to bring to nothing the things that are,* [29] *that no flesh should glory in His presence (I Corinth. 1:26-31).*

Remember my friend God will fix things up for you and indeed,

> *Every valley shall be exalted and every mountain and hill brought low; the crooked places shall be made straight And the rough places smooth;* [5] *the glory of the Lord shall be revealed, and all flesh shall see it together; for the mouth of the Lord has spoken."* *(Isaiah 40:5)*

The Lord will *perfect that which concerns you (Psalms 138:8)*. Surely God has more than enough power and resource to cause His purposes and plans for your life to come to pass just as His Word declares.

> *Have you not known? Have you not heard? The everlasting God, the Lord, the Creator of the ends of the earth, neither faints nor is weary. His under- standing is unsearchable.* [29] *He gives power to the weak, and to those who have no might He increases strength.* [30] *Even the youths shall faint and be weary, and the young men shall utterly fall,* [31] *but those who wait on the Lord Shall renew their strength; they shall mount up with wings like eagles, they shall run and not be weary, they shall walk and not faint (Isaiah 40:28-31).*

Staying Authentic to Your Purpose

We read from the opening chapter of St. Luke's Gospel how John the Baptist was to become filled with the Holy Spirit right from his mother's womb. The passage says,

> *But the angel said to him, "Do not be afraid, Zacharias, for your prayer is heard; and your wife Elizabeth will bear you a son, and you shall call his name John. [14] And you will have joy and gladness, and many will rejoice at his birth. [15] For he will be great in the sight of the Lord, and shall drink neither wine nor strong drink. He will also be filled with the Holy Spirit, even from his mother's womb. [16] And he will turn many of the children of Israel to the Lord their God. [17] He will also go before Him in the spirit and power of Elijah, 'to turn the hearts of the fathers to the children,' and the disobedient to the wisdom of the just, to make ready a people prepared for the Lord"(Luke 1:13-17).*

John without doubt, as the forerunner of our Lord Jesus Christ, received and did all that was prophesied about him. He became filled with the Holy Spirit, and there was no pretence about it. Even the Lord Jesus Christ Himself, who was filled and anointed with the Holy Spirit (Luke 4:1&18; Act 10:38) attested to John's greatness (Luke 7:26, 27). As a prerequisite to John's calling and ministries, he shunned wine and strong drink but fed on a very strange diet comprising locusts and wild honey (Matthew 3:4).

It is recorded that multitudes from Jerusalem, all Judea, and from the entire region around Jordan came to John confessing their sins, and were baptised. He touched and affected the lives of kings in his day. He had very interesting times with the Pharisees and Sadducees (religious leaders), and even had many of them baptised before baptising Jesus, the Lord. When the question was asked if he were the Christ, John himself humbly admitted that, he was not. Instead, John pointed to the Lord Jesus Christ admitting that Jesus was mightier than he was (Matt 3:11). However, John was the one destined with the grace and privilege to baptise the Lord, and the Lord Jesus gladly submitted to John's baptism in order *to fulfil all righteousness* as He said *(Matt 3:15).*

But here is the point; if someone were going to baptise the Lord Jesus, definitely, that person would not be self-designated, self-made, or just any ordinary person, so to speak. He must have been prepared and sent by God. He didn't necessarily have to be equal to God in any regard. But, to baptise the Christ, he had to be specifically anointed by God for that purpose. He needed to have the right spirit, attitude, and character; otherwise he could easily be overtaken by pride and other kinds of vices.

With John, even before he was born, he was already filled with the Holy Spirit. It took an angel to announce his birth, diet and purpose before he was conceived. His pedigree was unusual and definitely there was something special about him as a child. Come to think about it, how many of us had our birth and purpose prophesied even before we were conceived in our mother's womb? Just how many of us living today became filled with the Holy Spirit in our mother's womb?

Yet, John the Baptist knew who he was, the forerunner of Christ, to prepare the way for Him, and that he *must decrease while Christ increase (John 3:30).* John never confused his identity or his purpose, he knew exactly why he came and who he was. Even when people saw him differently and tried to thrust other roles and identity on him, he never budged and did not succumb to their temptation.

This character of John is key and very liberating for anyone who is confused about their roles, purpose or identity at the moment. Confusion in the area of identity is becoming so prevalent nowadays. It has become a haunting plague even among church leaders who from time to time want to preach like other people; build and model their ministries after those they admire or those they think are more successful. Without an iota of doubt it is good to imitate those who imitate Christ like Paul says (1 Corinthians 11:1), but is a sign of great confusion and deception if your main aim is to become copycat and photocopies of others. Being like others never brings anyone true success, so allow the world to appreciate your difference from others!

You can never be the best someone else, but only the best of you. It is so repulsively fake and inauthentic when you hear some preachers on television with voices, antics, and mannerism that are obviously unwisely borrowed. It is such a put-off and clearly defeats the very objective for taking the pain of picking what is not yours anyway. The greatest favour we can do ourselves on earth is to stay in our assignments and be content with God's plans and purposes for our lives. Just stay on your tracks and in your lane.

Clearly John did a remarkable job in sticking to his purpose and *job description* in Luke 1:16,17. And what he teaches us is the need for all people of purpose to be and to remain authentic to their specific lines of calling and ministries. It is disingenuous, and totally unwise to claim other people's line of purpose and assignments as ours just because theirs look glamorous or colourful in any respect. For the sake of remaining true to his particular assignment and purpose, John refused to imitate or to entertain any counterfeits, but was thoroughly satisfied with the wonderful infilling of the Holy Spirit of God Almighty. And as John faithfully fulfilled his purpose and assignment, so also will we do if we stay true to the reference of our call, ministry and purpose.

Chapter Sixteen

The Mandate of Purpose: Don't Be Deceived, Stay Focused

❖❖❖

Recognizing the Deception - An Ambassador or a Person of Trend

Unfortunately, an increasing number of people seem to think that unless church and Christianity are *glamorous* in their eyes, it will fail to entice and to attract crowds. Their argument for glamorising church and Christianity of course does not centre attention on the substance of church and Christianity as well as it does their forms. Part of that argument for a glamorous form is the need for church and Christianity to be "trendy".

With all the arguments for 'trendiness', one is left to wonder how John the Baptist survived his time and how he was able to fulfil his purpose in a 'trendy' society of his day without being 'trendy' himself. John the Baptist who was rather 'risky' than 'trendy' took a lot of risks and with a simple, passionate message of revival was able to reach the Pharisees, Sadducees, tax collectors, soldiers, governors, Jews and the Scribes, who were the very embodiment of 'trendiness' in their times.

In fact, John the Baptist was so out of 'trend' with the rest of his contemporaries that he called them, *brood of vipers,* and trees ready to be cut down. He did not motivate them as we do today. When addressing his 'trendy' crowd, he went on to say,

> *Brood of vipers! Who warned you to flee from the wrath to come?* [8] *Therefore bear fruits worthy of repentance, and do not begin to say to yourselves, 'We have Abraham as our father.' For I say to you that God is able to raise up children to Abraham from these stones.* [9] *And even now the axe is laid to the root of the trees. Therefore every tree which does not bear good fruit is cut down and thrown into the fire (Luke 3:7-9).*

Noticeably, in all the Gospels, John's peculiar message and style of presentation never changed. It is the same in all of the Gospels that recorded them. Yet, people came in their numbers and his crowd continuously increased (Luke 3:7). Certainly, there must have been something about John's approach that drove his message home, without compromising in the name of being *trendy, modern and contemporary.* That's what we need to find out.

If being 'trendy' is what we define it as today, meaning the situation in which truth and morality become relative, allowing people to do and have things their way to suit their taste, then we can easily say there were even more 'trendy' people in the days of John the Baptist, Jesus and the Apostles. For example, the Sadducees in Jesus' day and the time of Paul did not even believe in angels, spirits and resurrection of the dead, although they were deemed as highly religious (Matt 22:23; Acts 23:8). The very Scribes and Pharisees who were the doctors of the Law, and the Sadducees did not even know the Scriptures or the power of God. Jesus Himself told them time and time again that they were hypocritical, mistaken and in error (Matt 22:29).

As we have today, also in the days of John, Jesus, and the Apostles, people opposed the truth, they equally had religious extremists. Similarly, for many people religion really did not matter a great deal, to the extent that God's temple was turned into a profiteering market place (Luke 19:46).

When it came to religious questions, politicians were least interested (Acts 25:19,20). They allowed people to choose what they preferred to believe as long as it did not mean mixing religion with politics or joining church and State. As well as other moral laxities and confusion, there were enough debates regarding gays, lesbians, racism, segregation, divorce, marriage, equality, and teenage challenges. Equally, there were those in churches who wanted to be loud, others quiet, and for some, service was only service if it revolved around them. Others preferred certain kinds of leaders, and many of them did not even think leaders in the churches were necessary. These issues are certainly nothing new, and they form just a little portion of real 'trendy' issues that the books of Corinthians try to address in the old fashion way, using the Gospel of Jesus Christ!

The issue at hand is; it is grossly sad to dress up these misnormals in any suit that makes them appear normal and permissible. It is wrong to use them to one's advantage just to increase one's crowd in the name of God. When misnormals, leading from things and behaviour the Bible classifies as human depravity and sin, are being promoted in the name of being 'trendy', the church must not be deceived to fall for them. And it doesn't matter what name we give them, whether we call them modern, post-religious, youthful, or being 'trendy', biblical sin is always sin – *misnormals will always be misnormals* in spite of what time period it is.

Just because you find it difficult to personally break away from the grip of what the Bible clearly defines as misnormal, does not mean you should join, encourage or explain them away in order to make them appear acceptable. The problem is not with being 'trendy', but how 'trendy' relates to remaining faithful to Scriptural prescription, proscription and description of what things are right, expedient, or permissible.

John the Baptist, Peter, James and our Lord Himself lived in similar so-called 'trendy' eras, but knowing the truth, they never did campaign to endorse existing vices of their times.

Arguably their challenges might have been a little different in form, but in principle they are just the same as today's challenges. Paul for instance, once he came to know the truth after his conversion to Christ, made it his sole aim to expose and to stamp out ideas and practices that were contrary to the truth of Scriptures. He is simply one of the shining examples of how it is possible to turn from 'dead and unfruitful works' to the truth, and to walk in the excellence of God, even in a vile and broken society (see Ephesians 5:9-18).

Certainly, the Lord and His disciples didn't completely weed out the vices of their time, but they stood against the vile practices of those who denied godliness and the truth in the name of being 'trendy'. They offered those who were out of the way a better way, being light and salt in their times. That's our own challenge today; we can't weed out completely the vices accompanying what is considered today as 'trendy', but we can respectfully make the biblical position and alternatives known. We may not be able to eradicate those misnormals, but let us not campaign for them either through our acceptance of what we know to be biblically wrong and unacceptable.

Remember, we are in the world but not of the world (John 15:19; 17:16; Also see Romans 12:2; 1 Corinthians 2:12;5:10; 6:2;7:31). God has not called you to be 'trendy' but to be a true ambassador for Christ (2 Corinthians 5:20; Ephesians 6:20). No ambassador represents his personal interest or champions his selfish cause. Always bear in mind that as ambassadors, we are under directives, and represent a Kingdom whose dominion, ways and principles are not of this present world order, although we are sent to the world. To be truly trendy therefore is to espouse and propagate the unchanging truth and realities of our sending Kingdom to which we really belong, the Kingdom of God.

Trend and Behavioural Inconsistency

What has been will be again, what has been done will be done again; there is nothing new under the sun (Ecclesiastics 1:9).

The whole question of being 'trendy', as some would have you believe is about specific cultures and traditions tied to a certain era or epoch, past or present. As such certain periods, and the way of thinking and doing things associated with that period in time, can be strictly stratified and classified as past and old, or present and 'trendy' and 'with the times'.

On the whole, it is an argument for doing almost anything to be or to remain current but not necessarily relevant. *In such a world, currency and relevancy is not the same thing.* Hence, it is okay when whatever is deemed as 'trendy' is prevalent but not essentially appropriate or imperative especially with regards to issues of life, faith, virtues, moral responsibilities, and personal accountability before Almighty God.

Being 'trendy' is a subtle suggestion for blurring difference, an irresponsible shifting and in many cases, the removal of proven ethical safety boundaries in order to be and to feel acceptable in a 'trendy' world. For example, if an influential teenager suddenly became a global icon in such a world, as we have today with emerging stars, who command great powers and wealth due to the evolution of social media; such a teenager could potentially define 'new' morality and lifestyle that grandpas, grandmas, and even presidents and prime ministers would unquestionably adopt and sell to their citizens as 'trendy', for the sake of political advantage .

In this light, being 'trendy' really is denying true conscience and living without real convictions for the right things, but a having to shift, turn and swap, and shift, and swap again, and again for the rest of your life. There is actually no constant, no true reality and hence, no stability but only swinging fickle changes. The real problem of the so-called 'trendy' world, which also is the only constant it seems to have, is that change itself keeps changing. If you want to be 'trendy' therefore, you must do everything to remain with the crowd. Usually, this would mean a wholesale acceptance of whatever taste, preferences and perceptions in particular eras deemed to be generally acceptable, not necessarily by the majority, albeit it is made to appear so. Likewise, being 'trendy' does not necessarily suggest being right, although it intrudes upon and tries with every power to define what is right and acceptable. Hence a lot of people buying into being 'trendy' are fooled into thinking that to be 'trendy' is to be right.

In the end it remains the opinion and preferences of the few, who are capable of using their influence to make a good number of the population to buy into their way of thinking, and to prefer their preferences in style, taste or certain behaviour. These people often use a process of persuasion which is highly emotive, political and socio-religious to attract sympathizers and to drive a good number of the population to their side. But again, just because something is popular, looks attractive, and sells out well does not necessarily suggest that it is right and trendy in the true sense of the word. Similarly, books are not always "best sellers" because they are great books; they are, primarily because they sold well.

To help with our discussion about "being trendy", let's ignore for now the textual meaning and rather focus on the incredible profundity of Jesus' statement in a parable from Luke 5:39. In my view, the wisdom of His statement helps to resolve the tension and dynamic that exist between what is considered 'trendy' and what is not. It also shows the changing relationship that pertains to our preferences and perceptions of things past (old) and present (new). In that statement, Jesus said, *"And no one having drunk old wine immediately desires the new, for he says, 'The old is better.'"* Pay attention to the use and role of the words *immediately* and *desires* and how they form a bridge between *old* and *new* in the verse. As they are, they suggest there is a good possibility for someone who renounces a 'new wine' in favour of the 'old' to also with time, ask or develop a taste for the 'new wine'. One way this might happen is, they should keep having a go at it. So, time is a factor and of great essence as well in this case.

However, what is most apparent here is the fact that we have in this statement a reference to *new* and *old* as a judgment of taste, and perhaps personal preference, but not of enduring principle. If it is only a judgment of taste and preference, then it is also purely behavioural which is subject to change, given time and prevailing circumstances.

That means, in the likely event in which what someone had earlier desired should fail to taste or feel good, one could then change their mind to prefer the 'new' because now, it appeals to their sense of taste or feeling (let's call it desires). Hence they shift the post and lose their previous *centre* because their new desire has influenced their present choice. Evidently, they have acted and decided based on desires which are mainly behavioural. Their choice and the basis of it, falls short of the exercise of enduring principles. All of this is a good testimony that unlike God's enduring systems, human systems are flawed, and the campaign for "being trendy" is largely human capitulation to the enticement of their changing behaviour.

Now, a keen look at the Lord's statement regarding *new* and *old* with reference to our desires, preferences or behaviour leads us to conclude that, it appears He is addressing our conscious or unconscious response to change, but change based on the way we prefer things, instead of what ought to be. If that is the case, that our desires or behaviour play such a crucial role in making preferences for one thing or another, but meanwhile disregarding enduring principles pertaining to what ought to be, as we pursue change, then our conclusion about being "trendy" is right. After all, being 'trendy' as is presently espoused, is mainly about change but change based on taste or 'feel good' effect. It has nothing to do with honouring God or His Word. In most aspects, it is people arguing that "we should become slave to our shifting behaviour, and continue to vacillate in order to appease it."

There are others who think that being 'trendy' is about adaptation, but again it's all about adapting principally based on taste or a 'feel good' effect. However, the problem still remains. Just because I change or I must change and adapt to become 'trendy' doesn't necessarily make being 'trendy' right. It only makes me 'feel good' temporarily, and my whole effort to change and to become 'trendy' was only based on something very transient, and often intended to please so-called popular opinion about a rather interesting state of things and behaviour.

Clearly what we are grappling with is really about people's response and preference for the wine, *old* and *new,* which according to the parable has a lot to do with people's disposition and understanding. It has nothing to do with the wine's reaction to people. The wine does not necessarily change to suit people's taste. Whatever it is, *old* or *new,* it remains unavoidably and fundamentally the life and life cycle of the wine. But what is true about the wine, *old* or *new,* is that it satisfies and addresses the human need without having to change its principal composition and substance. People need the *wine*, and not the other way round.

Remove people's behaviour and preferences, and you are left with just wine under *new* and *old* label, as we presently have with *Old* and *New* Testament. One is never exclusive of the other. In fact, the Old runs-on to the New and the New looks back to the Old.
They share and have a common Source, a common thread and are intertwined, inextricably linked and flow from the same well, so to speak (see Mtt 13:52). We cannot tell what the *New* is in the absence of the *Old*.

The *New* does not necessarily invalidate the *Old.* They both work like the relationship and dynamics existing between *orthodoxy* and *charismatism,* in which *orthodoxy* or *tradition* checks and balances *charismatism,* while *charismatism* inspires and brings freshness to *orthodoxy* or *tradition.* One does not cancel out or replace the other. This cycle or strange *dialectics* will continue as part of church life and faith, affirming Solomon's wisdom about nothing being really new under the sun (Ecclesiastes 1:9).

So, what we are really faced with is the challenge of human behaviour, which is normally subject to change. This is the one thing that is not constant and so, in addressing people's behaviour, we use the one thing that is constant which is the Word of God, to adjust their inconstant behaviour if they must have a centre to their lives. Otherwise, we will be left with nations of people of relativism, without constant, without centre and without enduring principles.

It's Just the Same Devil in a New Suit

I find this difficult to understand, that we 'modern' preachers and believers tend to think that our challenges and the problems that we face today, are more than those of John, Jesus and the Apostles. Yet, we still use the very Scripture they gave us from the crucible of their challenges to address today's issues and problems. What an irony. If you can look a little deeper, you will find out that it's just the same devil in a new suit that we have to wrestle with!

If the truth will be told, our predecessors in the Faith had equally great challenges of their own or sometimes even greater than we have now, since theirs were a pioneering work. No one can deny that we currently stand on the shoulders of those great men and women of faith. Equally, generations after us will still be doing the same, drawing from the same enduring principles of faith faithfully passed on to us. *'for the Scripture cannot be broken' (John 10:35).*

The Bible we have, and the events and activities it records, were real life happenings in churches, within and without Christian communities. If it were possible to make comparison, the eras the Bible recorded probably had more idol worshipers than we have today considering demographical ratios. So, the human problem is the human problem with sin being its real roots. The same old Gospel message passionately and sincerely delivered by a Holy Spirit filled preacher or believer will bring about the necessary repentance from sin and dead works, and repentance toward God.

For John the Baptist, the Lord Jesus and the Apostles, the formula for effective ministry was the same; being completely filled with the Holy Spirit and carrying out ministry in the power of the Holy

Spirit (Luke 4:1,18; Acts 10:38; 1:8; 2:4;4:8). Our Lord even took the power of being filled with the Holy Spirit a step further when He persistently resisted and overcame forty days of unabated temptation from the devil, right at the beginning of His earthly ministry (Luke 4:1-14).

It is common to see and to hear people who usually have an advantage of considerable age and background trying to compare their experiences with present times, and they are inclined to conclude that their experiences were more valid, more riveting, and completely out-of-this-world. On the other hand younger generations also are deceived into thinking only their kind of experience must be counted for salt on the earth, and that previous generations are utterly out of touch and have no clue about the extreme challenges facing young people now on all fronts.

But, the truth is that every generation is going to equally have in principle and practice, relatively challenging and difficult issues and questions of their own to deal with. The bottom line is the human problem which the Bible calls sin. The problem of sin may present itself in different forms, but no matter the form or shape of it, sin is sin, and will always depict the general depravity of the fallen human species. For our part as children of God, let's get on with the job, preach and *endure affliction, do the work of an evangelist, and fulfil your ministry (2 Timothy 4:5)! Preach the word! Be ready in season and out of season. Convince, rebuke, exhort, with all longsuffering and teaching (2 Tim. 4:2).* Live out and up to your purpose.

That is what we have, a ministry and a purpose to fulfil. To *fulfil* means to *perform, execute, discharge, and to complete.* And our ministry and purpose is simply a service or an assignment we are called and sent to carry out and to complete. John had a ministry, "to turn many (*not all*) of the children of Israel to the Lord their God. To also go before the Messiah, in the spirit and power of Elijah, to turn the hearts of the fathers to the children, and the disobedient to the wisdom of the just, to make ready a people prepared for the Lord" (Luke 1:16,17). Focus on carrying out your God given purpose and beat the 'trend'!

The Place of the Holy Spirit in Purpose: Can You Do It Any Other Way?

❖❖❖

The Same 'Old Trick': Methods and Means

Clearly, it was going to take more than mere human endeavour, hard work, and theological expertise for John to satisfactorily fulfil his ministry. He needed what the Lord God first gave him while in his mother's womb, the infilling of the Holy Spirit. His job was going to be impossible without the great help of the Holy Spirit. And truly, this is the 'old trick' that works every time, everywhere, and in every generation; that those who genuinely have the infilling of the Holy Spirit for what God will have them do, will stand the test of time and stand out in their generation. Such people successfully manage to fulfil their ministries and purpose if, they remain submissive to the Holy Spirit who is our great Helper. He was given, and came, to help us to fulfil the purposes of God for our lives and ministries (John 14:16, 18, 26).

Now the truth is that, invariably every ministry that exists today, and probably all ministerial endeavours, will be unquestionably linked with those spelled out for John the Baptist, particularly the command to *turn people to the Lord*. Therefore, if we can learn from John, who faithfully fulfilled his ministry and purpose during a time of comparatively difficult circumstances, we too will be able to fulfil ours. This has nothing to do with the method, but the power and wisdom behind the method, which is evidently traceable to the fact that John was filled with the Holy Spirit for what he had to do; and he listened to the leadings of the Holy Spirit.

We have already seen elsewhere in this book that it was not so much about John's method that drew the multitudes that came to be baptised. For the times in which he lived, John's method was realistically unconventional, especially given how he referred to the Scribes, Pharisees, tax collectors, soldiers and Sadducees; calling them *broods of vipers*. That means, if we will have people to turn to God in repentance, it is absolutely pointless to begin this crucial task with first working on our personal communication skills. In fact some of the most effective people, who are doing great things for God, never went to regular schools; hence they hardly have all the linguistic sophistications of our time. Yet, they are so effective at affecting lives around them.

Getting people to truly repent, to change and to turn to God, is only by the power of the Holy Spirit. That is why it is so crucial that we ourselves, first and foremost, become filled with the Holy Spirit; so that He works through us, and speaks through us every time we stand before one or more people:

> *Nevertheless I tell you the truth. It is to your advantage that I go away; for if I do not go away, the Helper will not come to you; but if I depart, I will send Him to you.* [8] *And when He has come, **He will convict the world of sin, and of righteousness, and of judgment:*** [9] ***of sin**, because they do not believe in Me;* [10] *of righteousness, because I go to My Father and you see Me no more;* [11] *of judgment, because the ruler of this world is judged (Jn 16:7-11).*

With the Holy Spirit being in John the Baptist, working and speaking through Him, he had no need for the kind of the artificial antics and publicity stunts regrettably prevalent in some of our churches and with some individuals today. Obviously, John had no need for the *wine and strong drinks,* which in this case were symbolic of the inauthentic and counterfeit power and wisdom of this present world. He already had the real person, power and presence of God in and with him, having been filled by the Holy Spirit. He did not need the wisdom of the world in being drunk and high on *wine* and *strong drinks.* He already had the Spirit of Wisdom richly indwelling him and was too *drunk* in the Holy Spirit to have any need for other *supplements,* nor counterfeits.

> *And do not be drunk with wine, in which is dissipation; but be filled with the Spirit (Ephesians 5:8).*

Yes, that's what it is, we have just too many *supplements* these days, and the Holy Spirit needs none of that if we became truly filled with the Spirit. By *supplements,* I am talking about all the put-ons including false religious deep voices, or false hiccups coming through microphones, from preachers who look to be faking asthmatic attacks. There's nothing wrong with following a particular style with 'jerking', deep voices, hiccups and shouting, if they come naturally to you, but to deliberately bring it on oneself just because it seems fashionable and 'trendy' to jerk and to do all the other things often so commonly seen, are purely *supplements.*

All the manipulative publicity stunts and the hard work of special sound effects, deliberately calculated with the intension as it were to hypnotise a congregation, or cover one's own 'complex' become absolutely unwarranted when the Holy Spirit of God is truly present and in control. To hang onto these unnecessary 'extras' or *supplements* is as if the Holy Spirit is not enough, but He is always and everywhere more than enough. *Anything more than our total dependence on the Holy Spirit would be simply a move toward serving and glorifying our flesh.*

As you will observe, John was not tedious and complicated, yet multitudes came to repent and to be baptised, because the job of conviction was already done by the Holy Spirit, speaking through John directly to the hearts of his listeners.

The Spirit and Power of Elijah

Luke 1:17 says that John the Baptist, his going before the Lord as the forerunner, and ability to carry out his purpose, was going to be done with a certain quality; in the spirit and power of Elijah.

> *He will also go before Him in the spirit and power of Elijah, 'to turn the hearts of the fathers to the children,' and the disobedient to the wisdom of the just, to make ready a people prepared for the Lord."*

Well, to be able to describe what all this means, we need to visit Mount Carmel and to see Elijah in action; if truly we want to pin down the spirit and power of the man. As always, the spirit and power of a person are best seen when he is involved in some form of action. In this case Mt. Carmel is about the peak of Elijah's actions in the Bible. We know that he called a drought that lasted for three and a half years in Israel, but that was nothing compared to asking for a power and miracle contest against four hundred and fifty prophets of Baal and four hundred prophets of Asherah; men who ate at Jezebel's table.

I suggest that you read the entire narrative in 1Kings 18 for the full impact of the story. Upon Elijah's request, King Ahab of Israel summoned all the children of Israel together with the prophets to gather on Mount Carmel. When they were all gathered together, Elijah challenged them saying;

> *"How long will you falter between two opinions? If the Lord is God, follow Him; but if Baal, follow him." But the people answered him not a word. [22] Then Elijah said to the people, "I alone am left a prophet of the Lord; but Baal's prophets are four hundred and fifty men. [23] Therefore let them give us two bulls; and let them choose one bull for themselves, cut it in pieces, and lay it on the wood, but put no fire under it; and I will prepare the other bull, and lay it on the wood, but put no fire under it.[2]*

Then you call on the name of your gods, and I will call on the name of the Lord; and the God who answers by fire, He is God." So all the people answered and said, "It is well spoken" (1 Kings18:21-24).

For a fact, anyone with the audacity to throw an unqualified challenge like Elijah did, must either be mad or know something incredibly beyond what was immediately apparent to those he was challenging to the contest. What is even most puzzling was that the prophets and the people heeded to Elijah's invitation for a wild showdown. And so the time finally came, to begin what was going to ultimately be a contest between the God of Elijah on the one hand, and on the other hand, Baal and Asherah, the gods of the prophets convened by Ahab.

Each side of the competition had rightly done their initials, having prepared their bulls and the wood. Now, it was time for the invocation, and the prophets of Baal went first. They called on Baal all morning until noon, Baal had still not answered. Probably at this time, the prophets were beginning to think of a change of strategy as their faction grew anxious. They began to plead, *"O Baal, hear us!"*, but as the Bible says, *there was no voice* and *no one answered.*

It was now getting pretty serious, and as usual desperate situations call for desperate measures for those who follow something as dumb as Baal and Asherah. So, the prophets of Baal began to perform leap-jumps in circles, around the very alter upon which their pieces of bull were prepared and laid out. All of this was beginning to look like a well arranged, well-rehearsed piece of entertainment to Elijah who threw the challenge. One can imagine that he was beginning to secretly celebrate in his own heart the failure of Baal to respond to the passionate cry of his zealous prophets.

When noon came, Elijah then took his challenge a little further by taunting the prophets. The passage records;

Elijah mocked them and said, "Cry aloud, for he is a god; either he is meditating, or he is busy, or he is on a journey, or perhaps he is sleeping and must be awakened." [28] So they cried aloud, and cut themselves, as was their custom, with knives and lances, until the blood gushed out on them. [29] And when midday was past, they prophesied until the time of the offering of the evening sacrifice. But there was no voice; no one answered, no one paid attention (1 King 18:27-30).

Well, since the contest was about honour, glory and reputation, the prophets of Baal in the face of Baal's unmistakably loud silence had to make him speak, no matter the cost. It appeared that they were running low on strategies and innovations and now, as bizarre as it seemed, they were all too ready to take on any help from anybody, even their opponent. So, Elijah asked them to 'cry aloud' and they obediently 'cried aloud'. Very interesting! They soon remembered there was one more thing, which the text says, was *their custom.*

What was this custom? It was simply to lacerate their bodies and let their blood pour out presumably to nosh Baal. But, it did not matter how hard they tried, by evening they unfortunately had the same result, if not worse. Worse because, not only did Baal not answer, but the text says, no one else did, and *no one paid attention,* which meant, they also lost the support of their fans who had gathered since morning. It is okay for Baal to not answer, but when your supporters begin to boo and jeer, that's not a good sign for a possibility of any meaningful comeback.

After Baal failed to answer from morning to evening, Elijah, who probably now could see it was all his game, took his stand. He was still as confident as when he first called for the contest, and like a champion who knew his game and what he was about, he asked everyone to come closer.

So all the people came near to him. And he repaired the altar of the Lord that was broken down. [31] And Elijah took twelve stones, according to the number of the tribes of the sons of Jacob, to whom the word of the Lord had come, saying, "Israel shall be your name." [32] Then with the stones he built an altar in the name of the Lord; and he made a trench around the altar large enough to hold two seahs of seed. [33] And he put the wood in order, cut the bull in pieces, and laid it on the wood, and said, "Fill four waterpots with water, and pour it on the burnt sacrifice and on the wood." [34] Then he said, "Do it a second time," and they did it a second time; and he said, "Do it a third time," and they did it a third time. [35] So the water ran all around the altar; and he also filled the trench with water (1 Kings 18:30-36).

Note how Elijah goes about things, certainly there is 'wisdom in his madness.' He has all of a sudden even raised the bar, challenged His God even to a much more challenging task than the prophets of Baal had. But one thing was sure, if you read the text carefully, Elijah was playing his game to the rules of his God. His timing was apt because it was the time of the evening sacrifice. The manner in which he went about building and preparing the alter, the arrangement of the stones, and the Name to which it was built, are exactly according to the Old Testament regulations for an acceptable sacrifice unto the God of Heaven. Given that he followed the rules and prepared his sacrifice the way it delighted God Almighty, surely God was going to hear Elijah when he cried.

To begin with, the god of the prophets of Baal was no god, but it is the principle behind the whole episode, and how foolish the prophets were to have been led by Elijah into total humiliation. They allowed him to make them to do something totally presumptuous and outside their own scope and mandate. Even if Baal were able to answer, which indeed is utter impossibility for a false god, it really had no compelling reason why it should answer men who decided to take matters into their own hands by responding to Elijah's challenge in the way they did.

Anyone like Elijah who calls you up to a competition like that, might have already done his homework. In fact, this was a man whom, at the command of his God, went into hiding during the three years and six months of drought in Israel. He did not make any public appearance until his God asked him to present himself to King Ahab (1 Kings 1:18). So, Elijah was a man under authority and walking aright with his God.

Now, all said and done, the Bible says that

> *And it came to pass, at the time of the offering of the evening sacrifice, that Elijah the prophet came near and said, "Lord God of Abraham, Isaac, and Israel, let it be known this day that You are God in Israel and I am Your servant, and that I have done all these things at Your word. [37] Hear me, O Lord, hear me, that this people may know that You are the Lord God, and that You have turned their hearts back to You again." [38] Then the fire of the Lord fell and consumed the burnt sacrifice, and the wood and the stones and the dust, and it licked up the water that was in the trench. [39] Now when all the people saw it, they fell on their faces; and they said, "The Lord, He is God! The Lord, He is God!" [40] And Elijah said to them, "Seize the prophets of Baal! Do not let one of them escape!" So they seized them; and Elijah brought them down to the Brook Kishon and executed them there (1 Kings 18:36-40).*

The 36th verse holds the key to Elijah's victory and reason for the failure and demise of the prophets of Baal. It says Elijah prayed to the Lord his God saying, *let it be known this day that You are God in Israel and I am Your servant, and that I have done all these things at Your word.*

My friend, whatever you do at the command of the Lord God Almighty is bound to come to pass! Whatever He has promised you will surely come to pass! The Bible says, 'we have the sure word of prophecies confirmed, and we will do well if we heed to it as a light that shines in a dark place, until the day dawns and the morning star rises in our hearts' (2 Peter 1:19).

It is very dangerous to be presumptions and to follow blindly like the prophets of Baal. Those who do, will not only fail but may take on too much for their too little strength, which may lead ultimately to a disastrous end. God readily responded to His servant Elijah by honouring his prayer, simply because Elijah had not acted big-headedly or with arrogance. To have taken things in his own hands would have been a gross mistake, instead, he went at the word and command of God Almighty who watches over His word and is always ready to perform His Word (Jeremiah. 1:12). The wisdom here is that, God is only obligated to perform His word and to finish what He began.

"...I am ready to perform My word (Jeremiah 1:12)."

"God is not a man, that He should lie, nor a son of man, that He should repent. Has He said, and will He not do? Or has He spoken, and will He not make it good?(Numbers 23:19)

... For I am the Lord. I speak, and the word which I speak will come to pass; it will no more be postponed; for in your days, O rebellious house, I will say the word and perform it," says the Lord God' (Ezekiel 12:25).

Remember, God's word may come as revealed in Scripture, or through one of the ways He communicates to His people, for example in dreams, vision, or by personal revelation (*rhema* word) or prophecies. However, God may choose one of His appointed servants and messengers, and it could be a pastor of a church, or a prophet, to deliver His word to you. When that pastor or prophet then brings God's word faithfully to you, the word that is transmitted is not their own, but the word of God, which God confirms and performs.

Who confirms the word of His servant, and performs the counsel of His messengers; Who says to Jerusalem, 'You shall be inhabited,' To the cities of Judah, 'You shall be built,' and I will raise up her waste places (Isaiah 44:6).

The Lessons from Elijah: Mass Hysteria and Mass Psychology with Secular Society Agenda

Apparently, many things can be said about the outcome of the lively dynamics and relationship that often exit when the forces of personal faith, religion, society and the rhetoric of politics come together. However, the story of Elijah and the prophets of Baal particularly draws our attention to the crucial question of mass hysteria and mass psychology, as it relates to how the powerful forces of personal faith, religion, society and the rhetoric of politics interact, and negotiate with one another in an attempt to forge and to form a so-called new and 'trendy' world from the old.

Although this was not the main purpose for initially referring to Elijah's story, it helps those of us who are Christians, and church leaders who live in shared and so-called multi-faith societies. In this case, Ahab and Jezebel symbolize politics, who are deemed to be powerful and are able to sway and persuade a buck of the people for their own ends, like it has been said, *it's always the rich men's war but poor men fight.* Come to think of it, from a physical perspective, the prophets engaged against Elijah and his God were actually pursuing the agenda of their bosses, Ahab and Jezebel, who wanted to get rid of Elijah, the 'bad guy', and all he stood for.

The gathering crowd who were present at Mount Carmel, represent the real mix in our society who watch with largely spectator's eyes but often with vested interests. They are those to be pulled, polarised, and torn between opinions; helpless but still feeling like they have control. Their commitments are being tested at all levels. They desire change but just do not know what is right anymore; hence, despondency sets in so easily. This then leads many to settle for the easy option of allowing *others to run the show* while they spectate and look on.

Some also settle for an all-inclusive, all-is-good multicultural, multifaceted, multi-faith society in which truth becomes relative. Like the head of a standing fan, many people will vacillate and oscillate among various views and faiths countless numbers of times in their life time, and still not be satisfied. Such are those that are caught in the wave of seeking something new each time, when in truth, there is really nothing new (see Acts 17:21).

Typically, the prophets of Baal are the epitome and embodiment of religiosity, who are normally caught up in the hype, verve, and hysteria, but also the mere emptiness of the delusion of wonderful superstition. However, the vanity and porosity of their superstition overtime might become so obvious and blatant to common sense, but as the saying goes, *common sense is not so common*, in their case. As a result the prophets of Baal, for whom *common sense is not so common,* become almost irreversibly and helplessly strapped to their religious superstition, that it becomes almost impossible to shift their beliefs and loyalty to anything else, not even a clearly demonstrated truth.

The prophets of Baal, who clearly represent in this case religiosity, typically have what I call the *mars hill* phenomenon (See Acts 17:22, 23), having no real personal or organic relationship with the object of their belief, and yet are willing to defend and to die for it. Having not really seen their gods move or talk before, they still literally convince themselves into believing; and afterwards fence themselves into that belief as well. Although their belief is all it is, just a belief, without the attending power to even light a coal, they still expect what is not true to work and to perform the impossible. It is like self-hypnosis, and is a very extreme form of self-delusion and deception, which in my view is always more difficult to break free from.

It is difficult because the perpetrator himself is the victim; hence attempting to offer any form of deliverance will be tantamount to asking them to literally save themselves from themselves. This self-imposed victim unfortunately could easily rope others into the same circle of perpetrator-victim (self-harm) situations, because they provide, by their belief and practices, what seems an enticing, popular and generous alternative, albeit false, that keeps them reeling in a dangerous cycle (see Acts 8:11).

In addition, their uncommon commitment to their kind of belief and practices are clearly evident so as to be very convincing and self-validating to their unsuspecting on-lookers. They powerfully and openly exude persuasive passion that easily distracts an enquirer from examining the substance of what the prophets really have to offer, and instead rather get engrossed with the prophets' exhilarating performances.

Interestingly, society quite appreciates the prophets' presentation, because they are very skilled in the subtlety of packaging and marketing. Society, hence, buys into their superstitions and are not only astonished by the prophets, but also get captivated into believing that they are indeed presenting something new, trendy, popular and fashionable.

Elijah on the other hand, represents true faith; but the truth is no more trendy and popular in a society where the prophets of 'trend' loom high. Therefore to begin to assert the truth, Elijah needs to be very radical in selling the truth to an already otherwise 'captivated' crowd and audience who are now most sympathetic and orientated towards multi-cultural, multi-faith, and *multi-everything society.* Where will he begin in trying to offer the truth he bears to a crowd and people who want nothing else but what they already know and believe? He has a massive challenge to re-orientate all whom he is privileged to gather, toward receiving his truth; an 'alternative' which is by no means easy and popular in a 'trendy' and *multi-everything* society.

This time, reorientation will mean breaking from the popular norm that is already known, and in some ways imposed on the crowd. It is a process that is no doubt costly but it must be done, because *desperate times require desperate measures* (I really mean this in a positive way). Obviously, no change comes easy, especially where the agent of change is no longer popular, and has been labelled to be just one of the views among many others.

Now, in the face of stiff opposition to the truth, what will you do? No doubt, an *Elijah* alone against prophets of Baal (Religion), Ahab, Jezebel (Politics) and the crowd (Society) has a monstrous situation on his hands; almost likened to the proverbial *David-Goliath struggle* that will have to shift from the human realms and to be fought by the power of faith. It is a matter of what is real or unreal, what is true or untrue, but *the proof is always in the eating of the pudding* as they say. But many, easily and deliberately, avoid this style of proving anything in a sophisticated *multi-everything* society in which suspicion overshadows even the most innocent of things said or done. Avoidance, playing it safe on the fringes, or the superficial patronization of what we don't know is probably the best practice as people often want us to believe. Yet, the Bible says, *for the lack of knowledge My people are destroyed (Hos 4:6)*, and also *you shall know the truth and the truth shall make you free (John 8:32)*.

Like the proverbial Ostrich, some sections of society think, it helps probably to pretend that it's okay, just try forgetting whatever misgivings or promptings that may arise about what you believe, and things will take care of themselves naturally. *Denial is the best practice*, and hopefully one day the truth will eventually evolve. Unfortunately, by itself, that truth never emerges nor evolves. But in the meantime, the same people who acquiesce and subscribe to the wisdom of 'denial' might be really frustrated, desperate and in need of some real purpose and meaning to life. Their capitulation to 'denial' coupled with their frustration with life and the lack of true purpose in their own lives eventually let them to settle down for some other clever alternative, although empty and vague. In the end, if the grace of God suffices, such people will see that they too are trapped in false hope, and that nothing happens by chance.

Another interesting challenge that confronts an *Elijah* in trying to make his truth known is the academic, self-styled, critical Darwin generation equally trapped and engrossed in blatant dismissal and none-clinical method of proofs. Even most challenging for Elijah is the fact that this group of people oppose faith and a belief in God, disown religion, and falsely claim to be scientific. Although any reasonable person would quickly know that it takes even more faith to believe their principle claims than it does for example to believe in the existence of God who created all things.

Their curious behaviour and claims largely mimic those of the prophets of Baal whom we have already described.

Elijah knows exactly what he is coming against, with the spirit of religion, Ahab, Jezebel, and politics and society, and all their ramifications. His strategy is straight forward, to demonstrate the truth for its worth. Here is Elijah with a giant problem, and he is no giant, but a servant of the Almighty God of the belief which he champions as the truth. His God shows up powerfully after the politicians, religions and society have failed miserably. They finally see with their naked eyes that Elijah's God is the only true God and they worship Him, and then shrieked their distaste for empty rhetoric and vain drama by slaying the prophets of Baal.

But what happens in the end? We sadly end just as we began, only to start again because there's really nothing new under the sun. Things move in cycles and in circles, and life is really an array of successive events, sometimes related or unrelated, moving in their appropriate circles, and they start and end, and end and start again appearing to have a life of their own (Eccles. 3:1-22).

So, how can I make my circle or cycle last? How can I enjoy what I experienced as an event to prolong it? Can you see the crowd at Mount Carmel who have just seen and experienced true belief clearly demonstrated, they only got free to really be freed. One cycle has only ended for another to begin, but they have not as yet come around full circle. The job is not entirely done as long as they are still linked to and surrounded by what they have just been delivered from. The intoxicating rhetoric of politics, the confusion of religion and the gripping and enticing trenches of society still pulls strong and will not let go easily. These people find themselves in an endless cycle of being fish in another man's pond, and actually pawns and expendables, for a wild adventure seeking agenda called *secular society*. While so-called *secular society* seeks to be rid of religion, and to deny the one true God of Elijah, it after all inadvertently creates many more humanistic religions, and multiplies pantheon of false gods, recklessly heading in different directions as they aggressively scramble for followers.

Self-made "gods and goddesses" follow other gods and goddesses, and they in turn seek followers too in a *secular society*.

Now, the final retort of a very obstinate and sceptical crowd on Mount Carmel proves that an Elijah kind of belief is true, powerful and authentic. It is not necessarily attractive in a *secular society*, and a *multi-everything* society, but that Elijah's way demonstrates the facts clearly, and the God of Elijah hears, decisively acts, and He is alive. As a result, the crowd wants to follow Elijah and to follow His God. In essence, the statement people are making albeit by their action to follow Elijah based on what they have heard and seen is, 'I am only yoked to what I have because no one has shown me clearly anything greater and better. If I could afford the truth, then I would abandon the fake!'

Herein lies the problem of the 'trendy' majority, which the significant minority who have seen the light do not yet appreciate. Unfortunately, instead of being like Elijah, the significant minority want majority vote, so the truth is 'wonderfully' concealed and where possible, it is subsumed under glamorous display of dangerous publicity stunts that will not allow the light of the truth to be seen or realised. So, society is still largely unchallenged and mostly unchanged; the rhetoric of politics and the confusion of religion go on unabated and, true faith remains scarce and in some places well hidden. All we tend to see from time to time is a very short burst of splintered, and pockets of eventful cycle of change that do not last enough to effect meaningful and desirable long-lasting circles of positive trans-generational changes and spiritual revivals within our societies and nations as a whole.

Question; are we willing and ready to rise to the challenge of demonstrating true faith without compromise or fear for the 'powerful' as Elijah did in his time? Is it time to return to the true God of Elijah and ask for the spirit and power of Elijah for the change and spiritual revival long overdue, and which we urgently need today in our churches and societies? I believe it is time, and only through our sincere return to the God of Elijah, coupled with our genuine quest to walk in the true spirit and power of Elijah, as people pursuing relentless Godly purpose, can we begin to have the long awaited awakening and revival of nations, of our own faith and churches.

Even more crucial to our personal purpose and spiritual fulfilment is the fact that individuals who know and have the truth of God will be willing to stand for it and to live it out without guilt or shame; that God Almighty may be glorified through us as we allow the glorious light of the gospel of Jesus Christ to shine into the haunting darkness of our societies and nations. That way we, by the grace of God, can help our societies and bring positive change to communities in dire need of knowing the One true God and Father of our Lord Jesus Christ. And let's not forget, in addition to our prayer for revival, let's pray also that it would continue and last. A full circle of generational revival is better than a short burst, short lived event of revival as we have known.

Rediscovering the Spirit of Elijah for Purpose Fulfilment: Making it Easy and Doing It God's Way

❖❖❖

Where is the Spirit of Elijah?

We have seen the true spirit and power of Elijah clearly and vigorously demonstrated on Mount Carmel. We have seen how the host of Baal's prophets in no uncertain ways demonstrated what they were made of. They literally put up a great show, but it was an empty show with a significant amount of sincere, decisive antics, gimmicks, and ecstatic displays; but they were all false.

Obviously, they did not deliberately set out to deceive anyone, but the issue was that they themselves were deceived and as a result they put up a genuine religious show. The trouble is, had it somehow worked, it might have deceived the many who were present. Such is the problem with false religion. Most people who are involved are very sincere people, but at the same time, they are sincerely deceived without knowing it. Sometimes they only come to recognise that they are deceived when it is too late to quit. So they decide to just go on, remaining deceived even to their death.

The shocking news broadcast story of 1993 involving David Koresh's Waco Cult is a modern example of how the *spirit* of Baal still works even through genuine people today. Koresh and eighty-two of his faithful followers sadly died in what later became an all-out war between Koresh's cult members, the FBI and ATF *(Bureau of Alcohol, Tobacco and Firearms)*, near Waco, Texas. Koresh's members and followers included children, educated and professional people. It was reported that he fathered children by over a dozen of his female followers.[3]

Can the *spirit of Baal* still influence genuine and sincere believers today? Yes, it is very possible, especially in such times in which a good number of believers do not really prefer the solid Word of God but just a nice, glamorous environment where they can just sing and dance, meet friends and make business contacts. Unfortunately, there are church leaders who are all too ready to ignore the pitfall of the rampant spiritual corruption and ungodliness among believers and within our society today. They rather serve and provide for the gullible passions of members and potential members without any regard for what the consequences may be. *Judgment is turned away backward, and justice stands afar off: for truth is fallen in the street, and equity cannot enter (Isaiah 59:14)*, the Scripture rightly declares!

What the church and the people of God need today is not another *false spirit* according to the workings of Baal and his prophets. We need the true *spirit and power* of Elijah, and even more than that, *the God of Elijah who answers by fire. Precision and not gimmicks, simplicity of truth according to the Bible and not over embellishment of storytelling; love, loyalty and passion for God and the very people He loves are what we earnestly need in today's church.* Even more so, that we all would cast our eyes on our eternal hope that is in Christ, the salvation of our souls and the expectation of the second coming of the Lord Jesus Christ.

Such redirected attitude and expectations will drive us from the deceitfulness of Baal's *spirit* and its overtly suggestive persuasions of lies, falsehood, pretence, and empty but glamorous shows which often characterise some church services, some Christian television programmes, and the believer's life.

God's Purposes and the Spirit of Elijah

Elijah lived and ministered in some of the most difficult days, at the time when true faith was under massive attack. Societies and communities then were perfectly multi-faith and *trendy* as well. People had and were taken by many opinions about belief, just like in Britain, France, Russia, the US and other parts of the world today. Religion was only good if it accommodated other people's beliefs. Religious cocktailing and religious syncretism were the norm of the day.

The true voice of God became so scarce. So much that a once theocratic nation called Israel, considered to be primarily a faith community had to turn to politicians and unfaithful priests and prophets to make major decisions. That era was hugely depicted and dominated by what has come to be known as the *Jezebel spirit*, a terribly wicked influence whose main personification was Jezebel the wife of King Ahab, and the queen of Israel.

John the Baptist came on the scene in similar times in Israel. Some believe it was four hundred[4] years since the true voice of God was heard in Israel, and others think it was just a very long period of lull in prophetic activity. Whatever it was, Israel had real spiritual and social issues during this long haul of not being able to allow themselves to benefit from their relationship with the God of their fathers.

Those were truly difficult days, when the nation of Israel had gone too far from their faith in the one true God of Heaven. Instead of true faith, there emerged an elitist religion together with other practices of sects, including the Pharisees and Sadducees, who worshipped in highly sectarian synagogues.

They defined what was godly, religiously lawful or not. Those were amazing times of *political correctness* because of Roman rules and oppressions.

With all this going on, people began to get restless and to look for more than religion. They wished for a saviour, a *messiah* to restore hope to their nation amid the anarchy of politico-socio and religious difficulties. This was when John the Baptist came on the scene with his message of repentance toward God. He was not the *Messiah*, but he had to prepare the people and nation for the coming of the *Messiah*. Just how would he get such *broken* people and complex religious and political order to listen to him? Well, God as always would provide the method and means. In order for John to succeed in his mission, John must come *in the spirit and power of Elijah, ...to make ready a people prepared for the Lord"* *(Luke 1:17)*

John did according to the word of prophecies over his life, no gimmicks and the results were clear even up to today. According to Luke 1:17, the *spirit and power of Elijah* was granted to John specifically for the *purpose of turning the hearts of the fathers to the children, and the disobedient to the wisdom of the just, to make ready a people prepared for the Lord."* This 'spirit and power of Elijah' was never given for acrobatic displays, or for temporarily hyping up the emotions of crowds, visiting the symptoms of issues and not addressing the root causes so that people keep coming back again.

I think it was Dr. Myles Munroe or at least I heard him say, *when purpose is not known, abuse is inevitable.* That's so true. Give a child a knife and stand before them, soon they will be stabbing you or harming themselves in some way. This is not new, and problems relating to the abuse and misapplication of the power and gifts of God have sometimes been prevalent among gifted church leaders and Christian believers. It is now common scenes on television or in conferences and churches for the 'powerful man or powerful woman' to show up and all they do is to entertain. Well, entertain, but also preach the gospel of Christ!

Where is the *spirit and power of Elijah?* Wherever the *spirit and power of Elijah is*, there certainly is bound to be seen the fathers' hearts turning to the children, and the disobedient turning to the wisdom of the just, and the making of people ready and prepared for the soon and imminent coming of our Lord Jesus Christ. In the absence of this everything we do, whether in our churches or on television or even in our lives, are porous and hollow. This is so because clearly, the purpose of the *spirit and power of Elijah* inextricably ties into the very spirit, tenants and substance of the Lord's Great Commission in the Gospels.

And Jesus came and spoke to them, saying, "All authority has been given to Me in heaven and on earth. [19] Go therefore and make disciples of all the nations, baptizing them in the name of the Father and of the Son and of the Holy Spirit, [20] teaching them to observe all things that I have commanded you; and lo, I am with you always, even to the end of the age." Amen (Matthew 28:18-20)

And He said to them, "Go into all the world and preach the gospel to every creature. [16] He who believes and is baptized will be saved; but he who does not believe will be condemned. [17] And these signs will follow those who believe: In My name they will cast out demons; they will speak with new tongues; [18] they will take up serpents; and if they drink anything deadly, it will by no means hurt them; they will lay hands on the sick, and they will recover" (Mark 16:15-18).

Bringing the two gospel narratives together, we have a full commandment. There it is, all authority is given to the Lord Jesus, and in that very authority He also commands us to go into all the world to preach, teach, make disciples and baptise them. *"In My name"*, He says, heal the sick, cast out demons, speak in new tongues, nothing deadly will harm you, and the Lord of all authority is with us even to the end.

If we should attempt a summary of this commandment, it would be *make disciples, heal, and stop devils.* In my view, this is no different from what John in the *spirit and power of Elijah* came to do. John had the spirit and power of Elijah, and our Lord gives us power when the Holy Spirit comes upon us (Acts 1:8). In addition, we have His Name, His authority. The God of Elijah who answers by fire, whose Spirit worked in John is the same God of our Lord Jesus Christ, who works in us by His Holy Spirit. So, whatever John did in the spirit and power of Elijah, we can do, and even greater because our Lord Jesus is now exalted to the right hand of God Almighty, our Father (John 14:12).

So, what's the matter with us?

> *And from the days of John the Baptist until now the kingdom of heaven suffers violence, and the violent take it by force.* [13] *For all the prophets and the law prophesied until John.* [14] *And if you are willing to receive it, he is Elijah who is to come (Matthew 11:12-13).*

> *"The law and the prophets were until John. Since that time the kingdom of God has been preached, and everyone is pressing into it (Luke 16:16).*

John did such a fine job and completed his assignment and purpose elegantly as we see in Matthew and Luke. He preached, he prepared the way of our Lord for His first coming; called people to repentance and baptised them, and brought healings (*turning the heart of the father to the children*). Because of John's work, Luke acknowledged that *everyone is pressing into the kingdom.* Why is the church today still lacking? Why are we not as passionate and responsive and mission minded about preparing the way for the second coming of our Lord which is clearly our main purpose?

Maybe, it is high time we rediscover the spirit and power of Elijah, in the way that God has prepared and preordained, for ushering in our Lord Jesus Christ at his second coming.

Rediscovering the Spirit and Power of Elijah

Any church and people who intend to make any significant impact in our generation and to be part of those who are serious about their assignment of preparing a way for the second coming of the Lord Jesus Christ, will have to rediscover the *spirit and power of Elijah*. It is certainly the time to engage and to rely on the power of the Holy Spirit.

There is no other way we can do any good and effective job at preparing and hastening the Lord's coming except by and in the power of the Holy Spirit. This is the same Holy Spirit that was upon the Lord Himself during His earthly ministry, Who even quickened Him from death and caused Him to finish victoriously (Acts 10:38; Romans 8:11). He is the same Holy Spirit that came upon the disciples with mighty power (Acts 1:8), so that three thousand (Acts 2:41) people got born again in one service and were added to the church during Peter's first sermon.

Another five thousand (Acts 4:4) got born again and joined the church during his subsequent sermons. Others joined the church, including many thousands Jews (Acts 21:20), through the works of the apostles. Similarly, elsewhere believers were increasingly added to the Lord (Acts 5:14). Philip the evangelist alone by the power of the Holy Spirit through the demonstration of signs and miracles, brought great joy to the whole city of Samaria (Acts 8:8).

What was the secret of the early church? They had the power of the Holy Spirit, and were fearless and bold in testifying of the Lord Jesus Christ. In essence, this was no different from the *spirit and power of Elijah*. The good news is, the same Spirit is in and upon us today even for greater works just like the book of Romans says:

> *And if the Spirit of him who raised Jesus from the dead is living in you, he who raised Christ from the dead will also give life to your mortal bodies through his Spirit, who lives in you (Rom. 8:11).*

I heard a true testimony of a pastor who experienced what today is now being termed the *Lazarus Phenomenon.* He died and after three days, his life was miraculously restored to him during one of Pastor Reinhard Bonnke's crusades in a village in Nigeria. But this pastor, in recounting his supernatural after-life experience said, the only reason why the angel of the Lord who gave him a detailed tour of heaven and hell allowed him to return to earthly life was simply to warn people that heaven and hell are real and every Word of God is true.

He said, the angel told him that the Lord Jesus has already prepared the heavenly mansion He promised those who believe in Him, except that His people, the church He calls His bride was not ready yet. In a sense, we the church were delaying the second coming of Christ since we have not been faithful in preaching the gospel to all nations and making disciples for Christ.

There are some real Christian zealots who pray that the Lord comes quickly. But, what did Christ say about His second coming? Did He ask us to pray Him in? I guess for those who pray that the Lord comes quickly derive their clues from Revelations 22:17,20,

> *And the Spirit and the bride say, "Come!" And let him who hears say, "Come!" And let him who thirsts come. Whoever desires, let him take the water of life freely. He who testifies to these things says, "Surely I am coming quickly." Amen. Even so, come, Lord Jesus!*

Well, while it is a good thing to pray for the Lord to come, I believe it is even more expedient to do what Christ commanded us before His imminent return: *"And the gospel must first be preached to all the nations" (Mark 13:10).* We simply need to add some actions to our faith and prayers by reaching out to the nations with the gospel of Christ.

Surely, that should quicken His coming and cause Him to hear our prayer for Him to come when He sees that there is no reason for Him to hold back any longer.

But, as long as His bride, the church, is not ready and the gospel has not been preached to all nations as the Lord Jesus instructed, it is a selfish and fruitless exercise to pray Him in.

The question for the church is, have we already prepared our people or are we preparing our people and making them ready for our Lord? These are questions of foremost importance for every church and believer; it does not matter our unique area of emphasis in terms of our purposes, callings and gifts. Whether it regards healing evangelist, the prosperity or motivational preacher, the bottom line is the same for every one of us; to make a people ready for the return of the Lord Jesus Christ.

Let's not forget that there is a big difference between just gathering a crowd of people, and besides, making conscious effort to prepare the same crowd of people for the coming of the Lord. We can make people ready for this earthly life, but we must also prepare them for heavenly life, which is the inevitable destiny for those who hope in Christ. Surely, we must teach people Godly principles to be fruitful, multiply, dominate, and to subdue the earth (Genesis 1:28), but we must also remain true to the core of our calling, which is to make a people prepared for the Lord by helping them so that in the end, *"we all come to the unity of the faith and of the knowledge of the Son of God, to a perfect man, to the measure of the stature of the fullness of Christ" (Ephesians 4:14).* For this reason, He Himself,

> *... gave some to be apostles, some prophets, some evangelists, and some pastors and teachers, [12] for the equipping of the saints for the work of ministry, for the edifying of the body of Christ, [13] till we all come to the unity of the faith and of the knowledge of the Son of God, to a perfect man, to the measure of the stature of the fullness of Christ; [14] that we should no longer be children, tossed to and fro and carried about with every wind of doctrine, by the trickery of men, in the cunning craftiness of deceitful plotting, [15] but, speaking the truth in love, may grow up in all things into Him who is the head – Christ (Ephesians 4:11-15).*

If you are a believer in any church whose primary purpose is to prepare you for anything other than the Lord Jesus Christ, then it is time to unapologetically quit that church, move out and move on to another.

For many walk, of whom I have told you often, and now tell you even weeping, that they are the enemies of the cross of Christ: [19] whose end is destruction, whose god is their belly, and whose glory is in their shame—who set their mind on earthly things. [20] For our citizenship is in heaven, from which we also eagerly wait for the Savior, the Lord Jesus Christ, [21] who will transform our lowly body that it may be con- formed to His glorious body, according to the working by which He is able even to subdue all things to Himself (Philippians 3:18-24).

For what profit is it to a man if he gains the whole world, and loses his own soul? Or what will a man give in exchange for his soul? For the Son of Man will come in the glory of His Father with His angels, and then He will reward each according to his works (Matthew 16:26-27).

And as it is appointed for men to die once, but after this the judgment (Hebrews 9:27).

Therefore thus will I do to you, ...; Because I will do this to you, Prepare to meet your God, ...!" (Amos 4:12).

My friend, we have a *city which has foundations, whose builder and maker is God (Hebrews 11:10).* That glorious city is called Mount Zion, and it is the city of the living God also described as the heavenly Jerusalem. It is the city of innumerable company of angels, and of the general assembly of God's faithful, referred to as the church of the firstborn, who are registered already in heaven. Our God Himself is the Judge of all who is exaltedly seated on His heavenly throne. In that great city are of course the spirits of just men made perfect, and also our Lord Jesus who is the Mediator of the new covenant with His own blood of sprinkling, His blood which speaks better things than that of Abel's.

From His glorious throne above, Jesus our Lord still mediates and speaks for His people from that beautiful city (*My rendering of Hebrews 12:22-24*). That is where you want to be and to spend eternity, not hell. It is the place to be, and the church should be making us ready for that glorious occasion and the gathering of all the saints of God.

However, a church and people of purpose, who want to pursue the Lord's assignment in making a people ready for the second coming of the Lord, and to make this glorious city described above their eternal home, must know that it will take more than superficial gimmicks. We need the power of the Holy Spirit. That's why the need to rediscover the person and power of the Holy Spirit in our times can never be overemphasized.

John the Baptist had to prepare people for the first coming of the Lord Jesus *in the spirit and power of Elijah* bringing in multitudes from all works of life to turn to God in total repentance. We have the same spirit and power today in the person of the blessed Holy Spirit ready to sweep across the nations of the earth and to bring endless generations to God. He was given for the purpose of helping us to fulfil the Lord's assignments on earth, and as well as making a people ready for His second coming. The Holy Spirit is the ultimate power in God's Kingdom building agenda of which we are privileged to be servants, labourers and co-labourers with Christ. By the grace and power of the Holy Spirit, and us truly relying on Him to start, continue, and to finish God's purposes for our lives, I know we will succeed.

The Necessities of Purpose: Who is Your Mentor and Have You Been Anointed?

❖❖❖

The Power of Being with Jesus

This brings us to yet another crucial and exciting point about all that transpired between the Sanhedrin and the disciples over the healing miracle of the lame man. This part of the passage has always aroused joy in me and made me shout, Amen! I hope it does the same for you somewhere along our journey of unpacking the revelation of what the Holy Spirit wants to bring to us.

Again, the wisdom and power behind the passage is true for every person of purpose attempting to follow through on what they've found as their God-given assignment or purpose. For the main characters, Peter and John, this probably was the pinnacle of their entire incidence involving the Sanhedrin over the healing miracle, and was definitely going to be a defining moment for their future ministry in pursuing God's purposes.

The Undeniable Proof

The two men, Peter and John, held their unbroken commitment to the testimony of the lordship of Jesus Christ, refusing to deny Him in the presence of the Sanhedrin. They vowed to speak openly in the Name of Jesus offering to everyone the saving grace which comes only in the Name of Jesus. Peter and John, as the text puts it, were rather *uneducated and untrained (Acts 4:13)*. Equally so, they could not be ignored for their amazing level of conviction concerning their beliefs. The Sanhedrin also took note of their extraordinary boldness and of course their *eloquence* and power of erudition in reasoning their faith and issues of the Law.

This time, there was something definitely unusual about Peter. Remember this is the same Peter who not so long ago denied His Lord Jesus. On the night he betrayed his Master, it didn't even take him much to do that. All it took were few questions from ordinary bystanders, including a young girl, and Peter didn't think twice about what to say. But now, Peter and John are before what was considered the college of leading opinion leaders with elite status; men capable of sentencing them to death by a slow and painful process of stoning. Yet, this time Peter refused to deny Jesus.

We have already seen in other places when Peter became filled with the Holy Spirit, accounting for his extraordinary boldness to defend the Name of Jesus and to clearly demonstrate that He is alive and always willing to heal the sick and to save the lost. Through the power of the Holy Spirit, Peter was able to without compromise accuse members of the Sanhedrin for their rejecting of Christ and their role in the crucifixion of Christ. Peter and John quickly became a serious enigma for members of the Sanhedrin, and they did not know what to do with them, because both men firmly testified that Jesus is alive and Jesus actually healed the lame.

Although the Sanhedrin were a powerful people, this time they knew this was a case extremely difficult to simply dismiss.

How could they deal with men who were clearly not afraid of death and dying for what they believed to be true? The Sanhedrin will find it impossible to deny that a true miracle has taken place in the presence of many living witnesses. The living evidence is in fact right there before all to see, a man who was a lame for forty years stood up completely whole when Peter and John prayed for him (See Acts 4:14). How do you discredit the claim that the man was healed when he was right there *standing* not crouching, squatting or withered to the ground?

I find it incredibly interesting that the Sanhedrin because they could not disprove the miraculous healing that took place, they themselves finally confessed: *for, indeed, that a notable miracle has been done through them is evident to all who dwell in Jerusalem, and we cannot deny it (Acts 4:16).* Confessing to the effect that it wasn't just a miracle but a *notable* miracle was something totally out of character for members of the Sanhedrin.

Remember on previous occasions, especially during His earthly ministry, they strongly opposed Jesus, His miracles; tried in vain to refute His power, and continued to persecute Him, which later led to His crucifixion (John 5:1-18; 9:1-34). Even after His triumphant physical resurrection from the dead, the same authorities bribed the guards to misrepresent the facts (Matthew 27:62-66; 28:1-15).

It is clear that, there is always a point, beyond which no matter how powerful a people or systems are, they cannot continue to resist the truth or the will of God. For this reason even Pharaoh and his magicians after putting up stiff and long resistance against the purposes of God regarding the deliverance of the Children of Israel, they in the end were made to submit and were subdued, confessing that indeed the Lord is God (Ex. 8:19; 10:7;12:31-33).

If the opposition and resistance of the Sanhedrin, Pharaoh and His magicians were broken so that the purposes of God prevailed in the end, then also you must take heart to know that with God nothing shall be impossible. No devil presently troubling you, or trying to oppose your purpose now and anytime in the future will triumph!

The Anointing to Perform

There are few things that are noteworthy at this point. They mainly stem from the confession of Peter and John coupled with their bold authority and the reactions of the powerful Sanhedrin. Remember, how Peter and John confessed,

> ... *"Men of Israel, why do you marvel at this? Or why look so intently at us, as though by our own power or godliness we had made this man walk?* [13] *The God of Abraham, Isaac, and Jacob, the God of our fathers, glorified His Servant Jesus, whom you delivered up and denied in the presence of Pilate, when he was determined to let Him go (Acts 3:12-13).*

Peter and John were making a true claim that directed their hearers to the very source of their ability to heal the lame man. They credited that ability to a power and godliness beyond themselves. It came from God who empowers His servants to make the lame walk. And the power to make the lame to walk, just as it is to carry out or perform the purposes of God, is always the *anointing of God*. Acts 10:38, declares, *"how God anointed Jesus of Nazareth with the Holy Spirit and with power, who went about doing good and healing all who were oppressed by the devil, for God was with Him"*.

Simply, no one does the things of God effectively and efficiently without the anointing of God. If God will send you, God will anoint you. That is why it is always possible, no matter the opposition, for you to begin and to complete your God-given assignment if God will anoint you. In God's anointing there's ultimately no place for fear or failure, and you are at your best under the power of God's anointing. You have been anointed and you are anointed to do the job God called you to do! You can walk in the power of that anointing or you can allow your own fear to hold you bound. It really doesn't matter your area of calling or assignment, whether in the secular or religious world, God will anoint you sufficiently to perform His will and to finish His purposes for your life.

Twelve Reliable Facts about the Anointing

First of all, for Peter and John to effectively execute their God-given purpose, an anointing capable of helping them to carry out their particular functions was accorded them through the power of the Holy Spirit.

Second, every true anointing is unstoppable.

Third, every true anointing thrives under strife and oppositions.

Fourth, every true anointing becomes seriously problematic to the enemy, and no true anointing is quenched by opposition.

Fifth, every true anointing is from God, sufficient, capable and enabling for the particular assignment one is assigned to carry out. The same anointing contains all necessary provisions for fulfilling one's purpose without fail (Luke 4:17-21) .

Sixth, every true anointing is given to do God's determined will and purpose (Acts 4:27-28; Lk 4:18, 19). In 2Chronicles 22:7 Jehu was specifically *anointed* to cut off the house of Ahab. The anointing is never for show-offs and personal agendas, but to bring glory to the God who anoints us. In most cases, the anointing literally serves God's purpose by ministering to His people. In fact, the anointing although is the power to break burden, it is really for *bearing the burden of the people and leadership* (Numbers 11:17)

Seventh, every true anointing has a mandate, *charge* or instruction, and authorization. Jeremiah had one (Jeremiah 1:4-10), Joshua also had authorization (Numbers. 27:18-23; Deut. 3:28); Timothy had one (2 Tim. 4:2-5; 1:6); the Disciples had specific instructions from Christ (Matthew 28:18-20, Acts 1:4,8).

Eighth, the anointing is kept and maintained by the help of the Holy Spirit of God (2 Timothy 1:14).

Ninth, the anointing must be stirred. The best way to lose it is not to use it (2 Tim. 1:6; Deut. 3:28; cf. Matt. 7:19).

Tenth, the anointing can be imparted and it is easily transferable (Rom. 1:11;1 Tim.4:13-14; 2Tim 1:6; Numbs 11:16-17, 27:18-23; Deut. 3:28). In the case of Moses and the seventy Elders, it was the same Spirit upon Moses that was imparted unto the Elders (Numbs 11:24-30).

Eleventh, every true anointing can be transferred to others by intentionally laying on of hands and prophetic act (e.g. declaration) desirable for the purpose of impartation. The anointing is also attracted by proximity and association in the form of mentor-protégé relationship in which respect for the anointing is evident. Jesus and the disciples (John 20:22, Romans 8:10-11); Paul and Timothy, and Elijah and Elisha, Moses and Joshua.

Twelfth, true anointing literally *sets one apart* and sanctifies and it is easily identifiable. This is the reason why followers of Christ or the disciples were unmistakably identified for the first time as *Christians* in Antioch (Acts 11:26). That means they were Christ-like, because they bore and truly exemplified explicit traits and characteristics of their Master, Jesus Christ. They shared in His anointing and lived and did as Christ did. The anointing on the disciples demonstrated Christ-*likeness* and they were recognised as champions of His manner of life. Hence, they were Christians.

Note: *Christ* is never the surname of our Lord Jesus. *Christ* (Khristós) means *anointed* or the Anointed One. So, our Lord was Jesus *the Anointed One* (See Psalms 2:2; Acts 10:38; Psalms 45:7; Matt. 16:16, Luke 4:18-20).

Now, Romans 8:10-11 confirms that we have the same Spirit in us who raised Jesus from the dead, the Spirit of life who also gives life to us. And also we have Christ living in us by His Spirit. With this understanding, it is therefore easy to know that the true disciples of Christ do share in His anointing and are Christ-like (John 17:22; 1Cor 6:17). They tap into Christ's anointing and exercise the power of that same anointing. It is with this same understanding that Paul tells the Philippians that *you all are partakers of my grace (Phil 1:7)*.

Similarly, it is understandable that the Lord confers upon those who believe in Him and share in His anointing a 'greater work' status (John 14:12).

Two things that are key to understanding the anointing that worked through Peter and John: the Lord rose and ascended to be with the Father, and that He went so that the Helper, the Holy Spirit of the anointing, would come not to leave but to be in us and with us (John 14:17; Ephesians 4:10-12). No wonder Peter and John could speak with the audacity and authority with which they spoke and did the miracles they did in the Name of Jesus!

They spoke because they were filled with the Holy Spirit of anointing and healed in the Name of Jesus, because the Holy Spirit of anointing who was in them was also with them to glorify Christ Jesus (Mark 13:3; John 16:7-14).

The Anointing that Goes with Purpose

Something about the rather strange admission of the Sanhedrin concerning Peter and John forcefully establishes the nature, power and the workings of the anointing. The Scripture says,

> *Now when they saw the boldness of Peter and John, and perceived that they were uneducated and untrained men, **they marvelled. And they realized that they had been with Jesus** (Acts 4:13).*

The anointing that goes with our purpose will always bring about astonishment because most times it is thrust upon the most unlikely of people, a common and unassuming person but yet walking in a greater dimension of power beyond themselves. Paul tried to make sense of why things work that way with the anointing when he said,

> *For you see your calling, brethren, that not many wise according to the flesh, not many mighty, not many noble, are called.* [27]

> *But God has chosen the foolish things of the world to put to shame the wise, and God has chosen the weak things of the world to put to shame the things which are mighty (1 Corinth. 1:26-27).*

Similarly, Apostle James on the other hand agrees with Paul when he asked in a rhetorical fashion, *"listen, my beloved brethren: Has God not chosen the poor of this world to be rich in faith and heirs of the kingdom which He promised to those who love Him?"* (James 2:5)

Basically, it's just the way God chooses to do what He does. He wants to show forth His glory, His power and wisdom in the earth through the kind of things He does. But mainly that His signature will not be mistaken. When we see someone who was considered in the natural to be unable and unfit, but yet manages to do great things, we cannot but admit that God is at work through one of His own. Likewise, the one through whom God is working concords truly that God is working in and through them.

> *But we have this treasure in earthen vessels, that the excellence of the power may be of God and not of us (2 Corinthians 4:7). Now He who establishes us with you in Christ and has anointed us is God (2 Corinthians 1:21).*

The Sanhedrin *marvelled*, when they *realised* that surely, Peter and John had no personal background or advantage in life to give them the kind of boldness and eloquence they exhibited before them. Hence they quickly looked beyond the disciples and testified that, surely the source of their power of boldness and eloquence must have been because *they have been with Jesus.* Amen!

They were right; Peter and John graciously received what they had, and it was an anointing whose source was the Lord Jesus Christ (John 20:22; 2 Corinth. 1:21). They gained their anointing by association, through walking with Christ; by their positioning with Christ and having learned and followed the Lord Jesus Christ. The Lord gave them what He had in order for them to continue His purpose on earth.

Remember how He breathed on them (John 20:22) and how He asked the Father to send them His *Promise* so that they became imbued with Power from on High (John 14:15-18;16:7-15; Acts 1:4,8;2:1-4)! God can do the same for you my friend. Thank you Holy Spirit!

The Anointing from God Teaches

In admitting that the men have been with Jesus, the Sanhedrin rightly located the Source of every true anointing, Jesus the Holy One (1 John 2:20,27; Acts 3:12-13; 2Cor. 1:21). Secondly by saying the men were uneducated or unschooled and untrained, but also so bold, the Sanhedrin indirectly admitted the power of true anointing to adequately school and train the unschooled and untrained. In that they made such admission, they were confirming what the Scripture already teaches; that God's purposes and God's assignments are fulfilled in God's ways and through His power.

We don't need human approval or human certification to do what God asks us to do. God knows we normally feel inadequate for His job, He knows we cannot *talk,* are unschooled or not schooled enough, but yet He made the *mouth* and puts His *Rod* – His *anointing* in our hands and says to us, 'go and stand before Pharaoh' (Ex. 4:11-17). He says, like He told Moses *"I will be with your mouth"*, and like He told Paul, *"My grace is sufficient for you, for My strength is made perfect in weakness"* (2 Cor. 12:9).

> *But you have an anointing from the Holy One, and you know all things. [21] I have not written to you because you do not know the truth, but because you know it, and that no lie is of the truth (1 John 2:20-21).*

> *But the anointing which you have received from Him abides in you, and you do not need that anyone teach you; but as the same anointing teaches you concerning all things, and is true, and is not a lie, and just as it has taught you, you will abide in Him (1 John 2:27).*

Are you ever ashamed of your weaknesses and inadequacies? Do you feel like a fool before the schooled, trained and sophisticated people of this world? Is your problem the *Sanhedrin*; thinking you cannot face them to ensure God's purpose for your life is carried out? Well, you need not worry anymore. God who called you has also anointed you. You have an anointing from God that teaches you all you need for God's assignment.

That anointing is true and authentic and comes as a result of *being with Jesus*. Others may dismiss, discount, or even cancel you out, but they cannot ignore the fact that you have *been with Jesus*, and are anointed. They may know your background and pedigree, your past and failures – they know in reality that because of all your short comings, your lack of academic powers, you really don't qualify for anything substantial in life. But my friend, you have an anointing from the Holy One – you've *been with Jesus*! Just make sure you stay with Him and there is nothing that you cannot do!

Like the Apostle Paul puts it, he said, *"I can do all things through Christ who strengthens me" (Philippians 4:13)*. What a way to look at life's important choices, life's duties, pursuits and endeavours. You *can do* because first of all, you have a *Can Do* God who accomplishes all His purposes (Job 42:2), and with whom all things are possible (Mark 10:27). This God, is He who has anointed you to do all things through Christ who strengthens you. There is only one way out for you my friend, that you will believe what the Lord has said, you have the anointing that it takes -*"If you can believe, all things are possible to him who believes" (Mark 9:23)*.

I encountered the true impact of this phrase, *'been with Jesus'* during one of our church's end-of-year- fast and prayer day when we decided to read the book of Acts line-by-line and pray about anything the Holy Spirit prompted us about based on our reading. I never really noticed the phrase the way the Holy Spirit opened it up that evening. It became the true highlight of our prayer-time that day.

We later adopted it as our faith-response to true life's issues regarding matters of favour and the blessing from the Lord. I told members to answer everyone who asks them the reasons for their hope, blessings and good prospects by saying, *'been with Jesus'*. By that we were acknowledging the goodness of our God, giving Him all glory for all the good things He has done. It was a wonderful way of saying; *I know it took the Lord to get here, there or to have this or that, and to do this or that!*

For example, if someone doesn't understand why you are having so much favour even though humanly speaking, you don't qualify for such favour, your response should be simply, *'been with Jesus'*. That's all it took the disciples, Peter and John to confound the elite Sanhedrin of their time and to go ahead and to fulfil their purpose. That they had *'been with Jesus'* meant their time had come for them to shine even in the midst of darkness! That they had *'been with Jesus'* meant, they have been truly anointed to do the works of God and even greater works - *"Most assuredly, I say to you, he who believes in Me, the works that I do he will do also; and greater works than these he will do, because I go to My Father (John 14:12).*

Prayer in favour of Your Purpose

Realise, every true anointing for purpose is protected, supported, sustained and deployed by effective prayer. After Peter and John were released to go their way, having been severely warned and threatened never to speak in the Name of Jesus again, they refused to keep quiet about Jesus and His Name. However, they were aware that the warning from the Sanhedrin was not an empty threat. So what did they do? They immediately contacted and joined their colleagues, briefed them and then resulted to what I call *prayer for, or in favour of purpose*.

Together, the disciples asked the Lord to do and to continue to do exactly what put them into trouble with the Sanhedrin in the first place. The reason they were arranged before the Sanhedrin was basically because of the gospel of Jesus Christ, and the miracles, signs and wonders wrought in His Name. But, see what fervent prayer the disciples prayed to the Lord for their purpose in Christ against the threat of the authorities.

> *Now, Lord, look on their threats, and grant to Your servants that with all boldness they may speak Your word,* [30] *by stretching out Your hand to heal, and that signs and wonders may be done through the name of Your holy Servant Jesus."* [31] *And when they had prayed, the place where they were assembled together was shaken; and they were all filled with the Holy Spirit, and they spoke the word of God with boldness (Acts 4:29-31).*

They had no qualms whatsoever that the power and means of doing what they did was not of themselves. They knew it was of God and they needed to look to Him at all times for the continuing of their purpose. The disciples recognised that to protect, and to also sustain, the very anointing for effectively carrying out God's purposes, they must look to God in prayer. Not just any prayer, but one that was effectual, fervent, and constant (James 5:16,17).

In Acts 12 similar prayer was offered again when Herod the king harassed the Church, killed James and went ahead to arrest Peter, meaning to end his life as he did to James. Know that all of this was intended, not just to silence the Church, but to abort the purposes of God in the works and lives of the disciples. However, by the power of effectual, fervent and constant prayer offered by the Church to God on behalf of Peter, he was miraculously released. Upon receiving the prayer of His people, Almighty God swiftly dispatched His angel who loosened Peter's chains, opened the prison iron gates and escorted Peter to safety, and to join his colleagues who were still praying. It took prayer to set Peter free to continue his work of purpose, declaring the gospel of the Lord Jesus Christ and bringing healings to all in need. And, through his release, the evil hand of Herod was stayed and the wicked expectation of the Jews was disappointed (Acts 12:11,19).

We see similar incidents in Acts 16:16-40 when the intervention of effectual, fervent and constant prayer defused a bad situation for the disciples. Paul and Silas were arrested and imprisoned for casting out a spirit of divination from a slave girl who brought profit to her owners through fortune-telling. They were put securely in the inner prison, having been dragged, beaten, and their feet fastened in stocks. Knowing and doing what they knew was right to do in difficult times of purpose, they prayed and worshiped their God. The result was immediately evident. The Lord sent an earthquake throughout the prison, the foundations trembled, all the doors flung open and everyone's chains were loosed. What happened later was interesting.

It wasn't the prisoners that were afraid but the guard who was, for his dear life. He was going to take his own life before morning, knowing that he stood in serious jeopardy if the prisoners had escaped by any means. With Paul offering him assurance, this terrified guard, far from being afraid for his life submitted his life, together with his own family, to the Lord Jesus Christ. Afterwards, he showed Paul and Silas great hospitality. On the next day, Paul and Silas were honourably released from prison with apologies, and they went on to continue in their line of purpose.

Whenever God's purpose for His people was threatened in any shape or form, they prayed effectually, fervently and constantly, and the results never disappointed. The prayers for, or in favour of purpose, have always had literally *earth shaking* and *quickening* result. Without doubt, any meaningful purpose will require such kind of prayers that are effectual, fervent and constant. Prayer literally walks hand-in-hand with purpose, from the discovery of purpose to its pursuit and fulfilment.

A common mistake we usually make, as people of faith walking in God's anointing is; we take things for granted by ignoring the very nerve centre that supports and sustains the anointing we were given for fulfilling our God-given purpose. Remember even our Lord Jesus took time off in prayer, staying connected to the Father who provided the anointing while the Son was on earth (Acts 10:38).

At the beginning of His earthly ministries, just after His baptism, He was praying when the voice of the Father sounded confirming His love for the Son and affirming His purpose (Luke 3:21,22):

> *When all the people were baptized, it came to pass that Jesus also was baptized; and while He prayed, the heaven was opened.* [22] *And the Holy Spirit descended in bodily form like a dove upon Him, and a voice came from heaven which said, "You are My beloved Son; in You I am well pleased."*

The Lord Jesus so much understood the significance of prayer to purpose that when He was finally going to depart from this earth, He did not gave His disciples bags of money or things to keep them happy and on the move. He simply left them with prayer, attesting that prayer was indispensible to their purpose, and prayer is greater than money and better than things (John 17).

A few things about prayer and purpose come to light from our earlier reading of the above passage in Luke 3. First, true children of God and of purpose pray. Second, whenever they pray, they are bound to enjoy open-heaven, and to access favour with impartation and visitation from the Holy Spirit.

Before the Lord Jesus chose His twelve disciples, whom also He named apostles, the Lord continued in prayer to God all night (Luke 6:12-13). He always prayed, most times alone, and the Lord prayed so often with great results that His disciples could not help but ask Him to teach them to pray as well (Luke 9:18, 28, 29; 11:1). When He was going to face His final hours at the climax of all His purpose on earth, the Lord prayed effectually, fervently and constantly.

In Matthew 26:36-46, we have an account of how, towards the finality of the Lord's purpose on earth, real threat to His purpose emerged, with Him being *sorrowful and deeply distressed*. At Gethsemane He admitted that His own soul was exceedingly sorrowful, even to death. As a result He prayed while lying flat on

His face saying "O My Father, if it is possible, let this cup pass from Me; nevertheless, not as I will, but as You *will*." His spirit indeed was willing, but His flesh was weak, the Lord said. No doubt the burden of purpose can be so overwhelming sometimes. All you can do is to pray for or in favour of your purpose, so that you don't abort it or allow the constraints of situations to kill it. So, the Lord went again the second time.

Remember, it is about being effectual, fervent and constant in prayer. However, this time He did not say anything new, but the same prayer He offered just as on the first occasion. And He went again the third time, *saying the same words* (vr 44). Does it really matter if we pray the same words to God on more than one, two or three occasions? No, as the Lord Himself has shown us through His own prayer, we should only concern ourselves with praying effectually, fervently and constantly for or in favour of our purpose when it comes under threat in any form or shape. Whether it is personal issues or external oppositions to our purpose, the way to go about it is the same, pray effectually, fervently and constantly.

After the Lord had prayed, He was ready to rise to the occasion; although until now none of His closest friends, the disciples at the time could bear up under heavy sleep to stand with Him in the time of His true agony. In the end, He came to His disciples saying "Rise, let us be going…," suggesting He was now prepared to get on with His purpose. In prayer He received strength to go on.

Jesus, the Lord, encouraged His disciples to pray continuously without losing heart as well (Luke 18:1). Likewise, Paul contends that we should *pray always without ceasing* (1 Thess 5:17). Apostle James says, *"… the effective* fervent *prayer of the righteous avails much Elijah was a man with a nature like ours, and he prayed earnestly that it would not rain; and it did not rain on the land for three years and six months. And he prayed again, and the heaven gave rain, and the earth produced its fruit" (James 5:17-18).*

Surely we know that the Holy Spirit who dwells in us is able to keep the anointing we receive (2 Timothy 1:14), however the anointing works by prayer; is deployed in prayer, with tangible results and is without doubt sustained and protected by an effectual, fervent and constant prayer. If you need help or are struggling in the area of prayer life, ask the Holy Spirit of prayer (Zech 12:10) to guide you and to teach you to pray. Your survival and success as a person of purpose greatly depends on your prayer life. As you pray, you are literally digging and drawing from the unlimited wells of purpose and all that you need to faithfully fulfil God's purposes for your life. You can always press on into your God-given purpose through the power of effectual, fervent and constant prayer life. Always pray-in-prayers and pray with prayers!

Wisdom for Purpose: Twelve (12) important pointers from Acts 4:31-37. What Happens when *Prayer in favour of Purpose* is offered? After they've prayed in favour of purpose, there were:

- Shaking – *represents the incursion of the power of God* (vr 31)
- Filling with the Holy Spirit (vr 31)
- Boldness to Preach the Word (vr 31)
- Increasing Converts (vr 32)
- Oneness of Spirit and Soul (Love & Unity) among all (vr 32)
- Great Power in Witnessing (vr 33)
- Great Grace upon Believers (vr 33)
- Great Provision, Supply and Prosperity (vr 34)
- Great Giving and Generosity (vr 34)
- Great Collective Commitment (vr 34)
- Great Individual Commitment (vr37)
- Great Reverence and Loyalty (vr 37)

By the help of God and His wonderful Spirit, and through the grace, wisdom and power that our Lord Jesus, His precious Son supplies, we can do all things God has assigned as our purpose on earth. The good news is that you are never left to struggle things out on your own, although it might sometimes feel that way. I trust and pray that you will not die, but will live to declare His goodness, and that in the end you will have your desires fully met in your pursuit of God's agenda and purpose for your life. God bless you greatly and grant you every grace you need in order to finish faithfully. Amen.

Your Decision – Your Purpose!

◆◆◆

Did you know that you can make the Lord Jesus Christ your Lord and Saviour right where you are? Yes, you can. Your decision to turn to Him will make all the difference between a life with purpose and a life without one. Unfortunately, you don't have eternal life with God and you will never begin to live a life of true purpose until you first connect to God Almighty. His heart's desire in love towards everyone is that those who seek Him will receive God's gift of eternal life, and to also enjoy here on earth, a life with purpose and blessings.

Right now, you might be living a life far below your true potential and below God's expectation; but there's certainly a way out and a way up for you. God desires to give you a wonderful life full of love, joy, peace, and personal fulfilment through His Son Jesus Christ. Probably, you haven't known it this way, but God truly longs to help you and to lift your burdens from your shoulders in order to relieve you of your sufferings. You don't have to go through life wondering what life is all about – is it worth continuing to live?

The good news is that God who created you knows exactly what your life is about. He alone can help you make sense of life. Ultimately, God desires to be a great Father to you, to love you and to care for you in ways you have not known before, in anyone or in anything else. That means for the rest of your life on earth, you will also find a faithful friend in God whose ears are always open to hear you and to help you in times of your need. I will encourage you as you read this page; this is the right time you entrust your life and your future to God who wants to protect and to care for you in amazing ways. Here is your opportunity, and I gladly love to be a part of your new journey in Christ by you allowing me to pray with you right now!

This is how it is. The Bible (the Word of God) says, "that if you shall confess with your mouth the Lord Jesus, and shall believe in your heart that God has raised Him from the dead, you shall be saved" (Romans 10:9). That means that, if you don't know Jesus, and have continued to walk in rebellion to His love and ways for you, then you must first recognise your need for Christ. Know that He died for you, forgiving you your sins, and taking away your guilt and punishment, so that you may live, and may receive the life He designed for you. Just as Jesus rose again, so also you too can have victory in every area of life, and you can keep rising to the top with Christ Jesus. Most importantly, you will have eternal life with God, and heaven becomes your home after you physically die. If you receive Jesus in your heart and in loving relationship as your Lord and Saviour, you have no reason to fear being condemned to hell and everlasting punishment, because He has taken your punishment, and opened a new way for you to spend the rest of your life under God's grace, love, forgiveness and mercies (Rom. 6:23).

The truth is, that you can be forgiven all your sins, and God will not hold anything against you because Jesus His Son has already paid in full for your sins, together with all your guilt and shame and the eternal punishment that you should have had. For everything that you wrongly got yourself into, God wants to lift the weight off your shoulder and in exchange to give you His joy, peace, and a brand new life with a brand new start.

Just pray right now: Dear Jesus, I now believe and confess that you died for me and rose again in victory. I confess that I am a sinner. I have sinned against You, but I choose right now to give you my life and everything about me. Please forgive me and take away my guilt, shame and punishment for the bad things I have done. I need your love, peace, joy and blessings. Come Lord Jesus and be with me. Come into my heart and give me the assurance of your Holy Spirit. I vow to follow you for the rest of my life and to submit to You always. I love you and thank You, Jesus for receiving me right now. I believe my life has changed, and I will live to fulfil Your purpose for me, and my new life.

My dear Friend, you've just made the most important decision of your life. My particular prayer for you is, the miracle you've always looked for has begun! May the Lord heal your body of any disease or sickness, and may His unlimited power of favour come upon you, right now, right where you are. God richly bless you! Amen. Now, please feel free to contact me for further help and information. We love to help where possible.

About the Author

◆◆◆

Pastor Didi and his wife, Dorothy, live and pastor in England, United Kingdom. They both love the Lord Jesus Christ passionately and are the founding pastors of an all-inclusive people background church, the Good Word Ministries, UK. Together, they continue to enjoy God's unlimited grace and favour at various levels and in different aspects of their ministries. A core area of their own purpose is reaching out in faith and obedience to assist people to realise the love of God in Christ, and to help them discover their God given purpose and potential. They believe that every one of God's children is loved and has unlimited potential to become the best that God intends for them.

Their second book entitled; *Walking in the Light of His Mysteries: God's Supernatural Platform for Creating Miracle Moments, Change and a Glorious Future,* is an excellent example of practical Christian living, Christian commitment and victory, and also the inexhaustible blessings that await all who truly believe in the Lord Jesus Christ and His Word. In short, miracles are still very possible, even today.

Pastors Didi and Dorothy are presently both directors of Aleph World Ltd, and Pastor Didi holds a BA (Hons) degree in Theology, and a Master of Philosophy (MPhil) degree in Religious Studies.

****

To Contact Good Word Ministries, UK, Please visit
www.goodwordchristiancentre.org.uk

**Please include your prayer requests and comments
when you write.**
****

Acknowledgements

❖❖❖

We are truly grateful to Miss Julie Stubbs, our special friend and sister in Christ, who volunteered to proofread the finished work of this revised edition, for errors. Thanks very much for your time and commitment in helping to make the necessary corrections.

Also to my dear friend, Michael Roper, who I first met at work and thought I needed to write a book, and kept encouraging me thereafter. Thank you my friend, and thank God, He caused us to meet in the first place.

Last but not the least! Our ongoing gratitude and sincerest thanks go to all members of Good Word Ministries and our friends. Your friendship and support in various ways have been inspiring. You have all helped and have added greatly to our overall experience in one way or another. Together, we are fulfilling God's purposes, and thank you all!

EPILOGE

◆◆◆

What happens when you align yourself with the purposes of God? Well, the possibilities are limitless, and they include having your personal desires met, and getting the necessary provision to do what's next. It means having the right connections and meeting the right people to help you fulfil God's purpose for your life!

Beyond Me is a clear narrative about the power and dynamics of the purposes of God, locating the most unlikely candidates and then transforming them into God's effective instruments for extraordinary works and assignments in His kingdom, to benefit humanity.

This book is a master piece that sees everything including, the most impossible promise and prophecy; your present personal struggles and challenges, in the light of the purposes of God and allows you to appreciate how things stand from God's point of view.

It is essentially a good picture of how nothing truly makes sense outside of God's purposes and also how a person can conquer their world, personal fear and shortcomings to fulfil their purpose in life. Also, it truly matters how one responds to external oppositions!

Beyond Me seeks to answer important questions that normally baffle Christians who are trying to find and to pursue their purpose. For example, we need to know that having the right behaviour while pursuing purpose is as important as carrying out our purpose itself. Secondly, purpose can be a great motivator if you know what to do.

You will encounter statements like "purpose is everything" and "God does not promote quitters". God promotes conquerors! You will also come across life changing truths like "why God gives the cup before His water", and "Moving from despair to hope", and a "Church on a sinking ship – putting faith into action".

You are provided with strategies and practical guidelines into the power of faith to help you deal with time of frustration and to overcome obstacles in the course of pursuing your purpose.

You will also find help to understand the immense power and influence your decision wields in relation to your personal purpose and your life in general. Not the least, you will be blessed with an astounding truth about the relevance and the need for a present-day equivalent of the spirit of Elijah, to assist people and churches of purpose, to successfully navigate the 'busy lanes' of secular society.

____ An inspiring new book, and an accurate example of how you can successfully drive and negotiate God's promise and purpose for your life during storms of uncertain times.

End Notes

❖❖❖

[1]*Words by Miss* Fanny Crosby, 1868; first appeared in
Songs of Devotion, by Howard Doane (New York: 1870).

[2] BBC news network reported that this horrible 7.0 magnitude- quake,
Haiti's worst in two centuries, struck on Tuesday, 12/01/2010. Haitian
Prime Minister Jean-Max Bellerive told US network CNN he
believed more than 100,000 people had died. The Red Cross
confirmed that up to three million people wereaffected. *http://
news.bbc.co.uk/1/hi/world/americas/8456819.stm (10/05/2010)*

[3]http://www.time.com/time/daily/newsfiles/waco/
031593.html; (20/01/10)

[4]http://www.catholic.com/thisrock/1998/9803chap.asp, 23/01/2010

Lightning Source UK Ltd.
Milton Keynes UK
UKHW040657010223
416291UK00005B/583